# The
# Five-Ton
# Life

Our Sustainable Future

SERIES EDITORS

Ryan E. Galt
*University of California, Davis*

Hannah Wittman
*University of British Columbia*

FOUNDING EDITORS

Charles A. Francis
*University of Nebraska–Lincoln*

Cornelia Flora
*Iowa State University*

# The Five-Ton Life

Carbon, America, and the
Culture That May Save Us

Susan Subak

University of Nebraska Press
Lincoln and London

Library of Congress Cataloging-in-Publication Data
Names: Subak, Susan Elisabeth, author.
Title: The five-ton life: carbon, America, and the
culture that may save us / Susan Subak.
Description: Lincoln: University of Nebraska Press,
[2018] | Series: Our sustainable future | Includes
bibliographic references and index.
Identifiers: LCCN 2017043649
ISBN 9780803296886 (cloth: alk. paper)
ISBN 9781496208095 (epub)
ISBN 9781496208101 (mobi)
ISBN 9781496208118 (pdf)
Subjects: LCSH: Carbon dioxide mitigation—
Economic aspects—United States. | Carbon
dioxide—Environmental aspects—United States.
| City planning—Environmental aspects—United
States. Classification: LCC TD885.5.C3 S83 2018 | DDC
363.738/74—dc23 LC record available at
https://lccn.loc.gov/2017043649

Set in Garamond Premier Pro by E. Cuddy.

# Contents

# Illustrations

# Tables

# The
# Five-Ton
# Life

# Introduction

"The palm has not the means of covering the whole of the beast" is one of many analogies to the proverb of the blind men and the elephant. In the case of modern environmentalism and climate change, it is as though we are charged with a specific blindness, a specialized eye where some are trained to look at the rooftop (solar), the sidewalks (walkability), the shape of the building (passive solar), the traffic flow and parking (car alternatives), or the menu (reducing methane). But if we saw a place or a person that did well in the sum total of these characteristics, if their overall greenhouse gas emissions were very low, would we recognize it? How about the place that actually did the very best? Highly unlikely. It's no one's job to find this or describe it. Those who live it are getting on with their lives. And if they know it, they are unlikely to ride the proverbial high horse, and even less likely to ride the literal medieval high horse, that referred to the largest, most expensive of steeds. But is it in our interest to allow these parts of American culture to remain unknown and unheralded?

This book is about the lower emissions culture of America—what I call the Five-Ton Life. It is a general notion of emissions that are equivalent to half or less of the American average. I explore this notion for urban, suburban, and rural communities. Once we find where it is, what would it take to preserve and emulate it? These are questions that take us into the details of personal values, contemporary relationships, and architecture more often than the city, state, and federal policy levers that are more familiar instruments of climate policy. The five-ton project can also be a guidepost for individuals seeking to understand how their own choices might line up with this part of American culture.

For many people worried about the global warming problem, the best approach seems to be to aim for a clear goal such as zero emissions—to end fossil fuel use altogether. It's tempting to support long-term plans toward achieving a fossil-free future for a nation, carbon "neutrality" for an institution, and a "no-impact" life for an individual. A nagging problem with this approach is that the difference between zero impact and our present state of twenty metric tons of carbon dioxide equivalent per American is enormous. The difference is vast, but most people don't yet know how far they personally are from such a goal, let alone how far society is from making a clean break with fossil fuels. Americans who want to make serious improvements in their own emissions, hoping to help change society in general, are often left with the looming chasm between the likely triviality of doing "one thing for climate" and the daunting, if not impossible goal of bringing their personal emissions down to zero.[1]

An alternative to a target of zero is to set some other individual goal that can be achieved in the absence of a rapid transformation of the economic and political system. But what should that goal be? And why bother if most of America's emissions seem to be outside of our direct control? Electricity generation and heavy industry can seem distant from individual activities and are the most familiar bogeymen of our fossil fuel age because they are our only significant consumers of coal. These sources make up a majority of American emissions, but only barely, at 52 percent.[2] It is easy to forget that these sources are chugging out greenhouse gases day and night to produce electricity and goods for human beings, and mainly for domestic consumption at that, but they are, of course. In actuality, greenhouse gas emissions from American residences and personal transportation have been increasing at a faster rate than emissions from industry.[3] U.S. residential emissions grew by 20 percent between 1990 and 2014, compared with a drop of about 10 percent from industry.[4]

Calls for personal actions are often pitched apologetically as small measures that can be taken while we await a breakthrough in national policy or international fora.[5] But most of the efforts at the national level, such as former president Barack Obama's proposed Clean Power Plan, primarily aim to reduce emissions from electricity generation while suggesting that the economic impact for individual households will be minor, or even positive. Controlling greenhouse gas emissions from electricity generation through state and national programs as outlined in the Clean Power Plan was expected to reduce our total national emissions by about 11 percent from 2014 levels.[6] While such programs are promising—American power plants are gradually decarbonizing—they leave untouched the vast majority of American emissions.

Politicians and many environmental leaders often focus on the large concentrated sources of emissions, although doing so depends on resolving the wider political power struggles that have enfeebled efforts to enact domestic regulatory controls in the United States and to ratify international climate agreements. The closest we have come to a coordinated international agreement that includes the United States is the Paris Agreement, where participants make individualized "ambitious" plans for future reductions. But how can the United States make an ambitious plan in the absence of a change in American culture? American homes are among the largest in the world, our commercial sector the most overbuilt, and our habits among the most mobile.

It is tempting to blame inaction on partisan opposition, but all the major parties are associated with big consumption—when compared to the rest of the world—and have had little to say about how to change that course. Although American per-capita emissions are somewhat lower than they were a few years ago, they still stand at double the per-person European emissions.[7] American emissions are even higher than the per-capita emissions of people living in Canada, which is colder and more sparsely settled. In *The Carbon Code:*

*How You Can Become a Climate Change Hero* Canadian scientist Brett Favaro reminds his American readership that when they reduce their emissions the impact is equal to four people, because American per-person emissions are so much higher than the world average.[8] While European emissions have fallen by about one quarter since 1990, American emissions have increased in that time.[9] Because of these differences, Americans—more than Europeans and most other nationals—can make a difference in the global picture by shedding two, five, ten or more tons of carbon dioxide from their lifestyles.

Progress in developing renewable energy has been held up as a beacon of hope in a frighteningly warming world and our best chance for bringing our emissions down. Between 1990 and 2016, U.S. solar energy consumption increased by about tenfold and wind energy by almost a hundredfold. In 2016 these renewable sources contributed some 262 trillion British thermal units (BTUS) a month compared with a measly 8 trillion BTUS a month back in 1990.[10] This is a heady achievement except for the fact that Americans now consume much more energy—that is, 400 trillion BTUS more per month than we did in 1990. The renewable share has not made up the difference, let alone shifted us toward a reduction. Political scientist Ronald Mitchell has considered annual declines in emissions due to innovation compared with increases in emissions due to population growth and consumption, and found that historically, innovation just does not keep up.[11] Three decades ago, when global warming was just emerging as a public concern, homes were smaller, cars were smaller, and "binge" flying was less common.[12]

For the non-fossil fuel share of our total consumption to improve significantly, we will need to make changes in the underlying cultural drivers that effect energy consumption rather than hope for dramatic improvements in technology. For an account of why contemporary environmentalism has often made unrealistic claims for renewables while skirting the consumption questions, see Ozzie Zehner's book *Green Illusions*, in which he asks and answers the question: "Why do we seem to have a predisposition for preferring *production* over energy *reduction?*"[13]

In part because of the contagious optimism spilling over from growth in renewables, many Americans take up the view that the big picture is improving. And looking at some important trends, we can find some areas where Americans have actually reduced. Among the activities that drive greenhouse gas emissions, beef-eating habits have seen the biggest change. Per-person U.S. beef consumption fell about 20 percent since 2000 for many reasons, including concerns that beef can cause cancer and heart attacks, more widespread empathy for the suffering of animals, and growing public understanding of how livestock links to water pollution and methane emissions.[14] Cattle production is America's number one source of methane, which is released directly from the cattle gut. Greenhouse gas emissions from raising cattle also include nitrous oxide and methane emissions related to cattle manure, and nitrous oxide and carbon dioxide emissions from raising crops to feed cattle. But cutting beef alone will not make a large difference.

Maybe you have seen the bumper sticker that reads "Eating Meat is Worse for the Planet Than Driving this Car." Unfortunately, it is not true, because eating meat contributes less than 10 percent of American emissions, whereas personal vehicles contribute almost 20 percent. Taking beef and meat out of your diet and eating vegetables or fish instead will subtract—at most—about 1.5 metric tons from your emissions compared with 3.5 metric tons, on average, from not driving. In countries that source their beef from land cleared from forests, however, cutting beef will be a powerful option that can slow deforestation. In recent years the United States has not imported meat from these countries, not out of concern over the environmental implications, but because hoof and mouth disease has been found there. In the long term, however, eating less beef can help to free up valuable land for better uses than growing corn for cattle feed. Less beef can mean more land for nutritional grains or even more woodland that can, in turn, reduce atmospheric carbon. Less beef also translates into allowing more water to remain in dwindling aquifers.

Looking at transportation emissions, a convincing reduction in driving does not emerge despite generational differences in vehicle use. Whereas in 1980 about two-thirds of U.S. seventeen-year-olds had a driver's license, by 2010 fewer than half did, and a growing proportion of Americans have not obtained a license by the time they are forty.[15] Fuel efficiency improvements through Corporate Average Fuel Economy (CAFE) standards have progressed over the years, but personal vehicles have grown heavier and larger. In many, though not all social circles, Americans drive SUVs without embarrassment. Although the trend shadows economic output to some extent, emissions from all private vehicles and commercial trucks, buses, and trains are similar to what they were at the start of the millennium and about 17 percent higher than their 1990 level.[16]

The other major source of greenhouse gas emissions in America, of course, comes from buildings—homes, offices, stores, and schools. When we talk about climate change, the elephant in the room is the room itself. Floor space per person in America stands large against Europe, let alone against most of the rest of the world. Americans live in homes that are twice as large on average as British homes, and American homes are larger than Danish homes, which are the roomiest in Europe.[17]

A few years ago, it looked as though America was turning its back on larger houses. After the housing bubble burst in 2008, the size of new houses began to decline in America. A few years later, though, floor plans again trended larger for several years, and continue to rise. The future is uncertain, but the long-term trend has been upward, and underlying this has been a drop in the number of new small houses. In 2000, about 36 percent of new houses were smaller than eighteen hundred square feet in size, but this share had dropped to 24 percent in 2013. Even while the tiny house movement has presented its novelty to the public, the reality of small house construc-

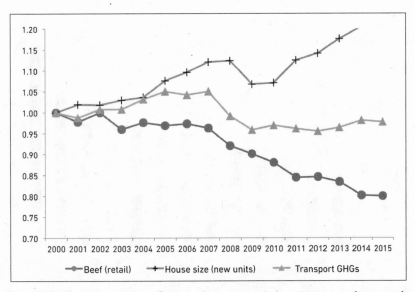

Fig. 1. U.S. cultural trends that effect greenhouse gas emissions. Larger new homes and heavier personal vehicles are raising U.S. emissions, while changes in diet are lowering emissions from agriculture. Compiled by the author from USDA 2017, https://www.ers.usda.gov/data-products/livestock-meat-domestic-data/livestock-meat-domestic-data/#Beef; U.S. Census 2017; U.S. EPA 2017, https://www3.epa.gov/climatechange/ghgemissions/inventoryexplorer/#transportation/allgas/source/all.

tion has taken a large dip. It appears that the suburb, or at least the "suburban house," is not dead after all!

Buildings, more than diet or even transport, offer the most potential for changing the course of our greenhouse gas emissions. In addition to the heating fuel and electricity used in buildings, which makes up about 40 percent of our total emissions, building construction demands energy investment, as do all of the furnishings and other items inside buildings. Purchase of these goods result in higher emissions from manufacturing and industry and are a good part of the reason China's emissions have grown so dramatically.[18] If we figure in the greenhouse gas emissions embodied in making and importing consumer goods, our American household greenhouse gas emissions expand by as much as 30 percent.[19] Reducing home and business sizes, and thus reducing the amount of interior

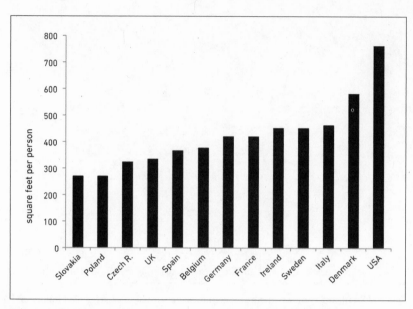

Fig. 2. U.S. and European floor space compared, compiled by the author from Enerdata of the European Union for 2008 and U.S. EIA, *Residential Energy Consumption Survey*, 2009.

items, would also lower emissions in the manufacturing sector and the construction industry. If large houses become less desirable and prestigious, fewer people will be willing to accept a longer commute to outer suburbs, where large houses can be obtained more cheaply. Reduced transport emissions are often a bonus that comes with smaller dwellings. Without a reduction in home size, traditional regulatory measures such as closing old coal plants and implementing higher fuel efficiency standards are unlikely to bring deep cuts in greenhouse gas emissions.

## A Personal Target

Given that household emissions have been on the rise, these emissions are important, and they are unlikely to be reduced much by renewables, what is in the cards to bring them down? Not much, as far as I can see. So we return to the initial question: What goal might

Americans strive for, short of a quixotic goal of zero emissions? A useful goal would have some practical characteristics: (1) The goal would be compatible with an historical standard of comfort and opportunity. (2) It would allow for individual preferences and personal expression. (3) It could be achieved anywhere in the country, even in colder climates. (4) It would be easy to count.

First, it is assumed that Americans will not make major sacrifices in comfort, that room temperatures will be pleasant, that living spaces will not be cramped, and that people will be well fed and clad.[20] Individuals will continue to be at liberty to pursue personal fulfillment. These goals rely on an assumption that the lives and communities that we are striving for already exist in America as desirable communities and households. Their existence can be discovered and emulated, and indeed they can be, as the following chapters describe.

Second, any individualized goal must allow for individual expression and endeavors. This may seem obvious, but striving for clarity, many climate leaders like to talk about the one thing that they have given up. I can think of thought leaders who say that they have decided not to have children, some who say they never eat meat, and others who are "off the grid." These ideas may be effective in establishing a personal brand or professional identity, but they are less useful for the broader American public, who are unlikely to manage to do all of these things at once. Getting to zero is an appealing goal, but it is possible to have low overall emissions while eating some meat, consuming some electricity, and doing some driving. The combinations of activities consistent with a low-emissions lifestyle are endless.

A target that could be taken up anywhere in the United States is presented here at the outset with the aim of simplicity. An ambitious target might be easiest to meet in the state of Hawaii because life on the islands requires no heating fuel, and many people already live in apartments.[21] Other warm-weather regions of the country including California, the Southwest, and Florida are more invested in single-family houses, but also require little heating fuel.[22] But a goal that is only viable in the parts of the country blessed with a warm climate implies migration as a climate policy rather than the adjustment and transformation needed throughout the regions of the United States. The five-ton notion presented here, however, could eventually be modified to take into account different regional climates.

While it may seem obvious, a useful personal target would be one that is easy to count and would not require specialized instruction, the help of consultants, or even new software. People could find out their baselines using utility bills that are at hand, knowledge of their diets, air miles statements, if any, and car odometers for those with vehicles. These numbers could be plugged into a good online greenhouse gas emissions calculator. It would be far simpler than the forms that people file by April 15. In this respect, a personal greenhouse gas emissions target would be different from some of the individualized metrics that have been proposed to address climate change. For instance, a group of influential scientists in Switzerland proposed that all people of the earth should strive to keep their energy use within two thousand watts per year.[23] By comparison, Americans consume, on average, ten thousand watts each year. Aside from the difficulty of achieving an 80 percent reduction in household consumption, the average American faces the challenge of trying to convert available units such as U.S. dollars, therms, vehicle miles, and kilowatt-hours (kwh) into watt units. A similar challenge with units and scale is faced with the "ecological footprint" concept that calls on participants to achieve the average of 1.8 global hectares of land per world citizen, which compares with an American average of 9.0 global hectares.[24] A target that needs only a greenhouse gas emissions calculator or a sheet with emission factors for converting from available units to $CO_2$ units is preferable. The best current example of a simple calculator is the U.S. Environmental Protection Agency's (epa) household calculator, which takes information from odometers and utility bills in dollar amounts or energy units and converts them into $CO_2$ emissions.[25]

Which leaves us with the question, what number would make a good target? Perhaps something "fair" like a per-person emissions target that takes into account the fact that different people and countries have different levels of historical responsibility for the problem? The scientific insight that a large part of the industrialized world's emissions linger in the atmosphere today has been much on the minds of developing countries that hope to catch up their economic output. This approach calls for greater sacrifices from countries like the United Kingdom, which began industrializing long before prosperous newcomers like the Asian tiger economies. I should add that I proposed such a thing in a 1990 study published by the Stockholm Environment Institute, the first on the subject.[26] In the following year, when the international climate negotiations began, researchers produced many similarly idealistic proposals that gave rise to current notions of historic responsibility, inter-generational equity and, eventually, global development rights.[27]

However, even a goal of meeting the *current*, rather than historic, global average per capita emissions has a utopian slant given how high American emissions were and are. That current target would imply about an 80 percent reduction in American emissions, similar to the two-thousand-watts idea. Instead, I propose that Americans seek to achieve a more moderate target, an amount equivalent to five metric tons or less. Currently, Americans emit on average about 12–13 metric tons $CO_2$ from residences, offices/schools, diet and personal mobility. In 2015, per capita greenhouse gas emissions as metric tons carbon dioxide equivalent were as follows: residences: 3.3, commercial 3.5, diet 1.9, and personal transport 4.0, summing to about 12.5 metric tons.[28] Five tons is less than half of the current American household emissions, but this emission level is already found throughout America, in urban, rural and even suburban settings.

Compared to our national average of Twenty Individual and Industrial Tons (TWIT) from all and everything, Five Individual Tons (FIT) sounds much better. For a person who is an "average"

American emitter, cutting that in half may seem like a formidable challenge, but in my own neighborhood in Washington DC it has happened many times in the last few years. It happened like this: Older individuals or couples decide to sell their three- to four-thousand-square-foot houses and move into apartments. After selling their houses, which happen to be solidly built homes from the late 1920s, the buildings are converted into multi-units of from two to four units. Before the conversion, one or two people were living in the large house, whereas now four to eleven people live there.[29] The amount of energy consumed for space heating and cooling per person is far lower than before, and electricity use is somewhat lower. Instead of a large home with endless possibilities for larger appliances, more furnishings, and heating and cooling mismanagement, the new space manifests into multiple cases of compact living and the original large house is taken out of circulation. An alliance of developers and affordable housing advocates supports these conversions, and if environmental organizations joined this cause, more such conversions would be achieved despite NIMBY, or not in my backyard, hostility.

## Success Is Here and Here

Aside from appreciating my own neighborhood's house conversions, I was driven by the question, who are the people who have succeeded in limiting their carbon output? And how did they succeed? To answer these questions I had to look in some obscure places and unearth data that has had limited circulation. I had to make comparisons that might not be considered polite. To understand how communities use energy in a given climate, I needed to know how different neighborhoods in the same metropolitan area performed compared with each other. Some of this information has been viewed as sensitive by those who work with it and it has been slow to be released. Using high-quality data from utilities and transportation studies, I am able to point out where in the Midwest you are likely to find the suburb with the lowest per-person greenhouse gas emissions (Berwyn, Illinois), the lowest-emitting rural areas (Holmes County, Ohio, and Lancaster County, Pennsylvania). Also, the four-year college with the lowest emissions (the New School, New York), and the category of urbanite with one of the lowest footprints in the country (central Washington DC families seeking bilingual education for their children).

The examples explored in this book are the best that I could find, but can be seen as a sampling of lower emissions culture. My examples are located in the eastern and midwestern regions, though interesting examples can likely be found in other parts of the country. In this book impacts from human activities are considered for the associated greenhouse gas emissions, not with other kinds of characteristics such as resource extraction, water consumption, and chemical contamination.

Solar, geothermal, and wind power did not figure into the low carbon culture explored in this book because I did not find much of it in any of the places that had low greenhouse gas emissions. Only one of the urban families taking part in the school survey had rooftop solar. The suburb with low residential energy use and low driving rates had no 2010 census-recorded renewable power sources. The university with the lowest emissions used no renewable electricity sources but was far more compact and had lower emissions than higher education institutions that have invested in renewable electricity. The highest-emitting university on record, Caltech, at more than 30 metric tons $CO_2$ per student, has one of the largest rooftop solar arrays in higher education. The solar array could not make up for the extensive floor space that provides Caltech students with the roomiest campus in America. Actually, I found that solar energy came up most often in the Amish community. I often found one or two solar panels on a horse barn roof, a set-up that doesn't generate much power, but most Amish use so little energy that these panels will go a long way.

My search for low-emissions culture really brought home to me the undeveloped state of individual and community knowledge about greenhouse gas emissions. Certainly, I could not expect to find who is succeeding at achieving a low carbon footprint by asking anyone. I tried it anyway, and talked to many college students majoring in environmental studies, professionals who make their living raising awareness about climate change, religious leaders who express a concern about the problem—and random people in coffee shops. Are your emissions much higher than the American average, about the same, less, or do you know? Has anyone ever asked you; have you asked yourself? The answer is almost always no. Despite the ease with which we can know ourselves, our own genes, our online social impact, and other data, the one number that will affect our grandchildren or our friend's grandchildren is the statistic almost no one knows, and that is our impact on the atmosphere.

Maybe so few people know this number only because there is no market for it, for thinking about the whole life as opposed to the customer for the hybrid car, the rooftop solar investor, or the carbon offset purchaser. Neither has the environmental movement in general found a way to tie membership and loyalty to their particular cause with important facets of consumption such as home size and flying habits. Science education does not usually include instruction on calculating carbon footprints within the hour or two devoted to climate change at the high school level.[30] Some college students will encounter a footprint assignment in a class, but it is at exactly the time in their lives when they are not likely to have utility bills. The absence of "carbon capability," as psychologist Lorraine Whitmarsh puts it, typifies the situation in Europe as well, but much of Europe is emitting at a lower and less variable rate.[31]

It took me a while to get around to doing a greenhouse gas inventory for my own household. Over twenty-some years of working as a technical researcher in greenhouse gas emissions analysis, I was never asked to volunteer my own emissions inventory. When I finally crunched the numbers, I was surprised that my family's emissions were about six metric tons per person, which was higher than I expected. The problem appeared to be the gas and electricity used in our 160-unit condo building, which consumed about $200,000 in condo fees each year. I spent as much on lighting for shared hallways and storage areas as I spent on electricity for everything inside our own unit. Our natural gas bills were lower than they would be if all my neighbors were living in single-family houses, but the building could have saved a bundle there too. The building was consuming energy at a level that surpassed an independent country in the south Pacific called Niue, an island located on a forested atoll where dolphins swim close to the shore and where the native vanilla orchid grows an especially succulent bean. The islanders worry a great deal about sea level rise and cyclones—the one that hit a decade ago wiped out more than a year of GDP. My condo building has about 250 residents compared to Niue's 1,400 and sits several hundred feet above sea level in Washington DC. I wrote to Niue's environment minister promising that I would try to reduce our building's emissions. I did not hear back but over the next year had some success in cutting emissions in my condo building.

These efforts helped bring my household emissions down to five tons per person, and then I wanted to find some of the other low-emitting households. I began working with several middle school science teachers in Washington DC to teach students how they can use their household data to calculate a greenhouse gas emissions inventory. With help from the students' parents, the project reached several hundred people. Although most of the families involved were of middle or higher income, about half lived in apartments and most drove far less than the American average. Many of the participants have emissions of five metric tons of $CO_2$ or less. The project thankfully disabused me of any notion of my family's singularity in carbon emissions.

The rudiments of an inventory are simple and include items like your gas and electric bills, odometer readings, frequent flyer statements, and recollections of beef consumption, but they can enable questions that are far more interesting. What value do these activities and products have in the first place? For instance, would I get more benefit from half a dozen trips to the beach over the next few years or from a one-off a trip to Alaska? Will the Alaska trip be less appealing if I acknowledge that my grandchildren may think less of me if I go? What is the real advantage of a three-thousand-square-foot home compared to a home half the size? And there remain the more traditional challenges of making our homes more efficient and less wasteful of energy and resources. These explorations may be the only way that the United States will make significant cuts in greenhouse gas emissions in an age when we can extract fossil fuels cheaply from the ground. Civic engagement and individual action are necessary for significant changes to occur, but are part of the post-Kyoto world, where actions are decentralized—more like silver buckshot, in the words of Gwyn Prins and Steve Rayner, than the silver bullet of a broad international treaty.[32] This book is also multi-layered in its approach. With our lowest-emitting communities as a starting point, the vehicle for change begins with autonomous individuals, but extends to local and state rule-making and federal policies.

In the United States, we have the example of the Amish, who have taken up technology and energy use selectively and only after reflection and deliberation. They have weighed the pros and cons of every machine, device and energy source with the question of whether it adds or detracts from family and community life. They found more negatives than positives regarding most of our technology and fuels, and over the years, going district-by-district, they prohibited much of it. Today their greenhouse gas emissions are as low as one-quarter that of the wider society. In the absence of the strong community goals of the inspiring Amish subculture, better self-understanding of household greenhouse gas emissions among mainstream Americans might propel more of this type of decision-making.

# Consumption Denial

A notion of a target could potentially offer a correction to some of the part-whole weaknesses of current environmentalist culture. Environmentalist aims of improving walkability, undertaking "smart" growth, and living in compact housing are all worthy and effective projects in themselves. But if participants are satisfied with the outside appearance of sustainability without the broader self-knowledge of their emissions, these projects can put a patina on a lifestyle that is anything but sustainable. One of the keys is a balance between residential emissions and transportation emissions. While reducing energy use in these two sectors can be complimentary—multi-unit housing making transit and walkability more viable—they sometimes are not.

For instance good transit, a new bike sharing program, and support for small independent stores have made several neighborhoods north of Chicago's Loop highly walkable, and yet while many residents are freeing themselves from dependence on the automobile, many of these same people are increasing their overall greenhouse gas emissions because they are enlarging their living space. In recent years these neighborhoods, including Lincoln Park, Lincoln Square, North Center and Andersonville, have seen a great many two-flat apartment buildings converted into single family housing.[33] In the Lincoln Park neighborhood, which is the closest to downtown and the most walkable of them all, even four-unit apartment buildings have been converted to single-family homes, and in many instances, two or more single-family lots have been cleared and mansions built on the site.[34] Although Lincoln Park is an historic neighborhood bordering one of Chicago's most important green spaces, these de-conversions have proceeded with little resistance from historic preservation, environmental and zoning commissions. The elephant in the room when it comes to American greenhouse gas emissions still enjoys a degree of undeserved invisibility.

A different but related trend is the proliferation of large-lot solar, or suburban houses with rooftop photovoltaic. The addition of solar panels may be commendable, but sometimes they are added only after a house expansion. The owners are set on bumping out their living room or popping out their upstairs, and while they are at it, they notice that the local and federal subsidies for solar power have become attractive. These homes may even get added to the town's sustainability house walk, but at the end of the day, the inhabitants are likely consuming more energy than their unheralded neighbors in the smaller home next door. The solar-project owners, like the mansion dwellers in the walkable, transit-friendly neighborhoods, tend to be subjected to little peer pressure about their environmentally unfriendly choices. Lacking the data on their own greenhouse gas emissions, they may even be oblivious to the impact.

Then there is the scenario in which the household energy use is very low, but the transportation emissions are extremely high. In this instance, a person or family lives in a small house or medium-sized apartment, uses appliances judiciously, and has impressively low energy bills. All looks great—the adults take transit to work, the children walk to school, and everyone likes to eat beans. I found many such families in the course of my survey work in Washington DC. But there was a big catch: the benefits of low-driving rates often paled in the face of extraordinary airplane travel. Although the driving rate was about half the national average, the flying rate was almost double the American average.[35] Many of the families did not fly at all, but the ones who did drove up the total, and a surprising number of these trips were students' educational and environmental service trips. Taking the cake was a family that recorded the highest number of air miles, many of those long-haul trips undertaken with the purpose of raising awareness of the dangers of a changing climate!

These tales of big-lot houses in an urban walker's paradise, solar atop suburban McMansions, and binge flying among city condo dwellers were a reminder of the contradictions between some of our current environmental planning and incentives, and the hard truths revealed by greenhouse-gas emissions inventories. For the most part, modern environmentalism had little presence in the low emissions communities that I discovered. Some of the environmentalists showed up at the high-emissions tail of the study because large houses are still tolerated among mainstream environmentalists, as is frequent flying.

The inhabitants of the rural, urban, and suburban locations that comprise this book had low emissions not because they identified as environmentalists, but because they were deeply engaged in some aspect of life in these communities. For instance, the Amish forswear flying not because they view it as environmentally harmful or too modern. They have adopted some appliances and gadgets, including gas-powered refrigerators, compressed air powered washing machines, fit-bit type sensors that monitor their vitals, and other things.[36] They abstain because they believe flying makes it too easy to spend time away from the family and community, and also too easy to develop an attitude of being above it all. Many of the urban families in Washington DC had embraced city living, a short commute, foreign language immersion education, urban parks and diverse neighbors in exchange for losing a private backyard. Most of the people living in Berwyn had private backyards, but less floor space than the average American house. Like the DC families, they were drawn to the historical look and the convenience of living not far from the city's main businesses districts. College students at the greenest university in the country had embraced the social life of the city at large while giving up on the idea of the roomy lounge and rec venues common in today's campuses.

The discipline of an individual target could help clarify the relationship between personal emissions and leadership on climate. While a lengthening list of celebrities, politicians, and authors are willing to make impassioned speeches calling for action on climate change, it is often difficult to understand whom these speeches are for apart from the minority of Americans who say they doubt the scientific basis of climate change. They certainly do elicit a great many tart comments pointing out contradictions between the message and the messenger's life. Familiar examples are the Hollywood star flying to the next climate rally in a private jet, or the environmental author living in a ten thousand–plus square-foot mansion in suburban Maryland. These folks are usually calling attention to at least one good thing they are doing, but they are drawing plenty of attention to the other stuff.

In a rueful opinion piece in the *New York Times*, author and passionate climate activist Bill McKibben, whose lifestyle may be reasonably modest, wrote, "My days in public have often involved cameramen walking backward and videotaping my every move. It's mostly when I travel.... To be watched so much is a kind of never-ending nightmare."[37] Unfortunately, few Americans prominent in climate careers are doing a persuasive job of showing that they can walk the walk. Decrying this problem, George Marshall points out, "In other areas, inconsistent behavior by decision makers is utterly relevant; the racial prejudice of judges, the tax evasion by politicians ... because we know intuitively that an internal conflict may undermine their judgment." Noting that many climate activists are binge flyers, Marshall asks, "Is it any surprise, given these internal conflicts, that there is so little mention of flying among the list of actions promoted by environmental groups and the U.S. Environmental Protection Agency?"[38]

The problem is both the lifestyle, including excessive flying, but also an incomplete narrative about what a sustainable lifestyle really looks like. A correction entails telling the fuller story, not just the one particular thing that someone is taking on. A target is also particular, but if someone debates its practicality related to their own life, they already have begun a process of self-education. To say that four or five or six tons is too hard or too easy would involve some incremental steps of learning of one's own greenhouse gas emissions baseline and what it would take to change. Taking on a target such as five metric tons or less can potentially change the dynamic of peer pressure and group association. Currently, personal actions to reduce consumption are so varied—if they exist at all—that it can be hard to feel a sense of camaraderie with others trying to limit their consumption. However, understanding that others are taking on a similar overall goal can potentially avoid divisions that come up when others' efforts seem quite different from one's own. An overall goal could potentially help a vegan automobile hobbyist to see they have something in common with a carless carnivore.

E. O. Wilson reminds us that as a species we evolved to live in this particular atmosphere, "We are confined to a razor-thin biosphere within which a thousand unimaginable hells are possible but only one paradise."[39] How successful we are as a species is tied ultimately to how well we live within these constraints, maintaining the admixture of atmospheric gases that sustain us. How distant is this notion from the fabric of social prestige, fame and wealth, the ascent of man! But the concept can help steer us toward a measure of personal success that is multivalent in its potential for self-identity.

In my search for the five-ton life, I found my most satisfying example of a climate leader not in the present, but in the first years of the nation. In contrast to his eighteenth-century peers, George Washington was a sequesterer of carbon and a mitigator of methane, but in this he led almost entirely by deeds rather than words. His field-cropping experiments replenished soil carbon, and his ornamental plantings lent prestige to native, fast-growing tree species. He sought also to elevate the prestige of the protein sources that do not release methane, not because he knew about the greenhouse effect, but because these animals used less precious grain, as did the mule, the draft animal that replaced more methane-intensive oxen and horses. In his farm books George Washington noted the input and output of many of his experiments in a process that has much in common with today's greenhouse gas calculators. While today we wonder whether peer pressure can affect a downward pressure on greenhouse gas emissions, some of George Washington's material and environmental legacy at Mount Vernon had an influence that lasted years, others lasted decades.

The low-carbon culture I describe in this book is a specifically American outcome, not derived directly from any other tradition. The Anabaptists who became Amish came to America seeking religious tolerance and were able to stay and maintain such a different way of life because of America's more informal social tolerance. Chicago's western suburbs with their compact housing, which makes for lower emissions than the city itself, can claim architectural forms that are uniquely American. Prairie School architecture rejected European historicism, and the bungalow was an American invention that reflected an egalitarian notion of housing opportunities. In American cities, many residents can find fulfillment without private land because they offer something not found in most world cities: a high level of preserved nature and biological diversity, thanks to the instincts of our nineteenth-century landscape architects and the commitment of the residents and leaders that followed.

George Washington's beautiful estate, Mount Vernon, is the most visited house in America, but then a strand of beauty runs through all of these examples of low carbon culture. Hordes of tourists visit Amish settlements each year, drawn by the picturesque buggy riding, rural folk amidst a setting of traditional farmland and verdant lawns and gardens. The Midwestern town hosts popular bungalow tours, and the cool apartment culture of Washington DC opens its homes to online house tours. Outside, city, and regional parks are looking better and meeting the deeper needs of urban residents. City transportation departments such as DC's are helping to make car alternatives more appealing in a feedback loop on carbon that makes apartment and small house living—the crux of the matter—more attractive.

## CHAPTER ONE

# Founding Mitigator

## George Washington

George Washington might seem to be an irrelevant subject for a book about reducing contemporary greenhouse gas emissions. He lived some years before the greenhouse effect theory was proposed and about two centuries before it became a topic of presidential discourse. Washington lived in an era when many Americans viewed the new country's resources as infinite, and Washington and his wife took no small part in enjoying the abundance that a man of his stature could afford. Today, more people visit Mount Vernon than any other house in America, a fact that also held true in George Washington's own lifetime.[1] From a contemporary perspective the hosting habits of George and Martha Washington can be a puzzle, an unusual degree of hospitality even for late eighteenth-century America. Was there something at Mount Vernon that George Washington wanted his guests to see? Something relevant for our own time?

In early 2014, Mount Vernon unveiled a new rendering of the mansion's largest room. In Washington's retirement years, what he called "the New Room" served as a reception area and art gallery. It was here that Washington, a confident and correct host, would greet his guests wearing the navy blue greatcoat with buff facings that he wore as general of the Continental Army.[2] The landscape paintings mirror the dark blues and sandy shades of the general's uniform. Below, the wainscoting is of a "buff inclining to white" per Washington's own description. The largest and most prominent works of art on the walls are six landscape paintings showing scenes of the Hudson, Potomac, and Shenandoah Rivers.[3] One of them recalls George Washington's first trip west when as a sixteen-year-old surveyor for Lord Fairfax he gave rare expression to his spontaneous enjoyment of the landscape: "Higher up the [Shenandoah] River we went through most beautiful groves of Sugar Trees & Spent the best part of the Day in admiring the Trees & richness of the Land."[4]

Landscapes were not a subject seen in many of the great Virginia houses.[5] In Europe and the Americas landscape paintings had a low place until the nineteenth century, and few serious renderings of American landscape were in existence. This is the first room that visitors saw when they arrived at Mount Vernon, and if they saw nothing else of the house they saw this spectacular room with the landscape paintings. A visitor to Mount Vernon in the 1790s arriving by horseback or carriage might also be privileged to see a mule, the curious long-eared draft animal that was stronger than a horse and ate less. The animal that George Washington introduced to the New World also happened to emit methane at half the rate of its equine cousin. Later, at dinnertime, the visitors would usually sit down to an elaborate meal of many courses, but one that was less methane intensive than the beefy meal typical to the Chesapeake region. George Washington diversified his protein sources, just as he had diversified his crops. In cold weather the room would be mildly heated using wood instead of the coal that many Virginia and Maryland elites preferred at that time. These differences alone would have dropped Mount Vernon's carbon footprint far below most of his peers and elite predecessors.

In the fields of Mount Vernon, Washington undertook soil enhancement experiments that were unprecedented in the New World—experiments designed to improve the fertility of the soil, and which incidentally stored more carbon. Above ground, Mount Vernon's walkways showcased some of America's fastest-growing tree species, trees that are now viewed as some of the most effective at carbon sequestration.[6] His hedgerows and live fences sought to replace the practice of clearing hardwoods for fencing. Although in the late eighteenth century the presence of western lands conveyed a notion of limitless resources in America, George Washington viewed the nation's resources as rare and precious, deserving of study and conservation. In his day fuel wood and coal were not very expensive relative to the price of other household goods, just as today energy costs make up a small share of American's expenditures. His discipline in conserving that which seemed abundant, today has a pointed message when it is all too easy to forget how our household energy consumption affects the atmosphere. Through Mount Vernon and a life whose motto was "Deeds, Not Words," George Washington left a legacy of actions and activities that had a tangible bearing on greenhouse gas emissions in his own time and afterwards.

A visit to the Mount Vernon mansion today does not begin at the mansion itself but at a small house next door where the servants of Washington's guests were provided room and board. Today, the building is used to orient visitors to the idea that the Mount Vernon mansion is very large despite its appearance, and despite the fact that many visitors own houses that are larger than the one that they are now touring. The current president's Florida residence happens to be more than ten times larger. The Mount Vernon guides inform us that even the small room we are standing in was larger than the average Virginia house, and the room we are about to enter in the mansion was many times larger. Mount Vernon was impressively large for its time, and we should be awed that Washington built such a house totaling about seven thousand square feet, including kitchen and guesthouse. Or should we? More likely Washington was trying to impress not with the size of his house, but with its vantage point on a hill overlooking the Potomac River, the verdant gardens, and the undulating, serpentine path through newly planted native trees.

The point may be rather that Mount Vernon was impressively small for its time, an era when, like most eras, house size corresponded with social status and wealth. In England in the eighteenth century new buildings were known for their scale, which was much larger than in previous eras. Blenheim Palace, Castle Howard, and others that belonged to aristocratic families but not royalty, were all over one hundred thousand square feet. Most of the English administrators who returned to England in 1776 and who had held positions of governor or lesser stations in the colonies were now returning to houses larger than Mount Vernon.

In the New World, George Washington had no peer. In Europe, Washington's contemporary George III had at his disposal Windsor Castle (484,000 square feet), Buckingham House, Saint James, Hampton Court, and Frogmore House. George III's smallest residence, Frogmore House, with its eighteen bedrooms and formal rooms, still dwarfed Mount Vernon. The largest, Windsor Castle, was much smaller than the royal residences of France and Spain. The Palace de Madrid encompassed some 1.4 million square feet. The English king expanded Buckingham House into a Palace that became one hundred times larger than Mount Vernon. It was inconceivable for a European head of state to live without multiple residences, vacation houses, and vast kitchens that could feed hundreds of guests at a sitting. George Washington did not aspire to a palace or even an aristocratic house in the European tradition. When he returned to Mount Vernon after the Revolutionary War, he put his attention to managing the estate's fields, landscape, and enterprises, not to house expansion or addition. During his retirement years after the presidency he put renewed focus on his agricultural endeavors and did not seek to enlarge his house despite his many visitors. While Thomas Jefferson responded to the crowds that flocked to Monticello by building Poplar Forest, his retreat in the Blue Ridge Mountains, Washington did not do likewise. Washington built a house that was about the size of the "great" Virginia houses, such as Berkeley Plantation, Stratford Hall, and Carlisle House. It was as though Washington built a house as large as was expected of his station, but not an inch larger.

## Common Fuel

When visitors to Mount Vernon step into the mansion's New Room, the sight of its high ceilings and spectacular furnishings draws the eye, so it is understandable if most visitors do not notice a cast steel and iron grate embedded in the fireplace. Beginning in 1797, the fireplace could use coal, which it burned with unknown frequency, and was the only site in the mansion outfitted for coal.[7] The rest of the mansion's twenty-two fireplaces were set up to take wood, which was Washington's fuel of choice.[8] Some visitors might be surprised that Mount Vernon would have used coal already in the late eighteenth century. But in Virginia, some of the elite of Washington's circle were choosing to heat all of their rooms with coal.

By the late 1700s, many Richmond and Williamsburg families were burning coal in their houses using fuel mined in Virginia as well as from the British Isles. More than ten thousand bushels were shipped from the James River and from England annually.[9] The Chesterfield County, Virginia coal pits near Richmond had been worked already since the early 1700s, and the coal was of similar quality to that mined in England and Scotland.[10] By the 1770s, coal fields were actively mined in Newcastle and Henrico counties, Virginia, in addition to the coal from Chesterfield. The last British governor of Virginia, Lord Dunmore, was also importing coal from his own holdings in Scotland and selling it to his Williamsburg neighbors.[11]

A preference for coal over wood knew no partisan boundaries and was used in Williamsburg by British loyalists and colonial rebels alike. In the American colonies, the British administrators often used imported coal and house inventories show that stoves and fireplaces were often adapted for coal use. The governor of Maryland, Robert Eden, had his Annapolis house outfitted for coal, and the Governor's Palace in Williamsburg contained some fourteen stoves and grates fitted for holding coal. Williamsburg merchants sold coal in their stores, and some Williamsburg residents such as George Wythe, who had hosted George Washington in his home in preparation for the battle of Yorktown, had coal shipped directly to his household and used it for heating.[12] Coal use extended to the middle class; Williamsburg printer and journalist William Rind, whose Virginia Gazette was critical of British rule, used coal for his family's home heating.

Coal was relatively cheap in the mid-Atlantic in the late eighteenth century. One hundred bushels of coal, totaling eight thousand pounds in weight, was worth as much as five hogsheads of "syder." Wealthy households typically spent much more on liquor than on coal or charcoal.[13] Even blacksmiths, who were the most invested in coal during that era, were spending relatively little on coal, which made up at most 8 percent of their household assets.[14] In the Williamsburg stores, coal typically made up about 5 percent of the value of their goods.

George Washington was, of course, aware he could buy coal mined locally. In a trip to the Ohio River Valley in 1770, Washington became acquainted with a coal site whose contents he knew to be superior to the bituminous coal of Virginia, and wrote of his visit that he "went to see a coal mine. . . . The coal seemed to be the very best kind."[15] But although he understood the capabilities of coal, he took little interest in coal for household use despite the fact he emulated many other aspects of British material culture. For the most part he confined his usage to the trade of blacksmithing on his estate.[16] The Continental Army used coal for a range of industries, but after the war Washington's interest in coal became tepid. Over the next twenty years, if he continued to rely on coal instead of charcoal, the orders no longer appear in the estate's accounts.[17] George Washington's long probate inventory issued after his death lacks any mention of coal stocks. The coal grate installed in the New Room in 1797 remained the sole fireplace in Mount Vernon adapted for burning coal.[18]

In England the scarcity of wood generally made coal a necessity for many households. It was thought to be more convenient than wood for chasing out the drafts of the castles and palaces, and for the work of ironmongers and other occupations that needed fire. Coal was excavated from underground mines in Scotland, often using bonded labor, and women and children often performed the dangerous work of digging and hauling coal. The hazard of explosions in the mines was a familiar one, and coal-bed methane was identified by the name "fire damp." Beyond the practical advantages of the fuel itself, the burning devices held a certain cachet. A very ornate, three-tiered model of a new coal-burning stove arrived in Williamsburg, Virginia around 1770 at the request of the governor, Lord Botetourt. The iron stoves, which the Virginia governor installed in his home and at the House of Burgess, were said by their inventor Abraham Buzaglo to "surpass in Utility, Beauty & goodness any thing hitherto invented in all Europe." They "cast an equal & agreeable heat to any part of the room, and are not attended by any stench."[19] However agreeable the heat from the stove, neither George Washington nor Thomas Jefferson purchased anything similar for their houses. Although George Washington took a keen interest in fashion when it came to English clothing and furniture, on the subject of natural resources and how to utilize them, he kept his own counsel.

By 1800 England's rate of burning coal resulted in about twenty-seven million metric tons of $CO_2$ annually, a much higher level than found anywhere in the world at that time. King George and his entourage were responsible for a large amount and Windsor Castle alone could use thousands of tons of coal in a year.[20] In per-capita terms, in 1800 the English emitted about 1.6 metric tons of carbon dioxide per person, surpassing the consumption level found in about eighty nations contemporaneous with our own time.[21] In the United States, coal was not commonly used in households until the 1830s, and the country's slowness to utilize coal resources was due in part to the example of the material culture of America's founding presidents. Using biomass instead of fossil fuels for heat and power has been a greenhouse gas mitigation policy in many parts of the world so long as harvested trees are not "old growth" and are replanted and allowed to soak up carbon over time. Although soot and the other solid components of smoke can contribute to global warming, the biomass is still preferable to fossil fuels in its net heating effects.[22]

In their choice of fuel, the other founders followed the example of Mount Vernon and relied on wood. Thomas Jefferson eventually used coal in the White House, but at Monticello, heating was done with wood, as it was at James Madison's Montpelier. The founders chose fuelwood because it was conveniently plentiful on their vast estates, or because they knew that it was well distributed throughout America compared to the few known coal deposits in the New World. Fuelwood could be harvested from the detritus of the land. Wood fuel fit into the worldview of resource stewardship and self-reliance, in contrast to the domain of coal, which was risky, exclusive, and left a black stain.

So considering the Washingtons' reliance on wood fuel through the winter months, I asked one of the museum guides where the wood was stored in Washington's day, because stacks of wood do not figure in the current presentation. The guide hesitated and said, "Good question. But wherever it was, there must have been a lot of it. . . . All those fireplaces!" The answer was, of course, a pretense to explain again that Mount Vernon was a very large house that used considerable resources. But the absence of wood stacks reminds us that today we treat energy as though it is invisible and cheap, in contrast to Mount Vernon's original owner, who managed his fuel and other resources judiciously as though they were valuable and dear.

In other aspects of Washington's material life, the exterior of his house, he chose a common building material—wood—instead of the more prestigious alternatives of brick and stone. Mount Vernon's walls are made from "rusticated" wood: that is, wood cut, painted, and coated with sand to give the appearance of a stone surface. George Washington made a decision to rusticate his home already in 1758 when he prepared the house for his new bride. The surface is very different from the elite houses of Virginia and the mid-Atlantic, which were usually made with brick.[23] Washington's choice of building material puzzles some—he could have afforded stately brick, and rustication was not a traditional style. But Washington's choice of surface can be seen in the context of the choices he developed later in life. He was willing to buck the trend and avoid exclusive materials in his house exterior just as he had avoided coal inside the house. Decades later, when rusticated wood seemed all the more unusual, he continued to rusticate, and Thomas Jefferson constructed some rusticated walls at Monticello.

In the eighteenth century and earlier, heating a room with fire was an uncomfortable proposition–"scorched in front, frozen behind." In the last years of the eighteenth century, fireplaces in Britain and Europe were refashioned to heat rooms more effectively. The new fireplace and chimney design, called the Rumford Fireplace, entailed a shallow, angled base that helped the heat from the fuel to penetrate the room. At the same time, the chimney was made to be more narrow and rounder to improve the escape of smoke. In the words of its inventor, Count Rumford, the design would "remove those local hindrances which forcibly prevent the smoke from following its natural tendency to go up the chimney."[24]

Contemporary analysis confirms that if the inventor's specifications are followed precisely, the Rumford Fireplace is highly efficient. In fact, the fireplace burns wood as cleanly as EPA-certified wood stoves, and building codes have recently been modified to allow for their construction.[25] James Madison had his fireplaces built according to the Rumford design and was able to make do with less than a dozen fireplaces in the house. Mount Vernon fireplaces have the large, square shape that was the traditional design for fireplaces in the earlier period. Whether Mount Vernon fireplaces were not changed because of timing—Rumford's invention predates Washington's death by only a few years—or for other reasons is hard to say.

Count Rumford had been born Benjamin Thompson in Needham, Massachusetts. A British loyalist, he had fled the colonies in 1776 and returned as a senior commissioned officer in the British army to fight against the continental army—all facts that would not have endeared him to Washington. But it is also true that Washington completed most of his improvements of the interior of Mount Vernon in the years before the Rumford design was published, and he may not have wanted to make new structural changes at that time, although his library holdings confirm that he had Rumford's essays describing fireplace design at his disposal.[26] In 1787 George Washington had ordered and installed four cast iron fireplace backs that did improve the efficiency of the chimneys.[27]

In any event, George and Martha Washington were not in the habit of overheating their house. A household manager would have the responsibility for lighting fires in only certain rooms that were occupied at specific times of the day for studying, sewing, dining and socializing. The founders' houses were often chilly and uncomfortable by today's standards and habits of dress. Jimmy Carter's "fireside chat," for which he sat in a cardigan and advised the American public to turn down the thermostat, has its parallel in a scene two hundred years earlier when George Washington would work at his desk in the early morning hours dressed in a woolen coat, sometimes in bone chilling conditions, and make a note of the indoor temperature for posterity. For instance, on the morning of December 7, 1785, Washington's weather diary records the temperature in his study at 52° F, fully sixteen degrees colder than the recommended minimum office temperature as suggested by US health and safety guidance.[28]

## Diversified Protein

A bucolic nineteenth-century painting by Thomas Prichard Rossiter commemorates the Marquis of Lafayette's visit to General Washington in his new repose at Mount Vernon, but it is a barely discernable figure in the background that hints at Washington's attitude toward animal husbandry. In the shadow of the trees, a slave shoos cattle off the manicured lawn. This detail is remarkably prescient of the

Fig. 3. *Washington and Lafayette at Mount Vernon, 1784*, Rossiter, Thomas Prichard and Louis Rémi Mignot, ca. 1859. Metropolitan Museum of Art, distributed under a CC-PD-Mark license, Wikimedia Commons.

American leader who raised cattle but kept them at a distance on his estate, ate beef but took pains to promote pig to the wider world. Two hundred years later cattle production is the number one source of methane emissions in the United States, and many Americans are reducing their beef intake. But George Washington left clues in his letters, outbuildings and trash heap that cattle husbandry took second fiddle to his interests in crops and trees, and that beef did not take pride of place at his table.

At Mount Vernon today visitors to the tidy outbuildings near the mansion can gaze into the smoky gloom of a replica of an eighteenth century smokehouse. The exhibit bears a quote from George Washington that says, "The Virginia Ladies value themselves on the goodness of their bacon." One might wonder about the self-esteem of eighteenth century women if this was the case, but the remark appeared in a letter George Washington wrote to the Marquis of Lafayette following up on a shipment of produce he had sent to the Lafayette family. Washington was anxious to find out if the goods had arrived safely. The shipment might have contained items such as the esteemed peach brandy from Mount Vernon's orchards, but it did not because in the end Washington chose to send only hams. "I do not know that they are better, or so good as you make in France, but as they are of our own manufacture . . . and we recollect that it is a dish of which you are fond."[29] Among the elite of Europe and America, pig was regarded as "poverty food," but Lafayette sent an effusively grateful response. "This present Has Been Most Agreable [*sic*] in the family, and it is difficult to Express How welcomed is a Mount Vernon produce at such a distance."[30]

Slaughter records and correspondence point to the preponderance of pig in the Mount Vernon diet. In autumn, after the swine were rounded up from the woods, most of the slaughter—fifteen thousand pounds of meat—was reserved for the Washingtons' table. In addition to pig meat, the Washingtons ate much fish and some wild animals, and birds and turtles as well as beef and mutton. The meals themselves are something of a mystery, because neither George nor Martha Washington kept records of their menus. However, Mount Vernon staff believes that he ate cornmeal "hoecakes" for breakfast, and especially enjoyed fish. Washington shipped in from London fine wines, coffee, chocolate, spices, tropical fruits and many other luxurious food goods, and he purchased vegetables and poultry from their enslaved workers.[31]

Mount Vernon's spectacular flowers drew guests to the gardens and once there, they would see a large selection of vegetables. Martha Washington oversaw this part of the estate: "Impress it on the gardener to have everything in his garden that will be ne[ce]ssary in the House keeping way—as vegetable is the best part of our living in the country."[32] The Washingtons' interest in vegetable gardening stands out from a colonial culture in which vegetables apparently played a small part in the diet. In the late eighteenth century, like the earlier era, most people relied on grains and meat, and ate vegetables sparingly. Cauliflower and artichokes were viewed as good additions for refined households, and lettuce was consumed across different income levels, but available evidence suggests that the growing and marketing of vegetables was a minor part of food provisioning.[33]

Thomas Jefferson had his own perspective on food culture, and his taste for French cuisine is well known, but at Monticello cattle were also given a marginal place on the estate. Outbuildings for ruminant animals, including the cows themselves, were placed further afield, and the household apparently ate little or no beef for long stretches of time. For instance, a visitor to Monticello in 1796 observed that "Beef cannot be had but in winter."[34] Jefferson's farm book confirms that over several years many hogs, but no beef cattle (beeves) were slaughtered for the Monticello table.[35] Although none of the founding fathers were vegetarians, they did much to promote vegetables and on this subject Jefferson has the last and best word: "I have lived temperately, eating little animal food, and that not as an aliment, so much as a condiment for the vegetables, which constitute my principal diet."

In some parts of eighteenth-century Europe the upper crust regularly dined on pig meat, but in England and the American colonies among those with the means to buy it the choice was beef. In England some of the grandest houses planned their grazing pastures so they could see the cattle and the sheep from the most important rooms of the manor. Beef figured prominently in the diet, and the regard for beef was so deeply ingrained in British culture that in the eighteenth century they were in the habit of singing its praises at the start and close of theater performances and in the dining hall of the Royal Navy:

> When Mighty Roast Beef was the Englishman's Food,
> It ennobled our veins and enriched our Blood
> Our soldiers were Brave and our Courtiers were Good
> Oh! The Roast Beef of Old England
> And Old English Roast Beef!
> —*The Roast Beef of Old England*, Richard Leveridge, 1735

America in the eighteenth century may not have shared the same anthem, but it had similar tastes. Although American colonists preferred to eat beef, cattle in the New World were not very productive meat producers. Most of the stock descended from the animals brought to the Americas in the early seventeenth century, before the eighteenth century breed improvements in European cattle. Christopher Columbus had brought cattle to the New World already in 1494 with the aim of relieving the Iberian Peninsula grazing lands, which were proving inadequate to fulfill the Spanish taste for beef. By the eighteenth century English grazing lands were also overstretched, and beef was increasingly sourced from cattle pastured in Ireland and Scotland.[36]

In the Chesapeake region as well, demand outstripped supply and beef became expensive by the late eighteenth century. In Washington's time even the landed and merchant classes were spending much of their household budget on meat. In the Chesapeake region meat took up about one third of the landowners' total budget and the greatest portion was for beef.[37] Already by the 1750s, as local plantation supplies were depleted, residents of Williamsburg and Yorktown were buying beef that was sourced from cattle raised as much as two hundred miles to the west.[38] In the face of population growth, Virginians were forced to slaughter immature animals by the late eighteenth century. Americans would have benefited from a more varied protein diet, but persisted in eating large amounts of beef.

Compared to cattle, pigs eat only half as much to achieve the same weight gain, and this difference would not have been lost on the First Farmer. Washington's diaries show that he knew a great deal about food intake and animal weight gain. He took note of the effect on the animals eating different fodder crops that he raised on his own land. He also knew the difference in productivity between a penned pig and a penned cow and that a higher proportion of the pig is edible, including useable entrails. The woodlands of the Eastern Seaboard that comprised America's first states were well suited to raising pigs and less suited for cattle, which was a focus of the western lands controlled by Spain. Washington always kept a large number of pigs roaming freely on his farms, although he became obsessed with the idea of keeping them out of his gardens using "living fences."

For many years, he experimented with using native trees and shrubs in a new way—to recreate the hedgerows that penned the cattle and separated the fields in England. The hedgerows of the English countryside tend to be centuries old, but Washington wanted to secure his gardens in a matter of years. It was a dream of a gardener and of a conservationist because wood suitable for building fences, which usually came from chestnut trees, was increasingly hard to find. As he explained in a letter to a British agronomist, "I am not surprised that our mode of fencing should be disgusting to a European eye; happy would it have been for us, if it had appeared so in our own eyes; for our sort of fencing is more expensive or wasteful of timber."[39] In the New World colonial fences used wood at an unprecedented rate, particularly the "worm fence" in which wood is stacked in a self-supporting zigzag angle. This type of fence used about five thousand rails and more than an acre of cultivable land for each mile of fence.[40] "The scarcity of Timber in the Neck for fences & the distance it is to draw at other places, are evils I have long foreseen ... impressed the necessity of raising live hedges upon you," Washington put it in an urgent letter to his farm manager.[41] Washington tried different combinations of plants and although he did not have the results he hoped for, after years of trials with different shrubs and trees he had achieved a live barrier to keep out cattle.

Washington's cattle herd, which was sizable, suffered from the genetic deficiencies of North American cattle that were descended from smaller, less productive animals than those developed through breed improvements in eighteenth-century Europe. George Washington made an effort to use bulls that derived from more recent English stock, but accounts suggest that his beef cattle and his milk cows were unproductive. "It is almost beyond belief, that from 101

Cows ... I am obliged to buy butter for the use of my family," he wrote to his farm manager.[42] Another ruminant, the "white cattle," or sheep, were present at Mount Vernon but had their problems too. Although Washington's flock of sheep numbered at least six hundred at one point, the animals were plagued by various diseases, especially foot rot, and the mortality of the sheep was apparently high. [43]

George Washington had enough cows to keep a dairy running, at least intermittently, but did he want to? His attention to crops and soil management was meticulous and innovative, but in comparison he took little interest in the details of animal husbandry. His livestock were consumers of his varied stock feed experiments and fertilizers of his fields but had little stature otherwise. His cattle herd was large—peaking at 300–350 animals—but not in relation to his eight thousand acres of fields and cropland, which could have fed a much larger stock. One of his last letters to his farm manager, which he wrote during a tour of his farms in late 1799, notes the poor condition of his cattle on Dogue Run Farm. He inquired whether the cattle on his other farms need more attention, asking the question because he had not taken the time to inspect them himself.[44]

The décor in the New Room at Mount Vernon hints at the difference between Washington's priorities, with crops being heavily favored. The frieze on the marble mantelpiece, a gift from English merchant Samuel Vaughan, depicts scenes of nature and farming, including plowing and tending to flocks. However, for the ceiling Washington chose to omit any depiction of animals. Here the raised plaster outlines the organic contours of arabesque vine scrolls, and further impressions reveal neither fleece nor sheep as in the mantel, but crossed scythes, a pick and shovel, and a sheaf of wheat, motifs from fields rather than flocks. Perhaps their absence reflects Washington's preference to omit cattle and dairies from symbolic display on the grounds of his estate. His sentiment about the mantel with its livestock imagery, "too elegant & costly by far I fear for my own room & republican stile of living" shows a distancing from the object, just as in his farming practices and diet he showed no special regard for cattle culture.[45]

In eighteenth-century Virginia plantation owners typically paid their overseers with enormous rations of beef, but George Washington's diaries confirmed that payday at Mount Vernon was mainly about pig meat. His overseers could look forward to receiving about 400–600 pounds of pork annually and only 100–200 pounds of beef, a reverse of the beef-to-pig ratio found in the rest of the region.[46] Preserved bones from trash pits in the Chesapeake region suggest that most of the meat consumed by free households was beef. Meat from cattle made up at least half the diet, and only about one quarter derived from swine.[47] The beef-heavy diet was followed by the gentry, free laborers, and professional and artisanal classes alike, and the reliance on beef grew heavier as the eighteenth century progressed.

Analysis of the trash pit at Mount Vernon affirms that the Washingtons used more pig meat and less beef than was typical. Although the post-1775 trash pit has not been located, archaeologists have concluded that over the period 1760–1775, less beef was being used at Mount Vernon over time, a reversal of the increasing reliance on beef found in most eighteenth-century trash pits in the region. The farm book entries and archaeological evidence suggest that the Mount Vernon household methane emissions would have been much lower, perhaps half as much as typical for an elite Virginia household.

Although Washington would not have known that cattle and sheep would become a problem for the earth's atmosphere because of the methane they emit, remarkably, Washington had specific knowledge about this invisible and odorless gas. He had set it aflame in an ad hoc experiment at the end of the Revolutionary War. One evening in 1783, George Washington, Thomas Paine and other inquiring minds had an argument over the origin of the "will-o-wisp" that is sometimes seen at the surface of wetlands. The argument was whether the gas originated in the swamp mud or instead from decaying wood. Paine's account was: "When the mud at the bottom was disturbed by the poles, the air bubbles rose fast, and I saw the fire take from General Washington's light. . . . This was demonstrative evidence that what was called setting the river on fire was setting on fire the inflammable air that arose out of the mud."[48] The casual observer would have observed a scene like a vision of Zeus setting fire to the water, but today, the story is a reminder of Washington's irrefutably scientific proclivities. How fitting that Washington's documented experiment, which might have been on any number of inquiries over matter, was related to none other than a greenhouse gas! When it came to ruminants, Washington understood that much of their energy was expended without contributing to his dinner table.

### Black Gold and Mules

Today a tour of the mansion at Mount Vernon ends in the large kitchen outbuilding with a spread of seasonal dishes on the worktable, such as asparagus in springtime. Across the path is the smokehouse, where as George Washington might have wished, realistic, synthetic hams hang from the rafters. That is the end of the story as far as outbuildings for food preparation. Nagging at the estate's archaeologists is a lingering mystery: Where was the dairy, a small clean structure for storing milk and churning butter? Such structures were ubiquitous in eighteenth-century Virginia and were usually found near the house.

Two hundred years later it is the privy, not the dairy that has pride of place among the ornamental gardens at Mount Vernon. Tidy white buildings with red roofs, the structures called "necessaries" proclaim the importance of a human being's relationship to the soil. For farmers wanting to restore flavor and humanity into animal husbandry, the key is to bring farming back to the relationship between animals as consumers and animals as fertilizers, using animal dung before it has a chance to pollute waterways. Innovative Virginia farmer and author Joel Salatin introduced these ideas to a wide audience through his book *Salad Bar Beef* and other writings Set against the diverse vegetable plots and fruit trees, the Mount Vernon outbuildings serve as a reminder of the essential cycles of nitrogen and carbon.

In the late eighteenth century, horses were taking on more of the draft work instead of oxen, but when George Washington heard about the attributes of mules—that they are stronger than horses and eat less—he was intent on raising them at Mount Vernon. In 1785 the King of Spain obliged, sending George Washington a donkey. Washington rented out "Royal Gift" as a "covering," or breeding, animal but the initial results were disappointing, as he wrote in a letter to the Marquis of Lafayette: "The Jack . . . cannot be less moved by female allurements." Eventually he learned to keep a female donkey nearby to inspire the animal in his "deliberative & majestic solemnity to the work of procreation."[49] The mule project received a boost in the next year when Lafayette, to the great delight of his old friend, wrote, "I shall look for them with much expectation & great satisfaction. . . . Words, my dear Marquis, will not do justice to my feelings, when I acknowledge the obligation I am under for the trouble & pains you have taken to procure & forward these valuable animals to me."[50]

Visitors to Mount Vernon were amused by the sight of the mules. With their large, floppy ears and stouter build, they offered a less-than-regal presence in front of the finely wrought carriages of the day. A person most interested in appearance would not have troubled themselves with mules, but that was not the character of George Washington. He was pleased by the animals, which he found to be calmer than horses and, as expected, consumed less grain. He used them both in the fields and to pull coaches. By 1799, mules outnumbered horses at Mount Vernon by about two to one.[51]

The mule emits about ten kilograms of methane per year, on average, compared with eighteen for horses.[52] In the next century, the mule became an important draft animal in the South and the population of mules in the country approached six million by 1925.[53] If we assume, conservatively, that mules replaced horses instead of oxen, the "royal gift" that began with mule breeding at Mount Vernon helped to achieve a greenhouse gas emissions savings in America of at least 1,000,000 metric tons of $CO_2$ equivalent per year by the early 20th century.[54]

A household circa 1800 that used mules instead of horses and oxen would have been among the lowest emitters in rural America. Domestic animals were the most important source of greenhouse gas emissions from American culture during the seventeenth and eighteenth centuries, so any changes in husbandry and diet would have affected the emissions of the times. Greenhouse gas emissions related to diet in the eighteenth century would have been similar to today's level of about two metric tons of $CO_2$ per person per year. Reducing beef intake and draft animal emissions would have dropped the entire household emissions by at least one half.[55]

If we compare George Washington's household to that of a more modest town dweller of the time, the Mount Vernon emissions also come out very well. Take for instance one William Rind of Williamsburg, Virginia. He was a well-regarded newspaperman, editor and printer of the *Virginia Gazette*, his paper being the mouthpiece in that region for sentiments critical of the British. At the time of his untimely death he had laid up fourteen bushels of coal for the approaching winter. If his family's diet was typical, he would have eaten about one pound of meat a day, including a half-pound of beef.[56] The diet, along with the coal, would have pushed the per-capita greenhouse gas emissions to over four metric tons. The direction that George Washington's emissions took considering diet, draft animals, and fuel, would have looked very different. Ignoring for the moment George Washington's accomplishments in improving carbon storage on his land through soil improvement, the advantage of George Washington's material choices can look like the following comparison that shows his household per person emissions were about one-third that of his contemporaries (see figure).

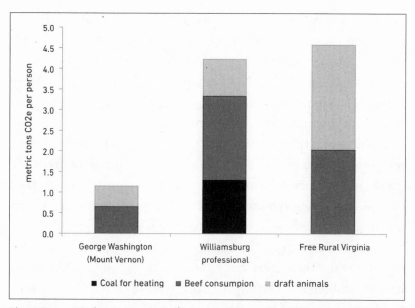

Fig. 4. George Washington's emissions compared with eighteenth-century plantation and urban households as assessed by the author. Draft animals assumes the following livestock: Mount Vernon mules, Williamsburg horses, rural Virginia oxen. Sources for other categories includes coal consumption: York County estate inventories, Colonial Williamsburg digital library; beef consumption: Mount Vernon ledgers and correspondence 1792–1799 and Walsh, Martin, and Bowen, *Early American Towns*.

## Carbon Above and Below

Tourists arriving at Mount Vernon today are steered toward the gate that approaches the serpentine path to the mansion. Several of the trees along the path date from George Washington's time, planted after his return to Mount Vernon in 1784 following the victory of the continental army. Washington used these precious months not to expand his house, but to improve his grounds and fields. Using tree and shrub species that he had personally selected, he directed the planting and replanting of seedlings that he monitored with such keen interest that he began to mark individual plants with notched sticks using his own code. From all accounts he was deeply, euphorically involved in this project.[57] "His simplicity is truly sublime, and he is as completely involved with all the details of his lands and house as if he had always lived here," wrote the Marquis of Lafayette to his wife upon the occasion of his visit to Mount Vernon at war's end.[58] Washington's prolonged absence from Mount Vernon and farming had been painful, and he had had to content himself with managing his farm from a distance, just as he had advised his troops to find comfort in planning their own home gardens.

Washington's keen interest in trees was unusual for that era. Even prosperous towns in the Chesapeake region had few trees in the late eighteenth century. A European traveler passing through Maryland in 1796 made the obvious point that, "They [Americans] have an unconquerable aversion to trees; not one is spared."[59] In Williamsburg, accounts from the late eighteenth century describe a dusty, treeless town: "There is no shade or shelter to walk under, unless you have an umbrella."[60] The few trees that were observed in town were the flowering catalpa trees along the Palace Green.[61]

Washington was always on the lookout for new tree species that he could introduce at Mount Vernon. He directed his slaves to plant more than one hundred trees near his house, most native in origin, and he hosted his largest parties in the springtime to show off his blossoming trees. For the serpentine, Washington chose fast-growing native species such as yellow poplar, American elms, and oaks, as well as ornamentals including redbud, dogwood, and sassafras. Surveying his progress in 1785, he wrote in his diary, "Finding the trees round the walks in my wilderness rather too thin I doubled them by putting (other Pine) trees between each."[62] Many of these trees thrived, and a century later renowned horticulturist Charles Sprague Sargent found that at least fifty-seven trees present at Mount Vernon were likely planted in Washington's time. By 2004, the original trees numbered only thirteen individual trees, half of which were American hollies. But in recent years, some of Washington's trees are enjoying a new life as a few trees have been successfully cloned and replanted.[63] Several of the two-hundred-year-old trees that can be found at Mount Vernon today are robust and continuing to store carbon, with the largest trees each representing over 40 metric tons of carbon dioxide that they have successfully kept out of the atmosphere.

Washington's efforts were the first wave in what would amount to a rediscovery of the ornamental power of native American tree species that merged the environmental benefits of trees in residential areas with their aesthetic benefits. In her book *Founding Gardeners*, Andrea Wulf describes how George Washington and the men who would become the other founding presidents took up the topic of gardening, cultivars, and tree species with unreserved passion. Correspondence between Washington, Adams, Jefferson, and Madison was peppered with references to various crops and ornamentals, and everyone received seeds and advice from Benjamin Franklin. Thomas Jefferson and John Adams had taken an English garden tour together in the spring of 1786. Although they could have used this time to also see the innovations of British industrial production they had interest only in gardening.[64] During their tour they made the revelatory discovery that many of the most impressive ornamentals were native not to Europe, but to North America. "My dear, we have seen Magnificence Elegance and Taste enough to excite an Inclination to see more," wrote Adams to his wife at the start of the tour.[65] But the tour only affirmed the Americans' love of their own landscape. "It will be long, I hope before Ridings, Parks, Pleasure Grounds, Gardens, and Ornamented Farms grow so much in fashion in America. But Nature has done greater Things and furnished nobler Materials there," Adams wrote.[66]

Cultivating and preserving a landscape more naturalized than the stylized gardens of Britain and France took shape in the minds of America's first vice president and secretary of state. George Washington was also inspired by Adams and Jefferson's discovery of the prominence of North American plant species in European gardens. He personally paid a visit to John Bertram's seed nursery in Pennsylvania, which was the source of many of the plantings in Britain's finest gardens.[67]

Washington's approach to land management at Mount Vernon supported a greater density of forest—and carbon sequestration—than practiced in either British or Native American land management. The indigenous tradition had been to set fire to the landscape from time to time, clearing the land for a better hunt. Different tribes were also adept at using the growing shoots for house construction, basketry and other uses.[68] The Shenandoah River Valley was a grassy route west, which had been shaped over millennia by controlled burning from Native Americans, as had the tidewater region of Washington's birthplace. The peninsulas along the Chesapeake Bay had been used for "fire hunting" by Indian burners whose fires helped to create the pine and oak savannahs found in the area.[69] Early diaries of Europeans exploring the Chesapeake Bay suggests that these fires could be seen from offshore, such as a 1607 account that reported "'great smokes' from burning woods on all sides."[70]

The brush fires were sustainable in that Native Americans conducted them at intervals to avoid a major buildup of fuel and, in contrast to tobacco farming, the burning did not cause erosion or major nutrient losses. But the intermittent burning meant that native practices served to lower the amount of carbon stored on the land. The acres that Washington inherited had been denuded of trees by the Potawatomi and other tribes. It had been depleted in organic matter and soil carbon in the seventeenth and eighteenth centuries through tobacco farming.[71] Therefore, George Washington's commitment to tree planting served to reverse the overall pattern of carbon loss practiced by indigenous and European inhabitants.

George Washington's influence on woodland preservation has a standing example in the Landmark Forest at James Madison's Montpelier estate. At about two hundred acres, the forest at Montpelier surpasses in size any remnant at Mount Vernon, which lost much land to housing tracts. A recent forest survey at Montpelier confirms that much of the land had not been intensively cultivated after the late eighteenth century, supporting Madison's observation that from his estate he could observe "red fields and pine covered hills." The topsoil had recovered much of its depth since the tobacco era.[72] Soil samples taken at Mount Vernon indicate that organic matter may have increased from around 10 percent during George Washington's time to 13 percent over the next century, after Mount Vernon's fields reverted to woodland.[73] As with the lands around Mount Vernon, in the Landmark Forest almost all of the oldest trees date from Madison's time and not before, revealing the turnaround in tree cover that the founding presidents achieved.[74]

George Washington decided early on as a young farmer in the 1760s to diversify his crops away from tobacco monocropping and to try to restore the fertility of the soils on his land, which had been depleted by erosion and the demands of tobacco production. Over time George Washington became one of America's premier agriculture experimentalists, a rarified enterprise whose adherents in the mid-Atlantic region during the late eighteenth century could be numbered on one hand.[75] Thomas Jefferson's remark that Washington only read books about agriculture and English history was probably an exaggeration, but Washington's study was well stocked with such books, and his correspondence with notable agronomists in Britain is abundant and highly detailed, especially on the subject of soil nutrients.[76]

In a 1788 letter to Arthur Young, one of Britain's foremost experts on agriculture, Washington wrote, "I am led to reflect how much more delightful to an undebauched mind is the task of making improvements on the earth: than all the vainglory which can be acquired from ravaging it." [77] During his retirement years, Washington pursued agricultural improvement as his main vocation. By this time, he had a well-formed view that American farmers were following wasteful practices that needed to be corrected. He believed that the notion of the limitless frontier had led to waste in America in contrast to England, which had benefited from coming to terms with their limited land area. "The aim of the farmers in this country (if they can be called farmers) is not to make the most they can from the land, which is, or has been cheap. . . . Much ground has been *scratched* over and none cultivated or improved as it ought to have been," wrote George Washington in 1791 in a letter to Arthur Young.[78]

We may now take for granted that Washington's perspective on soil conservation was a prudent one, but the outcome of the American Revolution was to open up additional land area. Three new states joined the United States during Washington's presidency and retirement years, and a leader more focused on the short term would have reminded his people of the new frontiers that he had already made available for homesteaders. Instead, his more persistent message was to make the most of the land they already had. He made no secret of his hope that his experiments would be expanded and taken on by the federal government and included this subject in his last address to congress as president: "In proportion as nations advance in population and other circumstances of maturity . . . renders the cultivation of the soil more and more an object of public patronage."[79] Washington did not live to see the realization of a national agricultural repository, which he advocated for, but in the long term Washington's dream that America would become "a storehouse and granary for the world" of course came true.[80]

When George Washington began working the lands at Mount Vernon in 1754 it had already been cultivated in tobacco for many decades. His first food crop was wheat, which also depleted the soil, but as time went on he further diversified into corn and hay and many other crops. He eventually developed a seven-year crop rotation with a schedule specific to individual fields. Many of the fields were planted with some combination of wheat, clover, buckwheat, oats, pasture, and potatoes, using a complicated schedule that aimed to restore nutrients to the soil. The actual work, of course, was performed by people who had little choice in the matter, but in the case of the slaves at Mount Vernon, many were unusually skilled because they had trained with the specialized farmers, gardeners, and carpenters that Washington recruited for his enterprises.[81]

He experimented with many soil enhancements including green manures, as he referred to cover crops that blocked weeds and returned nutrients to the soil, and tried other amendments including lime, dung, human feces, fish remains, and Potomac River mud.[82] Washington had his workers build a covered dung repository—a stercorary—in 1787, and it was active for at least a decade as Mount Vernon slaves were instructed to gather up dung for later spreading on the fields, a labor-intensive approach for fertilizing crops. In his use of green manures he may have accepted the advice that plant amendments may be preferred to dung because they would, according to one of his correspondents, "destroy rather than producing weeds."[83]

Already as a young man in the 1760s he had alfalfa planted on his land and persisted with the nitrogen-fixing crop for the remainder of his life, although it did not take to his soils as well as it did for his neighbors'. He also used clover because he was aware that as a leguminous plant it could replenish the soils, and buckwheat as a short crop to plow into the soil and block weeds. "The Buck Wheat if possessed of the properties of manure must in this field discover its powers . . . and in a very succulent state much of it sprang up," Washington fondly recalled from his presidential office in Philadelphia.[84] The effect of dung and green manure applications and the incorporation of crop residences would have increased the population of microorganisms in the soil and the accumulation of soil organic material and carbon. The green manures, especially, would have reduced wind and water erosion in the fields.[85] By preserving his soils, Washington was succeeding in storing more carbon in them.

The point is inescapable that Washington wished American agriculture to learn from his experimentation, and if he had had more time—more than the few years between wartime and presidential service and the brief retirement years before his untimely death, the public would have had a chance of hearing more from Washington himself about the results of his experiments. As it was, Thomas Jefferson took on many of the agricultural projects that George Washington had pioneered, and because the third president was longer lived and had more time to pursue agriculture, he was able to extend the experiments. In parallel with his comments about George Washington, Jefferson remarked of his own reading habits, "I have made researches into nothing but what is connected to agriculture."[86] At Monticello he grew some two hundred species in what became the largest vegetable plot in America. For his main crops he also pursued a seven-year crop rotation over multiple cycles. Jefferson had his steep hillside terraced to cut down erosion, and at Montpelier James Madison did likewise with his ornamental garden.

Like George Washington, organic farmers also use buckwheat, alfalfa, and other species in a complicated rotation that they modify according to weather conditions.[87] The crop rotation system aims to restore flavor to grains while replenishing the soil, but as in the eighteenth century, consumer habits do not take full advantage of the crops in the rotations. It is true to say, however, that American soils would have been further depleted in carbon and nitrogen by the nineteenth century were it not for the soil conservation efforts of George Washington and the other founding presidents. Considering George Washington's crop rotation and use of organic soil plant amendments, an upper bound of soil carbon accumulation at Mount Vernon might be at least 0.1 metric tons carbon per hectare per year.[88] At about one thousand metric tons of carbon dioxide per year taking into account all the Mount Vernon farms, George Washington's efforts added up in carbon terms and certainly provided a better example than a tobacco plantation.

## Population and the Republic

The choices that George Washington made for house size, fuel, soil amendments, animal husbandry and other parts of domestic life at

Mount Vernon reflected a disciplined intention. Other aspects of George Washington's life may be seen as exemplary but not the outcome of a conservationist's deliberations. George Washington was the rare head of state who never traveled to Europe or took long-haul pleasure trips or maintained a vacation house. His sole trip away from the continent of America was a voyage he made as a young man to Barbados in support of finding a cure for his brother's failing health. Today, the most destructive thing that an American can do to the atmosphere over a short period of time is to take a long-haul flight to a far-off land. Whatever urges Washington might have had to see foreign lands appear to have been satiated during his years working as a land surveyor, fighting the French and Indian wars, commanding the Continental Army and serving two presidential terms in Philadelphia. "I can truly say I had rather be at Mount Vernon . . . than to be attended at the Seat of Government by the Officers of State and the Representatives of Every Power in Europe," he wrote from his office in Philadelphia.[89]

On a recent visit to Mount Vernon I overheard a visitor with twenty-first century manners ask George Washington (official Washington impersonator Dean Malissa) whether he regretted that he hadn't had any biological children. "Biological children? You mean children? Of course, but it's God will that decides that." Malissa paused to look into the distance. "I suppose it's just as well, because in the tyranny of monarchy, how do kings pass on their power? Through their sons, primogeniture." George Washington had married a young, widowed woman and helped to raise the stepchildren, a course that James Madison eventually took as well. At that time, the assumption would have prevailed that the woman, not the man, was infertile, and history has well-known examples of how the social or legal mores changed to allow a head of state to beget a male heir. Henry VIII and others aside, eighteenth-century America had its examples of alternative family structures. In Washington's time, Native American groups and some European immigrant groups practiced polygamy, which was not illegal. If George Washington had chosen to do so, one could conjecture that it would have been tolerated. Laying any thoughts to rest that he would seek an unconventional relationship in order to procreate, George Washington wrote the following: "If Mrs. Washington should survive me there is a moral certainty of my dying without issue and should I be longest lived the matter, in my opinion is hardly less certain for while I retain the faculty of reasoning, I shall never marry a girl, and it is not probable that I should have children by a woman of an age suitable to my own."[90]

Today's climate policy discourse rarely mentions population, which is seen as a sensitive issue that that can offend people's view of their basic liberties and personal lifestyle choices. Statisticians, however, who make it their business to tabulate how our carbon legacies can play out over time into future generations, remind us that the decision not to have children is the most powerful action of them all.[91]

## Mount Vernon's Legacy

In the early years of the new republic, the other founding presidents also worked on improving their houses, gardens and fields, knowing that, like Mount Vernon, their estates would become public places one day. John Adams, who had been raised in a diminutive saltbox home, bought a new house that reminded Abigail of "a wren's house" compared with their spacious quarters in London and Paris.[92] But even after expanding their new house, Peacefield, it was smaller than Mount Vernon. Thomas Jefferson, who had the greatest interest and talent in building design, expanded Monticello, but at the end of the day Monticello was also about the size of Mount Vernon. At Montpelier James Madison expanded his house to include a separate suite of rooms for his parents, but when he finished the total size was about the same as the others.

The scale of Mount Vernon was approximated in the houses of all the founding presidents, and it conveyed a message about house size that was understood and accepted outside of the presidential circle. The largest house in the region, the unfinished Governor's House in Annapolis, Maryland, was completed after the American Revolution, when it reached about fourteen thousand square feet of space. George Washington certainly had no interest in living in it, and because of its size, it would not be appropriate for anyone else. Therefore, its original purpose as a residence could not be sustained and it became part of St. John's College. Mount Vernon was and is about seven thousand square feet of living space, and several thousand additional feet in an unheated basement, and these dimensions came to define for some time the upper limit of house size in America.[93]

In the early nineteenth century as American culture became more urbanized and industrialized during the presidency of Andrew Jackson, Americans turned to new forms of energy and technology. Reliance on the sailing ship and the stagecoach gave rise to the steamboat and the railway, and the Baltimore and Ohio Railroad was opened for business in 1830. American tool manufacturing took off, and goods became much cheaper. The changes in manufacturing and transport were fueled by exploitation of coal, especially the hard coal found in southeastern Pennsylvania. New grates were fashioned that could better use the Pennsylvania anthracite, and exploitation of this coal tripled to a quarter of a million tons during the few years between 1827 and 1831.[94] Nonetheless, American emissions from coal remained far below Britain's throughout the nineteenth century, and it was not until the 1860s that American emissions began to surpass those of British emissions circa 1800 (see figure).

American architecture also changed in the 1830s as older European styles came into vogue, especially the Gothic Revival. The symmetry of Georgian and Federalist architecture gave way to houses with features reminiscent of medieval castles and Greek temples. The Georgian houses had looked impressive in their small-scaled simplicity, an architectural form that was widely

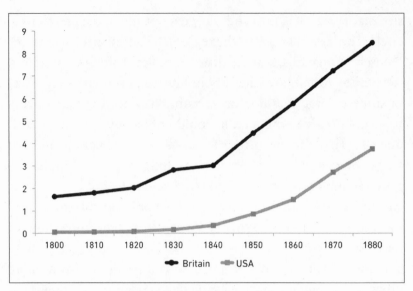

Fig. 5. Nineteenth-century per person $CO_2$ emissions trends (metric tons), United States and Britain. Carbon dioxide emissions before the 1884 invention of the steam turbine. Adapted from Etemad et al., *World Energy Production*.

appreciated two centuries after its demise, but the revival styles were a starting point for large-sized buildings that could give expression to the turrets, balustrades, and other details of revivalism. This style was flourishing by mid-century and by the end of the century was widely used in the homes of America's industrial moneyed elite in locales such as Newport Rhode Island. The American barons of industrial wealth built homes at a scale that had few precedents in Europe for those without hereditary title. In the 1860s one of the first large mansions, Ralston Hall, was completed in California (55,360 square feet) and by the 1890s many vast estates were built on the East Coast, including Biltmore House, which was finished in 1895 and remains America's largest house at 135,280 square feet.

But buildings erected during the first half of the nineteenth century retained much smaller floor plans. In 1837 Andrew Jackson expanded his own house, the Hermitage, in Tennessee in cold grey stone, and in New York William Paulding's home, Knoll, completed in 1838, heralded the arrival of the Gothic. But even these developments were not the end of the story for Mount Vernon. Both of these buildings—the Knoll (later known as Lyndhurst Castle), and the Hermitage—were of a certain size, and that size was of course about seven thousand square feet.[95] Conscious or unconscious, George Washington's Mount Vernon remained deep in the psyche of American culture for a long time.

Today, visitors can choose among several routes and several transport modes to Mount Vernon, but the one closest in spirit to the mule would be the bicycle path that wends close to the shores of the Potomac River, passing woodlands, small marinas, and tidal marshes. The path meets the George Washington Memorial Parkway, continuing on land that was once part of Mount Vernon's River Farm, before ending at the roundabout near the Mount Vernon mansion farm. The parkway along the Potomac was built during the dark days of the Depression to give Americans a beautiful arrival at Mount Vernon, and a renewed hope.

The numerous parking lots at Mount Vernon make the estate a convenient driving destination, although it should be noted that transit is also available using a Fairfax county bus from Alexandria that arrives and leaves Mount Vernon at a frequency of once per hour on a Sunday. In previous decades, ticketed visitors arriving at Mount Vernon could proceed directly to the mansion and grounds, but as of the early twenty-first century, visitors are channeled first into the lobby of a building called the Ford Orientation Center. The Center's auditorium offers a film about George Washington, but most of the building is devoted to an enormous, high-ceilinged lobby, so vast that it is never full. Because of its location, it cannot shelter visitors waiting to enter the mansion from the rain. And, of course, the huge space is heated and cooled the conventional way.

The Ford Orientation Center is joined by the Donald W. Reynolds Museum, which opened in 2006, and the two buildings comprise

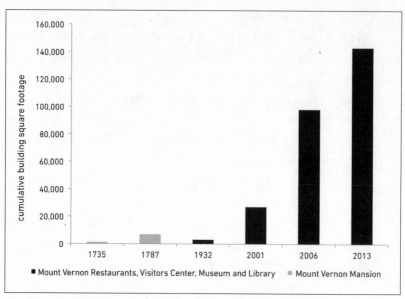

Fig. 6. Mount Vernon building size then and now compiled by the author from data posted at www.mountvernon.org and Frank, "Mount Vernon."

some 66,700 square feet of space.[96] A few years later, the new George Washington Presidential Library opened across the street from the entrance to the museums. The library houses fewer than one hundred original books, but its 45,000-square-foot space includes its own entertainment and meeting rooms separate from those in the building across the street, which also houses an auditorium, food court, restaurant, and gift shop. These additions total about 150,000 square feet and are the reason why Mount Vernon's annual fossil fuel bill is about half a million dollars today.

In the food court, visitors can buy bottled water and highly sweetened beverages, soft dough cookies, hotdogs, hamburgers, and salad with croutons. George Washington's hoecake breakfast, which he apparently consumed simply with butter and honey, can be ordered in the restaurant, but comes smothered with ham, crabmeat and hollandaise sauce. As a nod to both the eighteenth century and an alternative protein source, the food court and restaurant also serve peanut soup, but for the most part the menu of the day is ruminant animal. Six kinds of steak ranging from 8 ounces to 18 ounces, and pork and lamb chops of unspecified mass, are on offer at the Inn Restaurant.

From the parking lots on the perimeter to the huge, empty interiors of the museum and other buildings, as well as the greenhouse-gas-intensive food in the restaurants, the contemporary Mount Vernon experience uses resources at a scale vastly different from that of its founder. Ignoring emissions from the hundreds of automobiles that arrive daily, and the restaurant meals, today's Mount Vernon emits at least five times more greenhouse gases than the place that George Washington knew.[97] But perhaps more to the point, in the year 2000 and earlier, Mount Vernon's resource use had a fair resemblance to that of its eighteenth-century owner, and its greenhouse gas emissions were about one-fifth of what they are today. The difference in building scale and emissions is not independent of the fact that the historical site has accumulated new ideas, expertise, and exhibits over time, which it has chosen to present in airy spaces. These developments at Mount Vernon parallel the large growth in American educational and commercial buildings during the early twenty-first century. A question for the future is whether we can gain a clearer perspective on the real value added (or lost) due to further growth in the commercial built environment.

Taking to heart the founding president's own attitude toward natural resources and understanding the impact of a household, office, or school on the atmosphere becomes a question of vital importance. At Mount Vernon Washington promoted mules over horses, swine over cattle, diversified cropping instead of mono-cropping, organic soil amendments instead of new homesteading, native-tree planting instead of topiary, wood instead of coal, and restraint in home heating. The house itself was no larger than the houses of the other Virginia landed class—"Smaller than my cottage," remarked Elizabeth II during a visit. The amount of living space per person that Mount

Vernon embodied for the first family and overnight guests was about seven hundred square feet for each person. The presidents who followed built some of their own individuality into their estates, but the size of Mount Vernon was a line that they would not cross and neither, for many decades, would any other American. The large houses that emerged in the late nineteenth century were out of sync with the founders' intentions and practice, and it is this tradition rather than that of the founders that underlies the scale of much of America's contemporary buildings and consumption of fuel.

CHAPTER TWO

# Carbon Dissenters

## The Amish

The Amtrak train en route to Washington DC paused for a few minutes in a small West Virginia town, giving passengers a chance to stretch their legs. I chatted for a few minutes with a man standing on the platform wearing dark, suspendered pants, a straw hat, and a long beard, and who, like many of the passengers onboard, was Amish. He was traveling with his family back to their home in Maryland and was agreeable about answering my questions. His house was heated by two wood burning stoves, he told me—one in the kitchen, the other in the living room. This is a setup that is common among the Amish, but he added modestly, "That is what I have. Someone else might have something different." The trip had been delayed during the night as our train, the Capitol Limited, had been sidelined to make way for freight—csx owns the tracks. I noted the irony of the situation; a group of rural Americans who use the least fossil fuels—and especially the least electricity—was being delayed to make way for coal.

The Old Order Amish, a term that describes about 90 percent of all Amish, typically use about one quarter of the fossil fuels of an average American, and their life style places few burdens on public services. They don't own cars, fly in airplanes, or use air conditioning. Their use of appliances depends upon their own district's decisions, but to operate them they use Amish ingenuity that reflects a more deliberate relationship with fossil fuels and machines. Convenience and efficiency are not acceptable if they risk disrupting family camaraderie or widening the economic gaps among community members. At the same time, they are the most local of people. The Amish make decisions and conform to rules at the level of the district, or *gmay*, comprised of about twenty families who live close to each other. Rather than cliques or bloodlines, proximity outlined by roads or natural features such as creeks define the boundaries of the *gmay*. On average, they have much lower emissions than non-Amish Americans for every part of their life except for their meaty diet.

Like our historical antecedents, George Washington included, the Amish arrived at their lifestyle independent of concern over global impacts of greenhouse gas emissions. Among the Amish are independent readers of science who understand the dangers of climate change, but Amish society is unlikely to develop educators or formal role models for the wider world on this subject. I raised the topic with an Amish woman selling baked goods at a farmer's market. She replied that she knew about the idea of global warming, but that it doesn't come up much. Another person answered in a way that fell just short of a rebuke, revealing the *Gelassenheit* attitude of humility: "I thought that the climate was God's will. I didn't know that humans could change the climate." They are low emitters because they interpret scriptures as a guide to a specific material and community existence that is locally defined and maintained.

In the mid-twentieth century, observers of Amish culture predicted that their traditional ways would die out as they came to see the disadvantages of their strict rules and avoidance of modern inventions. Amish rules about technology vary according to district but all Amish accept prohibitions over owning cars. The backbone of Amish family transportation is the horse and buggy, a mode that is demanding of a family's time and skill. That fact alone would seem to make the Amish path a difficult one. But although the 1970s saw the dissolution of many communes and simple living experiments that had been enthusiastically and musically embraced by young people, no such fate befell the Amish. About 85 percent of Amish young people choose to be baptized and to remain Amish. The Old

Order Amish population has increased manifold since those predictions and as the non-Amish have become ever more plugged-in and tattooed, the Amish appear all the more different.

The Amish who once lived in a single settlement in Lancaster County, Pennsylvania, now live in at least twenty-four states with the largest settlements in Holmes County, Ohio, and Elkhart-Lagrange, Indiana.[1] Doubling about every twenty years, the Amish population in America now numbers more than a quarter of a million people.[2] On average, they enjoy a better longevity and a much lower incidence of mental illness, violence, poverty, and metabolic disease than mainstream Americans. Studies that try to compare the well-being of different cultures report that Amish individuals tend to be content with the material and other aspects of their life, that the Amish tend to be as happy as the rest of America, if not more so.[3]

The philosophical perspective of the Old Order Amish centers upon maintaining close ties with the family and the community, engaging in useful, wholesome work, and *Gelassenheit*, avoiding expansion of the personal ego or pride. This perspective has shaped the personalities of Amish individuals, who tend to be soft-spoken, modest, and patient compared to the non-Amish. Anyone who has taken a long-distance train ride between the East Coast and the Midwest and observed very young Amish children sitting quietly for many hours in a seat without electronic entertainment will know that these characteristics are shaped at a young age.

From an environmental perspective, *Gelassenheit* has provided an antidote to the contemporary pursuit of novelty, vocational specialization, and exceptional wealth. Amish culture, instead, is described by conformity, shared work, and small-scale enterprise that discourages status seeking. Shared work means that family members spend much of the day working together, and appliances that speed up housework are usually prohibited.[4] The Amish view television, movies, and the Internet as corrupting and a waste of time, and their use tends to be prohibited in all districts. An Amish bishop explained their rules this way, "Machinery is not wrong in itself, but if it doesn't help fellowship, you shouldn't have it."[5] The notion that technology thwarts interaction and reflection underlies practices found in other religions. For instance, many traditional Jews share similar observance one day a week, with a car-free and Internet-free Sabbath. Amish rules about technology and other matters apply to all families in a given district with the exception of teenagers and young adults, who may be allowed some years to explore the wider culture.

Decisions on whether to adopt new practices and technologies are in the hands of the adult district members, but a new proposal must win near-consensus because the idea fails if more than two members oppose. Scholars of the Amish attribute some of the stability of the Amish rules, or *Ordnung*, to the fear of weakening relationships with other districts where family members and close friends may reside. A given district would tend to match the rules of those nearby as well as districts where the members have close ties. For instance, a district considering whether to allow cell phones would be aware that taking them up would complicate their social lives, given that everyone would have relatives and friends who belong to districts that prohibit them. It is easy to see how the voting rules and broader community concerns would work to maintain the status quo. It is remarkable to contemplate how this outcome was achieved without regulations, legislation, or even national organizations.

## Heat and Light

From afar, an Amish farm in Lancaster County, Pennsylvania, can look more like a hamlet or compound than a simple farm. Some of the properties have elaborate, well-built wooden play structures for children, multi-storied birdhouses, neat vegetable plots, ornamental flower beds, and large expanses of lawn, in addition to a house, a barn, a horse shed and other outbuildings. For a lonely suburban child, catching a glimpse of Amish farms with long-skirted and suspendered children playing happily can be a glimpse of fairyland.

Such a life involves a great deal of physical labor, and hard work shared with family members is one of the givens of Amish culture. For many Amish, doing chores affords deeper satisfaction than what passes for entertainment and leisure recreation among the non-Amish. A letter writer to an Amish magazine put it this way: "It is important that children have work to do, that they feel needed and wanted and not in the way. Few things in life are simple. Certainly this problem is not one of them."[6] Much of Amish decision-making about technology aims to preserve these ideals of family life.

Amish houses in different locales can vary a great deal in external appearance, but regardless, Amish homes typically only have one or two stoves for heating, both located on the ground floor. The upper floor(s) are used less frequently and rely on ambient heat from below. These listings are for houses and farms in Steuben County, New York, offered at about $100,000. "This is a lovely working Amish farm with beautiful dark kitchen cabinets. There are 2 wood stoves used for heat and cooking.... There is no plumbing or electric in the house." Or, "Amish built home with 48 acres of land, barn, sawmill buildings . . . other extra building. . . . large country kitchen with oak cabinets. Heated by wood stoves. . . . Owner will pay for 1 smoke detector. No Sunday showing."

In their book *Living Without Electricity*, Stephen Scott and Kenneth Pellman provide evocative vignettes of Amish life that show exactly how Amish choices about technology play into family dynamics. Of course, it is not necessary to compare the social implications of this scene to one where family members are spread throughout the house staring at individual screens.

It was a cold winter evening and everyone wanted to stay close to the stoves. No one was off in another room or away at a meeting or social event . . . . Although they exchanged few words, the Millers enjoyed being together. There was something quietly reassuring about observing one another. . . . Ten-year-old Suzy was absorbed in a magazine article, and eight-year-old Dan struggled through a library book that was a bit beyond his level. Thirteen-year-old Andy sat on the opposite end of the table from Sylvia, intently figuring the profits from his last sale of rabbits.[7]

Such a scene underscores that although Amish households may heat their houses—usually with wood—traditionally Amish houses have used small amounts of fuel and the presence of a single stove has helped keep family and friends in close proximity.[8]

In summer, Amish families will gather in a similar fashion, but usually in a basement, since Amish households do not have air conditioning. Like the upstairs kitchen, the basement will have furniture, including counters for preserving and preparing food. Because they have a greater need for naturally cool rooms, the Amish have built rooms that provide respite from the heat of the day and that more closely resemble the subterranean spaces found in warm Middle-Eastern climates than the root cellars of Germany, their country of origin.[9] Nonetheless, the Amish tolerate heat much better than the non-Amish Americans, for we are among the top consumers of air conditioning in the world.[10]

Even in Amish homes that use more modern devices than a kerosene lamp, a flick of a switch does not suffice for turning on a light.[11] Fine wooden cabinets may give a clue to the presence of fuel tanks that power Amish lighting. Progressive Amish groups use gasoline or naphtha in lamps similar to the pressurized gas lamps that came into vogue in the late nineteenth century. A tank of compressed air at the base of the lamp forces the fuel into a state of vaporization and then into a mantle that glows at an intensity of a 100-watt bulb. Each lamp needs to be individually lit and many of the tanks are refilled or pumped manually, providing family members an incentive to save time and avoid wasting lamplight—and fuel.

The Amish approach to lighting serves family needs in much the same way as the limited heating. Before going to bed, this family congregates in the one room that is lit and heated, discouraging other family members from going off alone. This excerpt about a different family is again from Scott and Pellman:

> The clock struck nine, signaling the time for the family to settle down for the night. After the evening prayer the two oldest children, Joe and Rachel, took flashlights and led their brothers and sisters upstairs to the bedrooms. Rachel entered the girls' room and directed the beam of the flashlight to a lamp on a table beside the bed. She took the glass chimney from the lamp and got a wooden match from a small container. After striking the match she held the flame to the bit of kerosene-soaked wick protruding above the brass fixture. . . . The younger girls snuggled into bed in the unheated room, but Rachel spent a few minutes reading and writing before blowing out the light.[12]

The limited lighting may seem austere, but it helps prevent family members from dispersing, which would be advantageous if the family dynamic is strong and supportive, but perhaps challenging if not. Many Amish use flashlights powered by dry cell batteries as a transition from lamp to lamp. The batteries are not a very green aspect of Amish life, and the battery disposal may be as haphazard as it is in non-Amish life. Some of the convenience of batteries is purposefully altered—the batteries can be reused only if taken to a non-Amish business for recharging.[13] In any case, since the lit area is limited, the routine would tend to use less fossil fuel than lighting in conventional households.

Donald Kraybill explains in his book *The Riddle of Amish Culture* that Amish technological adaptations can seem confounding to outsiders but often show a strong internal logic and consistency. It can be puzzling to see that some Amish will use electricity but not in the voltage form that is standard in American households. Access to the grid is viewed to be a slippery slope that would make it easier for family members to covertly find entertainment from the outside world or to introduce noise and an unnecessary convenience that disrupts the camaraderie of shared work and leisure in the home. Therefore, Amish households are off the grid.

Uses of electricity apart from lighting are taken up or not as individual districts decide, and regardless, it is used in a different form than the lines running standard voltage. In the 1980s, the Amish started to use inverters that convert electricity from 12 volts—the standard current running through electric lines—to 110-volt electricity. Amish-style electricity took on a remarkably circuitous path, beginning with diesel, to a generator, to 12-volt, to invertor, to 110-volt.[14] The end result brings some degree of comfort and machine power while keeping cultural influences at more than arm's length.

## Amish Appliances

In the non-Amish world, of course, machines and electronic entertainment have become more common and numerous with each passing decade. While about 20 percent of U.S. households had microwave ovens in 1982, by 2009 more than 90 percent had them. In the Midwest, where many Amish live, about 60 percent of households had air conditioning in 1980 compared to 92 percent in 2015.[15] The average number of TVs per household is 2.5, but 24 million American households have four or more TVs, which may be indicative of the future. These appliances have all become more efficient but also larger and more numerous, and joined with a growing number of rechargeable plug-ins. Consequently, energy consumed in electronics and appliances has been increasing and makes up a growing share of American household energy use. In 1975 appliances and electronics made up 17 percent of American household energy use, but this share had increased to 31 percent by 2005.[16]

The question of how much of this is really necessary does not occupy the minds of many contemporary Americans. But the Amish, who have deliberated over the pros and cons of appliances for decades, have arrived at a general answer. Across the Amish world, only one appliance is deemed really desirable, and that is the washing machine. More than 97 percent of Amish districts allow their members to use them.[17] Even the most conservative groups such as the Swartzentruber in Ohio and the Nebraska Group in Pennsylvania, who avoid flush toilets and kerosene lamps, allow washing machines in some districts.[18] While earlier generations of Amish did not change clothes every day, contemporary Amish have become used to a fresh change of clothes, which they find complementary to their physically active lifestyle. The machines they use typically have an agitation basin and a wringer and are powered by compressed air or a form of petroleum energy directly. These machines tend to use less fossil fuel than a conventional electric washing machine. The wringer-washer's emissions may be as low as about 0.1 metric tons of carbon dioxide, slightly less than the most highly rated Energy Star washing machine running on conventional electricity.[19]

Clothes dryers are another story. Few Amish households allow them or use them. Most families simply line dry their clothing outside or use an inside line in bad weather. This can take the form of a wooden frame attached to the wall that can be stretched accordion-style across the room. Some of these wooden clothes drying racks are so well crafted that they bring an artistic, sculptural effect to a room. The air-drying habits of the Amish stand in contrast to the rest of us, who expend an average of 6 percent of our residential energy consumption on clothes dryers.[20]

Most Americans now have dishwashers, but this is an item that Amish consider undesirable.[21] Most districts have banned dishwashers and vacuum cleaners, and for the most part, power lawn mowers.[22] The dishes are washed by hand, the carpets are cleaned by pushing sweepers, and the grass is cut pushing mowers. Of these physical acts of maintaining the home and yard, avoiding power motors will save the most energy. Currently, Americans emit about 20.4 million tons of $CO_2$ through using power lawnmowers.[23] Vacuum cleaners in the United States lack Energy Star labels, because the EPA does not consider them to be important energy expenders. Dishwashers do have energy ratings because they can have a similar energy profile as refrigerators. By washing dishes by hand, Amish households are saving about 0.1 metric tons of $CO_2$ annually, and several times that by using manual lawn mowers.

When it comes to refrigerators, about 40 percent of Amish districts accept them. Since the Amish pickle and can so much produce and meat, they have less need for refrigeration. Some households will use blocks of ice or store food in a nearby stream. They will likely eat fewer dairy products such as milk and yogurt that are hard to preserve, or they will eat those foods mostly during the cooler seasons. An Amish family in a progressive district can leaf through a catalogue from Lehman's store in Ohio and choose a supersized, natural gas–powered refrigerator built and marketed with their needs in mind. The refrigerator will tend to be the largest appliance source of greenhouse gases, as it is in the non-Amish household. Typical emissions related to this item would be about 0.8 metric tons of carbon dioxide per year, one of the few instances where the Amish way means higher emissions.[24] Amish households do not have freezers because, although natural gas freezers exist, they are very expensive to use.

Modern toilets and baths are amenities that are acceptable to most Amish, but about 30 percent of the districts do not allow them, and even the progressive districts will usually make sure that their children grow up not to disdain outhouses and hand pumps. Even in Lancaster County, which is considered high tech in the Amish world, children attend one-room schoolhouses with hand pumps and outhouses in the back. An area of ambiguity and leniency is the use of telephones. Many Amish households have a telephone shed at the rear of the house and may use answering services. Other districts allow cell phones or allow them for certain uses, such as business transactions. In Lancaster County, more teens than not have cell phones, though not necessarily with the blessing of their elders.[25]

Along with fewer appliances, you will find much less "stuff" inside the home. The Amish furnish their homes with a generous number of chairs and sofas, but a traditional material culture points to a preponderance of wood rather than materials that require more fossil fuels to manufacture such as concrete, metal or plastic.[26] They often use natural fibers for their clothing instead of synthetics. It helps that furniture and clothing styles harken back to a rural simplicity dating from nineteenth-century America that never goes out of fashion in the Amish world.

Not only do they have fewer appliances, most of their goods lack the planned obsolescence found in today's electronic and other goods.[27] The Amish buggy, for instance, although a large piece of metal, usually lasts for several decades, much longer than an automobile. Amish furniture tends to be durable thanks to the large number of Amish who are competent at carpentry. Amish women preserve and store food in glass jars and cans that they can reuse. Some goods are used until they are beyond repairing or mending. If a bedsheet is worn out in the middle, it can be cut in half and the outer edges can be joined in a new seam down the middle. At least that is the advice on offer in the Amish magazine *Family Life*. Needless to say, Amish households have few imported goods, and unlike the non-Amish Americans, are contributing little to the growth in Chinese greenhouse gas emissions.

With manual labor often replacing electricity and with much less use for space heating and lighting, it is true to say that most Amish use little energy of any variety. Wind, solar, and geothermal may be high tech, but they are attractive to the Amish because they can be installed without participating in the public grid. Although conservative groups like the Swartzentruber do not use solar power, it has been accepted by most districts without conflict. In the twentieth century, many Amish households used windmills to pump water.

Though many farms switched to air compression pumps that are fossil fuel based, a drive through Amish settlements in Pennsylvania reveals that many old wind installations are still in use. Some Amish farmers also use an Amish invention that exploits geothermal heat to prevent water from freezing on livestock troughs.[28] Amish ingenuity brings to mind the concept of Intermediate technology, promoted by E. F. Schumacher, who would have approved of much taking place in this part of rural America.[29]

Much newer is the occasional gleaming solar panel seen on the roof of a horse shed or barn. Most households use so little energy that putting up as little as one or two solar panels can provide valuable electricity for a family. Although some outsiders complain that the solar panels mar the beauty of the Amish farmstead, an increasing number of Amish are using the source they call "God's Grid." Amish residents in Ohio use more solar on a per capita basis than any other community surveyed in the state.[30] Renewables can also come into play in small devices that the Amish use, such as solar-powered toys and water-powered digital alarm clocks.[31]

With the need for electricity being minor in much of the Amish world, the bulk of energy is used for heating and cooking, and in most Amish households fuel wood covers this need. Even in a district that allows fossil fuels, children will still be attending a school that uses wood and become competent in cutting wood, building fires, and removing the ashes. Even the skill of stacking wood is given attention, and some Amish learn to store wood artfully in the shape of giant beehives that repel water.[32] The Amish have a range of choices for stoves and as in the case of refrigerators, they can buy cookstoves designed specifically for them. Cookstoves continue to evolve, and some Amish inventors have contributed new models designed to appeal to large families while offering features to control airflow and improve efficiency.[33]

Burning wood emits black carbon that contributes to global warming, but also aerosols that counteract the effects of black carbon because they reflect light and thereby cool the atmosphere. At present, the warming and cooling effect of burning wood are believed to roughly cancel each other out, and as long as the forest is allowed to recover, wood fuel has substantial advantages over alternatives.[34] These advantages are related to sequestration—although fuel wood is removed—the growing trees store carbon and some wood products take a long time to decay. As a whole, American forestland is growing and storing more carbon than it loses, and the eastern and Midwestern forests near Amish populations are recovering from eighteenth- and nineteenth-century land clearing.[35]

Despite the labor involved, about 2.1 percent of American households use wood to heat their homes.[36] The motivation can be cost, or habit, or—as in the case of Pete and Toshi Seeger—environmental conviction. Like an Amish person, which he was not, Pete Seeger knew how to grow and prepare much of his own fuel. On his ninetieth birthday, he explained his Sunday morning routine in a *New York Times* interview. "I barely have time to split the wood for our fire. We heat one room with a fireplace and heat the other with a stove." "[Chopping wood], that's recreation. It's in our DNA to want to go 'Whack.' About two or three million years ago we started walking on two feet, and that's when we started swinging sticks. It's not an accident that sports like gulf and baseball and cricket are popular all over the world."[37] Pete and Toshi Seeger's use of wood was largely an environmental choice that can serve very well in a rural setting, if not in an urban locale with a large concentration of people.

The Amish tend to source their wood from small, privately owned forest holdings that are in a general state of renewal and carbon sequestration.[38] In Pennsylvania, forests cover about 60 percent of the state, and about one-quarter of the holdings are small, private lots of less than 20 acres. In Ohio and Indiana, which are not known for their trees, forests cover 31 percent and 20 of the land area respectively. These states also have important wood products industries, and families can often source firewood from industrial residue or from salvaged dead trees. In Indiana, about 70 percent of firewood is believed to come from dead trees and harvest residues.[39]

Health impacts of burning wood have been prominent in discussion over greater reliance on wood, and the EPA has set recent higher standards for new wood-burning stoves.[40] Air concentrations of fine particulate matter—parts per million of particles 2.5 microns or less—are monitored throughout the country, and particulate matter concentrations in counties with Amish settlements typically surpass national air quality standards. Holmes County, Ohio, has the highest proportion of Amish residents of any American county, making up about half of the county population. The widespread use of wood stoves there has contributed to elevated concentrations of particulate matter–13.5 microns/m$^3$ annual average in Holmes County, compared to the national limit of 12.0.[41]

We might expect to find higher incidence of chronic lower respiratory diseases like asthma and emphysema in these places. But despite all the wood-burning stoves in use here, the rate of death from these diseases is 35 percent lower in Holmes County, adjusting for age, compared with the nation as a whole. The cancer death rate is also lower, with 18 percent fewer such deaths in Holmes County. The pattern also holds true in Lagrange County, Indiana, which is nearly 40 percent Amish. Here the particulate matter (p.m.) 2.5 concentration is about 16 percent higher than the national average, but lung disease and cancer deaths are lower here as well. Lancaster County has high particulate levels at 15 microns, but respiratory deaths are lower by one quarter and cancer death rates are also lower.[42] This data does not prove that the smoky atmosphere in these locales is safe, but that the Amish do not seem to be suffering any marked ill effects from using wood fuel.

## Garden, Farm, and Commerce

Anyone who has been a guest at an Amish table will be struck by the experience, beginning with the quietude absent distracting sounds from refrigerators or distant LED screens. On a visit to an Amish household in Pennsylvania I was warmly greeted and seated at a table overlooking the garden, where the warm glow of the late afternoon sun provided the only illumination. The ubiquitous Amish vegetable garden tends to be a point of pride often sited at the front of the house in place of hedges or flowers. The products of the garden are typically canned or pickled, and the Amish basement will store dozens of jars and cans of ready-to-eat food. Amish women grow and preserve vegetables into advanced old age with help from younger family members, and in this way Amish households manage a level of food self-sufficiency that makes the absence of a nearby grocery store a matter of little concern.

An Amish evening meal begins with a moment of silence that reflects Amish religious practices and a quiet regard for the lady of the house, who has done the most to prepare the food for the table. A meal with an Amish family can seem like an idealized form of a Thanksgiving celebration, so it is telling that many Amish appreciate Thanksgiving Day by doing something different from their daily routine, like take a bus to Washington DC and visit Smithsonian museums at a time when many of the gawkers are watching football. During our meal, we were served at the start with bread and butter and a berry jam. The dishes that followed were mashed potatoes and buttered noodles, canned garden peas, and assorted pickled vegetables. The only meat that showed up with this colorful feast was a small dish of stewed beef and gravy.

The Amish diet harkens back to the pre–World War II American diet before novelty and culinary exploration were indulged. While vegetarianism is acceptable, it is not commonplace, and the Amish tend to eat more carbohydrates and processed meats but slightly less red meat than the average American.[43] Most Amish eat heartily and view body image as a vanity. Nonetheless, many Amish remain slender, supported by a physically active life, and Amish obesity rates are often low. In Holmes County, Ohio, the adult obesity rate is only 12 percent compared to the American average of 30 percent.[44] High caloric needs and culinary tradition mean that greenhouse gas emissions associated with the Amish diet resembles that of mainstream America.

Amish farming uses much of the machinery of conventional farming, but because they rely on horses to pull their machines, their farms are smaller. Horse centered farming—because it demands more time and labor—has helped to maintain a farm size of about 50 acres. If Amish farmers used modern tractors, farms could grow to a thousand or more acres, and Amish neighbors would be at a greater geographical distance, or they might be pushed off the land altogether. Larger farms would also mean widening gaps in wealth and perhaps greater discord among community members. The rules against rubber-wheeled tractors allow communities to remain compact and block the slippery slope toward car ownership. By keeping farms small and horse centered, Amish agriculture has contributed its greatest advantages for reducing greenhouse gases related to farming, allowing the Amish community to remain local and independent of car ownership.

The debate among the Amish whether to accept tractors was the deepest and most fraught of their community soul-searching over technology. When tractors became lighter and cheaper during the early twentieth century, many Amish farmers believed that they would not be able to keep up unless they used them. They worried that if they avoided tractors they would lose their farms, but accepting them meant risking the entire fabric of Amish community life. In Lancaster County, the community relationship with tractors turned into a protracted social experiment. They allowed them beginning in the years before World War I, then banned them in the 1920s, took up tractors again in the 1930s, and banned them again in 1940. That ban stuck until the 1960s when the Lancaster Amish settled on the present arrangement to allow some steel-wheeled tractors that are impractical for roads. Specialized equipment such as harvesters, balers, and blowers were permitted as long as they were dragged through the field using horses.[45] Actually, true to the dream of George Washington, many of the animals are mules. In any case, they are non-ruminant, four-legged draft animals that, unlike tractors, do not consume fossil fuels.[46]

The Amish took on the risk of denying themselves state-of-the-art agricultural machinery, but managed to remain competitive. In fact, with lower capital and labor costs and strong yields, Amish farmers tend to make much more money per acre on a variety of crops than do non-Amish farmers.[47] Many Amish believe they owe the success of their farms to their four-legged engines that can work in the mud and snow, conditions that could ground expensive machinery. Forgoing irrigation is another choice distinctive to the Amish, and it is interesting that Lancaster County is the most productive non-irrigated county in the United States.[48] Using horses instead of tractors on fields has reduced soil erosion, and compared to non-Amish farms, Amish farmland tends to conduct water well and is richer in organic matter, or carbon.[49] Although the Amish approach falls short of no-tillage or minimum tillage, their farming method has avoided the vicious cycle of soil impaction from heavy machinery. Horses replacing some machine power also means some minor improvements in greenhouse gas emissions, with lower diesel use in tractors and more carbon storage in the soil. While the Amish took on the economic risk of avoiding some functions of agriculture technology in order to preserve their community goals, their approached has reaped economic benefits as well.

Although being Amish may seem synonymous with farming, Amish farmers have shared in the challenges facing family farming in America, and now only a minority farm full time. One of the largest Amish settlements in America is in Elkhart-Lagrange, Indiana, where about 95 percent of Amish households do not work in farming, and where many earn a living making recreational vehicles for the non-Amish. It might seem that this much proximity to mainstream culture—let alone something as un-Amish as the RV business—would put a serious strain on their traditional ways, but this community is managing without major changes or defections. In fact, without the distance of fields to separate houses, the move to non-farm work in Indiana and elsewhere means that many Amish now live closer to each other. Instead of a farming community spread out over ten or more miles, some of the newer districts are as compact as one square mile. Mobility without a car would be a challenge for a mainstream resident of northern Indiana, but in the heavily Amish Lagrange County, about 27 percent of the residents carpool, about three times the national average.[50]

The Amish working in businesses can use many more types of machines than allowed in the home or on the farm. Many of those working in offices may use adding machines or even computers, so long as software is limited to word processing and spreadsheets. While the Internet was once off limits, some businesses now use it for ordering supplies and advertising.[51] Amish workers may avail themselves of coffee made in coffee makers or water from water coolers. They may even heat up their lunch using a microwave oven.[52] Generators are permitted for welding, and most districts allow the use of pneumatic power tools and chain saws that are typically used for construction, although these same districts may prohibit many farm instruments such as rototillers and pickup balers. Although only about 35 percent of districts allow machines such as bulk milk tanks and mechanized milkers for dairy farming, at least 70 percent of districts permit the use of pneumatic tools and chainsaws.[53] But all this electricity will originate with a different voltage than the standard 120 volts.

Although the Amish have fewer restrictions on technology used in the office and business than in the farm and home, the Amish commercial sector is much more streamlined than that of the wider American culture. The businesses themselves stay small, rarely surpassing a workforce of twenty-five people. Aside from small enterprises, the Amish have not developed the institutions of commerce and government found in the wider society. America's commercial and institutional sector is an enormous employer and consumer of energy, and added up to about 2.9 metric tons of $CO_2$ per American in 2015.[54] The Amish rarely use mainstream educational, civic, or correctional institutions. The rate of violent crime in the Amish world is much lower than the national average—about 80 percent lower in Holmes and Lagrange counties.[55] The Amish build and supply their own schools, and formal education ends at the 8th grade. They use a variety of stores and restaurants but not as frequently as the average American. The famous community barn raising keeps the household in good stead when a barn burns down, because the Amish tend not to own insurance. Although the Amish are American citizens and pay federal and state taxes, they tend to ask very little of their government. They rarely lobby, and litigation that has defended their rights on matters such as schools and zoning allowances for horses and *Daudy Haus* (grandparent's house) permits has tended to be pursued on their behalf by sympathetic outsiders.[56]

## Plain Mobility

Within the Amish World, the prohibition against owning cars has a special place. The rule about car ownership is universal, all districts have agreed to it, and it has come to define being Amish. The Amish have drawn a de facto line around their homes, and that circle is less than a twelve-mile diameter for most routine tasks and socializing, the distance that a horse can pull a buggy without being overworked. Short distances might be covered by scooter or on foot. Amish youth and adults, male and female, use sturdy scooters. The broad platform for standing makes for a stable ride experience and has won over some non-Amish, including Manhattan commuters. Most Amish do not use bikes because they cannot be practically used by women wearing ankle-length skirts, and Amish transportation is intended to allow people to travel together, not alone.

Although Amish buggies are built to a good standard, Amish throughout the country often face hazardous conditions on rural roads, due to their vulnerability to speeding or errant automobiles. Amish pedestrians often make do with using the edge of rural roads that lack sidewalks or even generous shoulders. Rules of the road, including required front and rear lights, also apply to the Amish, who have their own manual for sharing the road with vehicles and riding defensively: "Being respectful and courteous on the road is an excellent opportunity for us, in our small way, to be a light to the world," reads an official buggy rules-of-the road written in collaboration with the county sheriff.[57] Children as young as ten enjoy riding on public roads using pony carts and small horses, but like their parents' buggies, the carts bear a state-issued license plate. Despite precautions, the Amish are not immune from collisions. In 2012, at least fourteen Amish were killed in collisions with vehicles nationwide, and at least one hundred were significantly injured. The casualty rate is unfortunate, but because the Amish spend less time in vehicles on the whole they have been safer, and their mortality rate from road accidents is about half the rate of the wider society.[58]

Most Amish had the perspective early in the twentieth century that cars would weaken the fabric of family and community life and opposed them. It helped that public transportation was still important in America, including in small cities like Lancaster, which had a well-developed trolley system and several intercity train lines. In the early days of the automobile some Amish bought vehicles, but by 1920 the Old Order Amish had banished the car.[59] In 1927, some of the Amish in Lancaster and Somerset defied the ban, which resulted in their removal from the Old Order Amish. The breakaway car drivers came to be known as Beachy Amish Mennonites, the rare group of Anabaptists who remained Amish in many ways but could not give up the car keys.

As the Amish population grew and expanded to settlements further west, families had more cause to visit relatives in distant locations. But the transport that had served them well, especially trollies and inter-city train service, was eroding. New highways began to cut through Amish settlements, making horse travel to nearby counties difficult or impossible. Alongside the changes in infrastructure, longer life expectancy meant that more communities had elderly members who could no longer climb into buggies. In response, bishops began to allow members to use cars as long as they were owned and driven by the non-Amish, and not used on a Sunday. Today, many Amish make use of vehicles for business trips, and more than half of Amish businesses use a vehicle service regularly.[60]

Families may also hire a vehicle for an excursion. Amish culture provides opportunities to pursue hobbies and intellectual interests, and many Amish are avid hikers, kayakers, birders and visit state and national parks. I was reminded of this recently when visiting a state park on the Delaware coast on a summer evening and seeing an Amish family whizzing by on scooters along the bike path in gathering darkness in the direction of the shore. They were probably eager to see the sand flats at low tide, but they had such an air of exhilaration that the non-Amish standing in a nearby parking lot were transfixed.

Since Amish are passengers and not owners, however, the car is not a means to unlimited mobility or independence and is supposedly not a status symbol or a means of pleasure in itself. I once asked an elderly Amish woman about whether she enjoyed the convenience of hiring a car to visit family members. She replied that it had become a necessity because it was difficult to climb into a chassis and handle the bumps on the road, but that she missed the buggy a great deal. Her eyes shone as she described her favorite springtime pleasure trip with a horse and carriage along "a ridge with blooming hedges," a trip that she could now only make in a hired car where it is hard to smell the flowers. The experience of riding in and even driving cars, which is permitted for some young Amish before they are baptized, is usually not life altering. Many Amish districts allow their young people a time of less restrictions called *Rumspringa*, intended to allow youth to try and then dismiss as fleeting and trivial, the pleasures of the wider world, which may mean driving cars.

Given the rules, Amish car use is not terribly convenient. They are not likely to find a taxi to hail on the rural roads; they must make arrangements in advance. But since telephone use is often restricted, they might need to make several attempts to find an available driver using an answering machine in a telephone shanty. The hired driver is likely to be someone with a special license to serve the Amish. But without a meter in the vehicle, prices might need to be negotiated for each trip that is not routine, and finding a driver for the right time and price can be time-consuming.

For all these reasons, the limited need for cars and their lack of convenience, the Amish assuredly use cars far less than the 11,287 miles per year that denotes the American average car miles per year.[61] International jet travel is never part of the life of a member of the Old Order Amish, and although transatlantic crossings can be made by boat, few do so for the purpose of recreation. Among the non-Amish, much business travel involves airline flights—about 16 percent of all trips—but the Amish are able to succeed in business without ever using airplanes.[62] Between the lack of air travel, the prohibition on owning a car, the proximity of work and social life, and their car pooling habits, it is easy to see that Amish carbon dioxide emissions related to mobility is much lower than that of the general population.

## House for Prayer

Touring the countryside around an Amish settlement it takes only a little experience to recognize an Amish house. Telling details at close range are the presence of a horse shed and a vegetable garden, and the simplicity of the windows. But most Amish houses can be spotted from far off; a giveaway is a large house with an oversized main floor. Amish houses tend to bulge at the base for a specific reason. Many houses were originally built to host the Sunday morning prayer service. The Amish district members get together every other week for the service, and all the families are expected to take their turn hosting if they are able to do so.[63] Given the size of an Amish district, families must be prepared to seat more than one hundred people in their home, yard, or outbuilding.

How easy would it be for a non-Amish household to provide seating for an entire community? When I consider all my friends and acquaintances, even the largest houses would be insufficient to provide bench seating for 70–150 people.[64] Even with every stick of furniture removed, all but the McMansions would come up short. This requirement would seem incompatible with the idea of living in a modest-sized house. An Amish grandmother I interviewed in Lancaster County had this to say about it: "We older people ask, why do young people need to build houses that are so big and fancy? They are not necessary. It seems to be in style and in ten years it will change again."

In greenhouse gas terms, oversized houses and outbuildings of course are a problem when inhabited by the non-Amish. American electricity use, and space heating and cooling needs tend to increase proportionately with floor space. However, so much is different about the Amish, including how they use their homes, that the relationship between house size and energy use is of a different nature. The Amish prayer space may require little energy because a crowded room means that little or no heat is needed. When they are not hosting, these same rooms may be unheated or unilluminated, or temporary wall dividers may be used to break up the space and insulate the heated area. Nonetheless, it is hard to dispute that the size of an Amish house will have some bearing on its footprint, especially if the house uses petroleum products for illumination and heating.

Curious whether I could spot a trend in Amish buildings, I took to the small roads throughout Lancaster County over a spring weekend. I did spot new construction throughout the area, but the new projects were not new houses, but expanded horse sheds. This was quite clear—all over Lancaster County, many Amish families had recently added second levels to their horse stables. The new floors were slightly larger than the first, and many revealed one or two solar panels on the roof. My Mennonite host explained that these second floors were built to host the Sunday service. The trend seems to reflect more trust within the community, because the hosting tradition had been designed in part to allow members a chance to see that their neighbors are actually adhering to rules and not keeping prohibited items inside their houses. It becomes difficult to hide a large, flat-screen TV in your home if you are playing host to 120 people. By decoupling the prayer space from the resident's house, however, the Amish community is introducing the possibility that in the future, smaller houses will be viewed as more practical than they have been in the past.

## Low-Carbon Loyalty

This chapter has been concerned with describing the material life of the Amish and its bearing on greenhouse gas emissions. The rules and practices described here apply to the Old Order Amish who make up most of the Amish population. But a small number of Amish, the New Order, based in Ohio, defy most of these rules. Except for car ownership, much less separates the New Order from the wider society. The New Order participates in much of mainstream American material culture, including flying in airplanes and using conventional electricity. They also accept modern conveniences that the Old Order rejects, such as freezers and vacuum cleaners. The carbon footprint of a New Order Amish member may be as much as three times higher than that of someone who belongs to a traditional Amish district.

As a piece of the grand experiment of the Amish, one might speculate on how life is faring with the New Order Amish. Are they as a community as stable as the Old Order? The Old Order enjoys a loyalty to the Amish life that continues among the generations of

Fig. 7. This Amish horse barn in Lancaster County has a new upper story to accommodate Sunday prayer service. Low energy needs are covered by rooftop solar. Courtesy of the author.

Amish. The average defection rate for the Amish as a whole is only about 15 percent, meaning that the vast majority of Amish young people choose adult baptism and remain Amish. Oddly enough, the New Order is a different story. Defections are much higher, at 40 percent of the population. And higher defections are also found in other groups that allow adherents to use more technology. The Elkhart-Lagrange communities in northern Indiana include both progressive and conservative Amish, but the progressive districts experience more defections, with about 30 percent leaving the community as compared to about 20 percent among the conservative districts who avoid most contemporary technology. Members of these progressive districts no doubt have an easier time joining the mainstream because their material culture was not vastly different in the first place, but it may also be the case that their adoption of contemporary technology has diluted the social glue and sense of fulfillment that the more traditional Amish enjoy.

At the other extreme to the New Order are the stricter Amish communities such as the Swartzentruber and the Andy Weaver groups, which forswear petroleum products, flush toilets, and many other technologies that the Old Order has accepted or adapted. It might seem that a group that strict would have a difficult proposition in sustaining itself. But on the contrary, among the communities with relevant data, the defection rate is lowest—below 15 percent—for the Indiana-based Weaver group, whose members live a nineteenth-century material life.[65] They may be staying due to other reasons, but it is certainly true that the rigors of living a life that abstains from most technology and use of fossil fuel has not of itself led to many defections. Perhaps it is the absence of fossil fuels and appliances that drives a large part of the loyalty that young people feel toward their community and culture, impelling them to remain Amish.

### Lessons of Gelassenheit

If we consider an Amish Old Order household that uses some petroleum products but uses them in an Amish way, we can draw a general picture of what their greenhouse gas emissions might look like. For instance, a progressive Amish household with a natural gas refrigerator, petroleum-based lighting, and a wringer washer would be a source of some carbon dioxide emissions. But because the Amish pay much attention to when and where they heat and light a room, and use fewer appliances, cultural factors will reduce emissions. The greatest wildcard is transport emissions, because some individual Amish may hire cars frequently to visit far-flung residences, while others do so rarely. On a household level, Amish emissions may be a quarter or less of average American emissions. If we draw the picture at the societal level, the difference becomes all the greater. The American commercial sector is unprecedented in size compared to most of the rest of the world. Many of these

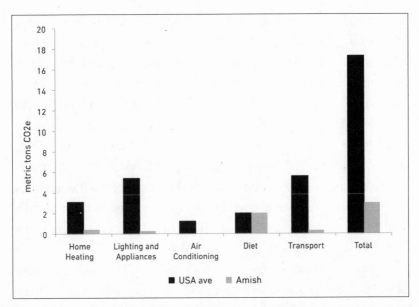

Fig. 8. Amish greenhouse gas emissions per person compared with the American average. U.S. average emissions are drawn from the U.S. EIA *Residential Energy Consumption Survey*, 2009, Table CE4.1, and diet- and transport-related emissions from U.S. EPA 2017, ES-25. Amish emissions are based on author's calculations drawing from Scott and Pellman, *Living Without Electricity*.

functions of government, retail, and education the Amish find inessential to their existence. Comparing our combined residential and commercial sectors to Amish society makes the contrast quite stark indeed.

The contrast in emissions between the Amish and non-Amish changes somewhat when we consider Amish family size. Amish couples have about seven children on average, compared to 2.1 in the rest of America, and the difference in fertility is augmented by the fact that the Amish tend to marry young and start their new households quickly.[66] If the Amish continue to have large families, the emissions projected for future descendants as a group would overtake average American emissions, but that point is not reached going forward one generation. Amish emissions are still less than the American average on a per capita basis as well as per household. Still, the Amish demography and culture reminds us that the ideal carbon dissenters live like the Amish but are vegetarian and have small families.

As greenhouse gas mitigators the Amish may be unprecedented. Imagine having so much control over the machine—the noise, information and convenience that comes with it. Never passing through airport security, no fights with children over screen time, mainly face-to-face interactions with your friends and family. No parking tickets, little junk mail. A quilting circle, not a decluttering support group. A pantry full of canned and pickled homegrown vegetables, no ingredients list necessary. On the flipside, horse flanks to brush, feed grains to acquire, and horse stalls to de-muck. Some measure of natural curiosity that goes unfulfilled.

What is possible for a non-Amish to take on? If the answer is none of the particulars, the answer can still be one or more of the general principals of durability, deliberateness, community connections and local. The Amish have avoided much of the obsolescence and materialism of contemporary society, and their selectivity is a shining example of a life with less stuff. Their goods tend to be well made, and by avoiding fashion, they avoid a degree of cultural obsolescence. Their deliberateness over space heating and lighting means that some effort is necessary to bring comfort to a room. Wood stoves need to be restocked, and petroleum lighting requires lifting, pouring, and pumping fuel. It's a small fraction of time out of a busy day, but enough effort that using fuels is never as casual as it is in the wider society. Supplying only one or two rooms with heat and light gives fuels a certain emotional acumen; social life becomes concentrated rather than dispersed. Amish deliberateness over transportation is so sweeping that it is hard to replicate exactly. But many Americans already deliberately make vehicle use less convenient by using car sharing or parking their vehicles some distance from their homes. Such actions are a light reminder against making short trips. Others make frequent use of the mainstream counterpart of the horse and buggy—the bicycle.

In the Amish world, the social and the geographical proximate are merged, and in the rest of America the possibilities of improving the localness of life are endless. Transplanting their example to mainstream society in the absence of large family size and a compatible religious fellowship, givens of Amish life, however, introduces unknowns. Their achievement is the product of an interconnected web of relationships and a shared belief of what makes a good life. Large family sizes mean a built-in social life and a momentum toward rules and routine. What if you took these away? For instance, a single person living alone would not have the incentives to conserve lighting in the way that the Amish do. Leaving the lights on has little social implication if there are not children around who need to be discouraged from spending too much time alone. In the absence of family and company, screen time becomes more compelling. If your local neighborhood does not provide satisfying personal connections, national and international travel become more attractive.

How many Americans can say that they are content to spend most of their time close to home? Perhaps few, but changing urban form expresses the yearning of the younger generation to live in compact, interactive, walkable neighborhoods. Curbing energy use can improve relationships among neighbors or at least reduce antagonisms. Want to live in a rural idyll but avoid noisy neighbors? Move to the countryside near an Amish settlement, a neighborhood where most of your neighbors don't have cars or motorcycles, a neighborhood without motorboats and power lawn mowers. The quiet countryside has its counterparts in urban neighborhoods where car traffic is marginalized and directed into slow, narrow streets. Pursuing more satisfying ties with one's neighbors is also a step that the non-Amish can take on at any time. It is in the reach of any American to adopt some of the habits of the Amish to keep more of our relationships and activities local.

The Amish shine a new light on our own helplessness about our fossil fuel dependence. Their needs for energy are so modest that solar and wind do a lot more for them than they would in a non-Amish household. They did not need national programs, laws, or incentives to avoid fossil fuels. They have used both the carrot and stick of peer pressure to guide their dependence on technology and energy. While districts have many rules about how individual families must live, in turn they provide a degree of support and companionship to their members. While our norm is to refrain from criticizing people for their possessions, the Amish have had an open dialogue with each other for some one hundred years about how technology adds or detracts from a good life. They have achieved a level of local consensus on these questions that may seem unimaginable, but is real and unique to America.

# CHAPTER THREE

# Urban Families

## Washington DC

A nineteenth-century essay about a picnic in the Kalorama neighborhood of Washington DC describes "towering heights, blooming valleys, purling streams and woodland groves."[1] Much of this greenery remains in adjoining Rock Creek Park, but remarkably, Kalorama Triangle and the nearby neighborhoods that make up zip code 20009 are now the densest in the East Coast south of northern New Jersey. Near the undulating valley of Rock Creek, about thirty-four thousand people live here per square mile compared with only ten thousand people per mile in the city of Washington DC as a whole.

Walking along streets in Kalorama Triangle, or Adams Morgan, and Columbia Heights, all part of 20009, it is easy to miss the density as lines of row houses with Georgian, Mediterranean, and Arts and Crafts features provide little clue to the compactness beyond. On the main streets, commercial spaces disguise the apartment buildings that rise above. Fully 85 percent of the residents live in multi-units. It is from the vantage point of the narrow, quirky alleys that the residential form best reveals itself as the brick buildings stretch to the edge of lots, leaving little space for cars or yards. Here and there, new stairways that access back doors on each floor are the main clue that some of the houses have been converted into multifamily buildings, allowing for radically lower energy consumption.

If 20009 were a county it would be the fourteenth-wealthiest county in the United States.[2] Here the median household income is $92,702, rivaling that of nearby Loudon, Fairfax, and Howard counties, which are the wealthiest in the country. Wealthier households tend to have more floor space, and no region of the United States surpasses the East Coast in the average size of its houses and its wealth.[3] In the 20009 zip code, however, many households have other priorities than space and high headroom, yards, and extra rooms. Many of these priorities are familiar, and proximity to work and cultural amenities come up a lot. But this chapter takes a different tack, looking in particular at affluent families who have turned their backs on elements of the traditional American dream that are presumed non-negotiable, such as single-family houses with private backyards and off-street parking. Living here, as well, are a better-known group of high earning individuals and couples without children who have foresworn traditional status symbols such as weekend houses, large floor plans and even car ownership.[4] These residents may be one of the United States' best examples of a population of affluent people who use very little energy in their homes and cars, and unlike peers in New York City, Chicago, and Boston, these residents are less likely to own a weekend house, with its attendant energy and gasoline demands.

The neighborhood gas station in Kalorama Triangle was razed recently to make way for a thirty-unit apartment building—it does not seem to be missed, about 46 percent of households here don't own a car.[5] A dilapidated store around the corner was demolished to make way for an apartment building with a gym on the floor level, the kind of amenity seen in many of the new mixed-use developments in DC. Maybe the most dramatic conversion can be found at an historic mansion in Dupont Circle—the former home of Chicago publishing magnate Richard Patterson. The original house, along with a new one-lot wide building, is becoming a ninety-unit apartment building. The "micro" units average 375 square feet, and the building developers envision a unique project that will offer social connections through a stimulating speaker series, a communal dining room, and smaller meeting rooms. The ground floor parlor will be refashioned into a lounge with undoubtedly very different décor than the stuffed moose and mountain goat heads that adorned the premises during the Gilded Age. A bike repair facility and free car-share and bike share memberships complete the picture for a car-alternative residence.

Like this apartment building, most new construction in these central DC neighborhoods seems aimed at young or youngish professionals, or at least people without kids. You don't find playrooms or outdoor play structures in the brand-new buildings. Many of the residents drive rarely and have low electric and natural gas bills because they live in apartments and condos. Their low carbon culture has been made possible by multi-unit investment, and a reversal of city codes that once required all new developments to provide a set amount of parking per unit. But the question for the five-ton life is similar to the hard question one can ask of any very small dwelling: Will people live here throughout their lifespan, or is it a temporary posting on the way to a large house and a growing family? Will the lives parallel those commonly found in affluent Manhattan, i.e. students and young professionals living in small apartments and eventually moving to larger condos or suburban houses, and second homes upstate in the woods or at the beach? Seeking an answer to that question, I ventured further into the culture of apartment living in Washington DC.

A better answer seemed worth the effort because the lowest carbon footprints anywhere tend to be found with families living in multi-unit buildings. It's easier for a family of four to achieve a low per person footprint in, say, a fifteen-hundred-square-foot condo than it is for a single person living in an apartment half the size. This situation of children growing up in apartments, of course, is not typical to America. Nationwide, only 26 percent of America's children live in multi-units or mobile homes. The state where you will find the most children living in multi-units is New York, at 43 percent. But Washington DC, as a compact city, can boast an even higher percentage of children living in multi units, at 47 percent.[6]

In the dense central DC neighborhoods where apartment dwelling families are commonplace, not everyone seems to feel that their choice is always well regarded, and some are engaged in assertively defending their lifestyle and the pedigree of the residents, such as this anonymous contributor to an online parent forum.

> In our building, I am one of the very few adults that we know that does not have a doctoral degree (I have two master's degrees). . . . So, to those that are scared that the apartment buildings ruin the quality of the local school, you might want to actually look at the demographics of who lives in those buildings. . . . And, even if the demographics of the 'apartment buildings' weren't so well-educated, I really hope you don't pass your snotty attitudes about Single-family houses in wealthy neighborhoods on to your kids.[7]

The online parent discussions on this topic, however, generally progress to broad statements of acceptance, such as the following: "No one cares where anyone lives – Gaithersburg or a condo in DuPont. It just isn't a conversation and that's nice." And from another contributor, "Now that you mention it, I have seen suite numbers in the addresses in our (Big 3) [private] school directory. Not a big deal. I don't think anyone cares."[8]

### A Cognitive Motivation

My work with middle school students in Washington DC's public school system on a carbon footprint survey that I conducted has given me a particular vantage point on how culture and emissions pan out here. The school is located in 20009 DC and draws primarily from two neighborhoods dominated by row houses and apartment buildings. The results of the carbon footprint survey showed dramatically low emissions for more than half the students' families. Emissions from driving were only about one third as much as the American average. Considering driving and home heating and electricity, about 85 percent of the families had emissions that were lower than the American average. In fact, nearly half of the families had emissions of about five tons each or less combined from their residences, cars, and diet. About 40 percent of the students surveyed were living in multi-unit buildings, and about 15 percent did not have a car available at home. These facts, as well as proximity to work, school, and shopping explained the low emissions rate. Only one household had electricity generated from rooftop solar, a source that currently generates about 1.7 percent of the electricity that Washington DC consumes.[9]

The students, none of whom lived in houses with significant lawns, let alone white picket fences, looked like they were doing okay. Their posture certainly looked more engaged than the listless, slumped-over sitting I remember from my suburban middle school days. I recognized some of the kids from a walking school bus or walk pool that passes through my neighborhood for which parent volunteers take turns escorting the kids to and from school. The school community is so cohesive that many of the parents had joined together to coach each other's kids on various practical skills like changing tires, investing in stocks, or cooking for a dinner party. Academically, the school's multilingual strength propelled several to represent the city in the Scripps National Spelling Bee and to achieve the college equivalent proficiency on the advanced placement Spanish test already in the 8th grade.

Many of these families were living in expensive apartments and condos and enjoyed relatively high income; only 20 percent qualified for free and reduced lunch.[10] Condos in central DC can be similar in price to single-family houses in many parts of the city, including the parts of the city that enjoy low crime rates like DC's far northwest section. So it is reasonable to assume that many apartment dwellers could afford to live in a house if they were willing to move. An anonymous contributor to a DC parent forum points out that for some people, such as herself, this is not a dilemma. "I recently realized that we could actually afford a SFH [single-family house].... We considered that possibility for about half a second before realizing how much we would be giving up in quality of life by having to take care of a house and yard."

But I have a hunch that many of the families were not living in multi-units as a first choice, since prices for single-family houses near the school started at $1.5 million. If cheaper houses were available in this location, some of the families would surely have snapped them up. There is another reason why many of the urban families are living in these dense neighborhoods rather than in the less expensive parts of the city. Many of these families are here because the central city offers something that can't be found in the less dense neighborhoods or in the suburbs—bilingual immersion schools. This reasoning comes up again and again in casual interactions in city parks, and playgrounds and wherever parents congregate. And the amenity of bilingual schools plays out in demographic data. Kalorama Triangle, which is in-bound for a well-regarded Spanish-English immersion school, has seen a 140-percent increase in children in the census tract between 2000 and 2010. In a neighboring tract that is not in-boundary for a bilingual elementary school, the share of children in the neighborhood declined by almost 50 percent during the same period.[11]

A half-dozen public language immersion schools can be found in 20009 alone, and fourteen such schools in the city as a whole. These programs are usually offered in Spanish, but French, Hebrew, and Mandarin public immersion charter schools are also present in the city. Parents may prefer a bilingual experience for their children not necessarily because they speak the second language themselves, but because they want their children to use their innate capacity for language acquisition before the capacity diminishes. Recent research about bilingualism and its potential benefits for brain development, avoiding Alzheimer's, and other advantages seem to have struck a chord for many Washington DC parents. Seminars on the cognitive advantages of bilingual education have become a mainstay of the

evening parent-teacher program at DC bilingual schools. An anonymous contributor to an online forum at dcurbanmom.com asked
why families would make sacrifices for a bilingual program and
received a typical response: "The research on the elasticity of the
brain and early language acquisition swayed us, and as a family can
support it at home."[12]

Many middle-class families left Washington DC for the suburbs
during the 1960s and 1970s to seek better schools for their children
and safer neighborhoods to live in, trends that played out throughout
the nation. The white flight created the very learning environment—
monolingual—that many well-educated Washingtonians now consider undesirable. As the crime rate declined in Washington DC,
dropping to half of what it had been in the mid-1990s, more families began to think twice about living in the suburbs.[13] In nearby
Montgomery County, Maryland, only about 5 percent of elementary
schools are bilingual, and gaining enrollment depends on the luck
of a lottery. In some of the more distant suburbs, you will not find
immersion schools at all. Even if more suburban schools started
immersion programs, many would lack the native-speaking population that enriches the bilingual experience, so many families whose
priority is languages choose to live in the central city.

One of these bilingual, apartment-dwelling families, Andrea Egan,
her husband, and three kids, is a recent transplant from Dallas. "We
looked into moving to the suburbs but decided it would be too hard
to navigate," explained Andrea. "Our priorities were accessibility to the
metro and to a bilingual school." The Egans left their custom-built,
three-thousand-square-foot "dream house and oversized detached
garage" and SUV for a twelve-hundred-square-foot apartment and
converted bike they call Liberty. The bike is outfitted with a metal
frame for holding groceries and providing extra support for the
youngest family member riding in the child seat. The children make
peace with sharing one bedroom by choosing their own decorating
theme—on one wall each. The dining room table also serves as a

Ping-Pong table, but the family spends much of their time in their "backyard": the 4.4 square miles of Rock Creek Park, whose western edge can be found directly across the street from their building.

That's where I met the family, at a friend's annual birthday hike that starts in Rock Creek Park and passes through four different woodland parks, before ending up at a kids' feature film at a Georgetown theater. The end of the hike in tony Georgetown may be a strange sight, with some twenty kids carrying sticks that they toss into the canal, but it seems every year more kids come out to hike. The human race surely was more likely to have evolved playing in this way than staring into a backlit screen for hours at a time or hanging out in a simplified version of nature's splendor, such as a suburban back yard.

## An Urban Evolution

The apartment-living lifestyle of the Egans and others like them may appear challenging in a nation where subsidies, zoning, and pricing seem to favor the suburban house more than the urbanized multi-unit. It can be hard to visualize dramatic changes amidst a widespread tendency to defend a status quo low density. But these Washington DC neighborhoods, located just north of the original L'Enfant city plan drawn up in 1801, show just such an evolution from suburban to dense urban. These neighborhoods, part of Ward 1 and centered around zip code 20009, including Kalorama Park, Adams Morgan, and Columbia Heights, are the densest in the city, but some of the sections began as large-lot mansion developments similar to present day Potomac, Maryland.

In fact, less than a century ago the Kalorama Triangle neighborhood was suburban in every sense except that it was within the city limits. All of the green space was enclosed in private backyards behind stone mansions or along the steep valley of Rock Creek Park, which was so sheer in this neighborhood that it was called the Badlands. An 1891 ad in the Washington Post describes a house for sale in what is now Kalorama Triangle: "Picturesque views are had in every direction, especially up the magnificent Rock Creek Valley. Immediately adjoining are the finest suburban residences in the District."[14] The "finest" residences in fact were the extremely large houses favored by the upper classes during the gilded age, such as Mintwood, a thirty-room mansion owned by land developer Lawrence Sands.

But Sands and several of his neighbors could see profit ahead, and the change from mansions into apartments and row houses was remarkably rapid. In 1901 Sands and his wife sold the Mintwood land parcel and moved into the first apartment building in the neighborhood, a Beaux-Arts–styled building called the Mendota. In the next decade, the largest landowner in Kalorama Triangle, George Truesdell, razed his house and built a new fifty-unit luxury building on his lot. Many of Washington's elite, including Supreme Court justices and members of Congress, were showing few qualms about moving into apartments. Within two decades the largest mansions were gone and most of the neighborhood residents were living in multi-units. After 1910, the smaller side streets filled in with attached row housing built in the Wardman style with two stories and a front porch. Over time, the insides of the large apartment houses also changed to accommodate more residents. Public spaces inside the buildings, such as restaurants and small shops, were gradually converted into additional residential units. Surface parking lots disappeared as new apartment buildings went up in their place.

A progression away from the large lots of the upper crust of the Gilded Age can be seen in other urban neighborhoods of America's older cities. The demise of the Victorian house accompanied declining family size and a change in attitude and hosting convention. In some ways, it was easy come, easy go, because when the mansions were built in the late nineteenth century, they were a relatively recent phenomenon in America. They had not been built here during the colonial period, the federal period, or even the Jacksonian Era. The large house, as it had evolved on other continents, appeared less relevant for European settlers in the New World. The most respected people in America in the seventeenth and eighteenth centuries through the first half of the nineteenth century did not think that it was necessary or desirable to own a very large house. It was harder to maintain a larger house in America than in Europe because the climate in the areas of early settlement demanded more heating fuel. America was not a polygamous society and did not have a need for housing multiple families under one roof. Nor did Americans have the British tradition of manor houses belonging to a hereditary aristocracy with hosting obligations. In Britain, the word "mansion" referred to the chief residence of a lord, but in the late eighteenth century American colonists began to use the term "manshon" to describe a house that could be occupied by anyone.

In the late nineteenth century, Americans enjoyed greater wealth and lower childhood mortality and built houses that we now call "Victorian." These houses often contained far more rooms than would be used for family bedrooms or routine family activities. To show off the family's finest furnishings, the upper classes developed an elaborate practice of making social calls that, according to participants, bordered on the tedious: "Probably Mrs. X wasn't any more pleased to have her activities interrupted than the caller was to interrupt them," wrote May Estelle Cook, describing the social obligations of the upper middle class in the 1880s Midwest.[15] A detailed code of American parlor etiquette rapidly evolved to fulfill a need for handling different types of social occasions. The demands on the wardrobe were also elaborate with a change of clothes required for breakfast, morning, walking, and evening dresses.

In the 1890s, as women started to join clubs and activities outside the house in greater numbers, the practice of trading cards and hosting mere acquaintances began to wane, as did the excuse for the very large house. The size of families also decreased. While about half of all households in 1890s America had five or more members, by 1930 only about 30 percent of American households were this large, and the percentage had shrunk to 10 percent by 1990. Amid the trend of

Fig. 9. Kalorama Triangle multi-unit converted from a single-family house. The house on the left was converted into four condos from a single house in 2011 before the DC city zoning rules were altered to limit such conversions. Currently, the building has eleven residents compared with two previously. Courtesy of the author.

declining family size, many forms of smaller house, especially the bungalow, took root in America's expanding cities during the early twentieth century. The changes that took place in Kalorama Triangle were echoed throughout American cities as Victorian houses were demolished to make way for apartments and commercial buildings. Sometimes the painted ladies were converted into multi-units with streamlined exteriors.

Today, with ever-smaller families and fewer expectations about receiving guests, the purpose of the larger house is less obvious. While in 1975 about 40 percent of married Americans said that they entertained in their home at least twelve times a year, by 1999 this number had declined to less than 20 percent.[16] According to the author of *The Not So Big House*, Sarah Susanka, the majority of people who live in single-family houses say that they never use their dining room.[17] Therefore it is not surprising that more people are meeting their friends in restaurants instead of in their homes. In fact in 2015, according to Department of Commerce data, Americans spent more money in restaurants and bars than on groceries.[18]

A few years ago, it looked as though America was beginning to lose interest in larger houses and suburban locales. According to a 2011 survey, 77 percent of millennials said that they planned to live in an "urban core."[19] A study from the National Association of Realtors similarly reported that 62 percent of young adults wanted to live in a neighborhood with transit and mixed-use development instead of in a residential neighborhood without sidewalks.[20] Innovative planners like Andrew Duany, Elizabeth Plater-Zyberk, and Jeff Speck, authors of *Suburban Nation*, have influenced the spread of the mixed-use idea intended to marginalize the automobile. Instead of commercial areas separate from homes, New Urbanist ideas advocate mixing these functions to place people near desirable walking destinations and near transit. These goals, businesses near transit, walkability, and density, characterize much of the new development found throughout the Washington DC metropolitan area. The subway is still expanding, and most existing metro stations are in the center of a growing hub of residences and buildings. These trends, however, appear to have had limited impact at the national level, as yet, because apartment construction still lags much behind house construction. In 2014, 620,000 single-family houses were completed, compared with 264,000 units in multi-unit buildings. More than twice as many Americans are moving into new houses each year compared to multi-units, and instead of shrinking, house size is still gaining.[21]

At the same time, an indisputable shift in attitudes is taking place that has the potential to transform the built environment and the average carbon footprint. Bolstering the alternatives to traditional suburban scale is the growing prestige of the smaller space, where inhabitants appear less materialistic, more organized, and clutter-free. People who live in small spaces can appear to be more experiential than acquisitive, and inhabitants are usually happy to explain to the media that they now have more time and money for recreational pursuits, community service, and relationships. Social scientists tend to agree, explaining, "Experiences make people happier because they are more open to positive reinterpretation, are a more meaningful part of one's identity and contribute more to successful social relationships."[22]

And then there's the challenge of the tidy house. A century ago, the problem of clutter was too minor to have much of a presence in the house and garden section of a paper such as the *New York Times*, but now, according to *Times* contributor Pamela Druckerman, "Everyone I meet seems to be waging a passionate private battle against their own stuff, and they perk up as soon as you mention it." The column, of course, attracted many comments that explained why the problem is more than a conversation starter. "Clutter is the expression of a culture that has replaced meaningful pursuits with shopping. We've plundered the earth for this clutter and now we're like King Midas. We wanted wealth and what we got was death. Getting rid of clutter is about something much bigger than creating a restful living space."[23]

Clutter contributes to carbon emissions through the goods themselves, which are often made overseas using coal. Recent estimates of the greenhouse gas emissions embodied in manufactured goods that Americans buy and use but that were made overseas suggest that this is a large and growing part of the American footprint. Using detailed data on manufacturing and trade, Christopher Weber and Scott Matthews of Carnegie Mellon University suggest that as much as 30 percent of total U.S. household carbon dioxide occurred outside the United States in the form of goods that were imported and consumed by Americans.[24] This amount is in addition to emissions related to products manufactured inside the United States. Many households are boosting the energy related to their possessions by renting space in a storage building that may require energy for temperature moderation and gasoline for visiting the site. In this way, the carbon footprint of the original house is extended into emissions related to the goods inside the house, storage away from the main house, and extra mobility in passing back and forth.

Even residents who don't keep their homes spotless will be shouldering a great deal of housework and upkeep, the more so with a larger floor area. Far fewer households retain the live-in servants that were a given of larger houses in the nineteenth and early-twentieth centuries. House owners tend to take on the tasks that apartment building owners usually employ others to do—roles such as building manager, desk clerk, engineer, cleaner, and gardener. In America, workers in multi-unit buildings make up a huge employment cadre. About 686,000 people are employed as building managers, rental agents, and maintenance workers for apartment buildings, not including the thousands of people employed to fulfill these roles for condomiuns.[25]

The concept of the clutter-free, beautiful, small apartment and its aesthetic and existential advantages can be found in a growing number of blogs, including Andrea Egan's *DC Urban Experiment* (dcurbanexperiment.com), where photos of her living room reveal not a single trace of clutter. The Egans host large (vegetarian) dinner parties as well, although her apartment does not contain a dining room or other features that a suburban realtor might claim are necessary for entertaining. Other bloggers pitch the concept of small is beautiful in the fields of philosophy, activism, and physical fitness: Tammy Strobel's "Go Small, Think Big, and Be Happy," at rowdykittens.com; Leo Babauta's zenhabits.net; Colin Beavan, or No Impact Man, at colinbeavan.com; Annie Leonard and the Story of Stuff at storyofstuff.org; and Graham Hill, founder of LifeEdited.com and treehugger.com. The original small apartment blog, Max Gilligan-Ryan's apartmenttherapy.com, is "saving the world, one room at a time." Joshua Becker's becomingminimalist.com offers advice for getting rid of sentimental possessions by photographing—"shoot your stuff"—scanning—"put it in the cloud"—or capturing memories in a personal journal and throwing the mementos out. Wisconsin architect Virge Temme likes to talk her clients into scaling down their plans. "They might start with a plan for a 4,500-square-foot house. I ask them to reassess and they start thinking 3,000, but settle on around 2,000 square feet." Temme often counsels her clients to rent a condo for a year before they pursue building a house. "Then they might decide they don't need the space."[26]

The small, cool apartment concept has helped to drive the growth in demand for micro-units of less than 400 square feet and new construction projects have gained official support in New York City (Kips Bay), San Francisco (Cubix), Portland (the Shoebox), and Washington DC. In a neighborhood of northeast Washington, you can find a cluster of tiny houses. The smallest one is the familiar tiny house of 65 square feet made by the Tumbleweed Tiny House Company, and can be transported like a mobile home. The larger two-hundred-square-foot Minim House won an award in 2013 from the American Institute of Architects. It passes the national building code minimum of 135 square feet and is a model in multifunctional furniture and built-ins. The full-sized bed in the Minim House is on castor wheels and can be rolled away to fit under the floor of a small raised area of the room that serves as an office. The storage space under the sitting area includes a water tank and fuel tank. A table that seats six people can collapse into coffee-table size. A screen can be pulled down over the windows to present the image from a projector. This highly versatile house was built for only $77,000, about one tenth the cost of nearby houses.[27] Such a house models low energy use but it stands on land close to the city center, a site desirable for multi-unit housing. Given the demand for land close to city centers, it may seem more logical to stack the Minim House, which in fact begins to describe what multi-unit buildings are and why they exist.

# House Alternatives

The advantages of location, cost, low maintenance, and for some, the aesthetic edge of apartment living have all contributed to the increasing de m and for apartments in America. Adding to the demand is the large number of older baby boomers who want to age in place, but in easy-to-maintain, easy-to-navigate dwellings. Given that retirees make up an increasing share of the U.S. population, the demand for apartments will only grow larger over the coming decades. These seniors seem to be more attracted by "small cool" than by exurban models. According to surveys from MetLife Mature Markets Institute, few seniors (14 percent) express a desire to "move away from crowded cities," and relatively few express a wish to move to a warmer climate (18 percent).[28] The majority say that they prefer a dwelling with low maintenance (63 percent), suggesting a growing demand for living in cities and towns and for living in apartments.

While the demographic cohort interested in apartments—including older baby boomers—has increased, new apartment construction slowed dramatically after the 2008 loan crisis. For some people, aging in place alone in a large suburban house is not a first choice, but a practical result of limited alternatives. People who wish to rent or buy apartments, particularly in locations distant from the Eastern and Western Seaboard, can be frustrated by a lack of supply. Multiunit construction dropped off rapidly in 2009. By 2010, only about 124,000 rental apartments and about 31,000 condo/co-op units were completed.[29] Apartment construction began to tick up in 2012 but remains below the projected need, which Harvard's Center for Joint Housing puts at three hundred thousand new units each year.

To finance multi-unit buildings, investors tend to rely heavily on government-sponsored loans instead of private loans and insurance, but federal lenders abandoned many projects at a time of sore need after the 2008 housing bust. Although federal lenders Fannie Mae and Freddie Mac financed 85 percent of multi-unit projects in 2009, this support dropped to 43 percent of loans in 2012.[30] The federal lenders restricted credit despite the soundness of many multi-unit applications. Whereas single-family house loans translated into a loss of $209 billion for the federal lenders, they scored a net gain of $7 billion from the multi-units. Only 0.5 percent of multi-unit property loans defaulted compared with 8.7 percent of single-family mortgages. Given their credit worthiness, a logical response would be to expand credit for multi-unit lending.

Home ownership—especially large house ownership—is heavily subsidized through the mortgage interest tax deduction. High income households are the main beneficiary, and Harvard tax economist Edward Glaeser has long claimed that instead of making home-ownership easier for the middle class, this deduction drives people in high tax brackets to buy larger houses.[31] Analysts at conservative think tank R Street Institute have estimated that the mortgage interest deduction has supported an average house size increase of 540 square feet in the Chicago area and a whopping 1,424 square foot increase in the Washington DC area.[32] The environmental impact of this deduction was unforeseen but of enormous consequence, and likewise for the tax deduction on vacation homes, which faces similar problems in its environmental and equity ramifications. In *The Agile City* James Russell suggests, "When America is not adequately housing people with severe needs, it cannot afford to underwrite luxe digs on beaches and in mountains."[33]

Overhauling the mortgage tax deduction could cast a shadow on the allure of the very large house. An alternative to doing away with the deduction altogether would be to modify the deduction so that it only applies to smaller homes. One possibility is that the deduction would only apply to first homes and those 1,500 square feet or smaller, about the dimensions of the median American house constructed circa 1970. The smaller house is of more relevance to the lower-middle bracket seeking home ownership and such a cutoff makes a clear statement about both the social and environmental impacts of the deduction.

Supporting smaller houses and apartment construction certainly would be a cheaper way to cut carbon dioxide emissions than many of the proposals and programs that have received federal and local government support. Apartment floor plans have been maintaining their compactness despite the trend toward supersizing new single-family houses. New multi-unit dwellings were 1,187 square feet on average in 2016, down from a high of 1,300 square feet in 2007.[34] The trend toward smaller apartments and larger houses point to widening differences in America in energy consumption and carbon footprints. The difference is largest in the Northeast, the region with the largest new houses and apartments, but also the most small and tiny old apartments, and swank new apartments in walkable neighborhoods.

Aside from their lower energy requirements, multifamily homes can offer an edge in energy conservation because features can be applied to scale over many units. Therefore, it is disappointing that incentives for improving energy efficiency in multifamily homes often lag behind what is available for single-family houses.[35] In Arizona, for example, apartments and condos make up about 5.9 percent of the housing stock but only 0.1 percent of the energy efficiency investments. In only a few states—California, Massachusetts and New York—is spending for multi-unit efficiency improvements commensurate with the share of multi-unit housing compared with total housing. The most far-reaching program for multifamily housing is a program called the National Grid, located in New England and New York and managed by a private company that offers free audits and incentives for installing more efficient equipment such as different lighting, lighting controls and compressed air. Between 1998 and 2010 their program reportedly reached about a quarter of a million households and achieved accumulated savings of about four metric tons of carbon dioxide per household, about a 20 percent drop in energy use.[36]

In the recent past, central DC did not retain many retirees and seniors, a cohort with a high demand for multi-units, but a demographic shift can be seen in the latest census data with an increase in the proportion of seniors in the neighborhoods near Rock Creek Park and a decline in the commercial-centered U Street and Columbia Heights neighborhoods. Between 2000 and 2010, the greener neighborhoods of Kalorama Triangle, Adams Morgan, and Lanier Heights saw a 50 percent increase in the proportion of seniors living in these areas. Aspects of green culture such as bike sharing and car sharing have been absorbing an older demographic as middle-aged residents and retirees find value in them.[37]

Some of the older residents in Kalorama Triangle and other DC neighborhoods are a dynamic force in the growing interest in urban naturalism. Some have become "weed warriors" in Rock Creek Park, trained and licensed to remove invasive plants from the national park. Each warrior has a given territory and instructions not to work in another volunteer's turf, and a few have become so vested in the project that they have accumulated many hundreds of hours on the task.[38] Others have been involved in tree-planting through the Casey Trees Foundation, riverine plant establishment through the Anacostia Watershed Society, or native seed collection through the Potomac Conservancy. Recently, hundreds of volunteers contributed to Rock Creek Park's once-a decade BioBlitz, the species inventory weekend that began in Walden Pond and has engaged thousands of people in rich enclaves of biodiversity throughout the country. Many people who get a taste of these experiences of urban nature, constructive work and camaraderie find them irresistible, not to mention the sports and recreational activities that traditionally take people outside.

Like many other American cities, Washington DC has a good bit of nature preserved. On a recent visit to Rock Creek Park, biologist E. O. Wilson described the park, "Original forests. It's a little beat up but it's the real thing."[39] Wilson's term for a deep biological need for wild nature—biophilia—has endured and inspired a DC-area group by the same name. Parallel efforts can be seen throughout urban America as people find a personal connection with public lands preserved in cities, be they public forests, prairies, or estuaries.[40] According to research by the Trust for Public Lands, about two-thirds of all American urban dwellers live within a half mile of a public park.[41] The psychic value that many suburbanites have gained by working in their own private garden is being dynamically transformed in these biologically rich, urban spaces. Some of Washington DC's newest housing developments aimed at seniors are mid-rise apartments in commercial zones that back directly onto Rock Creek Park.

Since so many American residential neighborhoods are already built and zoned to encourage houses instead of apartments and condos, a hopeful prospect for more compact living are house conversions. The act of converting a house into two or more units can cut greenhouse gases more effectively than putting up an apartment building nearby because the conversion erases the original, larger floor plan. Such conversions can also undermine the excuse some people use to justify a large house. Anyone who has engaged anyone in a conversation about urban-versus-suburban living has most likely encountered this defense. Moving into a smaller residence is futile, the argument goes, because someone else will move into the big house and resume a high carbon footprint lifestyle. The conversions contradict that point because, when they subdivide the large house, they are subdividing the per-person carbon footprint, and the higher-carbon lifestyle is no more.

In a typical conversion in Kalorama Triangle, a row house built in the early twentieth century for a single family gets gutted and rebuilt and goes on the market as a two-, three-, or four-unit condo building. The original front exterior will remain the same, but a new stairwell and sometimes more space may be added on the alley side. The energy use per square foot will typically go up after a building is converted, but since more people are living in the building, the overall footprint will go down.[42] For instance, a three-thousand-square-foot attached house in DC converted to three separate apartments would typically change the number of people using the space from 1.5 persons before the conversion to at least 5.0 after the conversion. Converting the building drives up the energy use per square foot by about 50 percent, but with the added people, the per-person carbon footprint is cut in half.[43]

The conversions would seem to be unobjectionable, but they have fueled bitter opposition. A minority of conversions, which have been called pop-ups, have involved adding an unsightly upper floor that does not blend in with the older building fronts. But much of the opposition is not about aesthetics, and conversion opponents have charged that the projects will make the neighborhood less "family oriented." The family values argument and stereotype seems to hold enough weight that residents of the converted buildings sometimes make a point of attending local meetings to explain that they are human too and even have children! A few homeowners have put a new twist on the NIMBY stance, arguing that a planned conversion will limit sunlight and affect their ability to benefit from solar energy in the future should they decide to install panels. Some homeowners in Washington DC have even threatened to lobby for legislation that would prohibit conversions in the vicinity of houses that already have rooftop solar panels.[44] Supporters of conversions have countered with at least one example of a converted building that volunteered to host their neighbor's solar panels. The whole debate underlines the problem of perceptions toward renewable energy versus consumption. Converting a house will bring far steeper cuts in carbon emissions, but the perception remains that rooftop solar is the greener option.

A less controversial kind of conversion consists of projects that create accessory units. These spaces entail converting a basement or a garage to make an apartment on the property, usually for a parent or child. Changes are afoot to zoning rules in Washington DC that would give residents the right to use such spaces. These projects will increase the number of people living in given neighborhoods and are considered complementary to smart growth because they can create more dynamic sidewalks and walkable communities, especially if the aged parent or young adult does not drive. Unlike outright house conversions, however, these projects will not necessarily reduce per-person energy use. Instead, they may maximize space and privacy for all family members and extend the living area that is consuming energy—a different situation from the old days when relatives moved into the den or spare bedroom.

The debates about conversions have fielded many topics, including architectural aesthetics, affordable housing, parking scarcity, and real estate values, but energy conservation tends not to be one of them. An exception, such as this example in a local newspaper, rarely makes in onto a hearing transcript. "How do we get enough density to leverage the transportation assets and walkability, so we minimize GHG emissions?"[45] It might seem that the conversion controversy would attract national environmental groups such as the Natural Resources Defense Council (NRDC) and the Sierra Club, which have energy conservation programs. However, these organizations, which also have DC advocacy programs, have been sitting this one out. The voices in favor of conversions in DC have been led by the developers themselves and some affordable housing advocates. The lack of involvement of environmental organizations in density controversies such as this one is a topic that transit advocate Benjamin Ross takes up in his book, *Dead End: Suburban Sprawl and the Rebirth of American Urbanism*. He argues that neighborhood groups that are the most local tend to be the ones most vociferously against residential density. True to Ross's point, the most local of Washington DC's government bodies—the Advisory Neighborhood Commissions—have voted soundly against the conversions. The citywide historic preservation commission has been more divided with some members proposing that the aesthetic concerns with some pop-ups could be handled through design rules or by detailing that the height of the conversion must conform to the average building height on either side of the property. These kinds of debates and accommodations have been far from the agenda of climate change advocacy, but they are the stuff of greater compactness and ultimately, a lower emissions culture.

## Car Alternatives

The first large-scale bike-sharing program in the United States, Capitol Bike Share, was launched in Washington DC in 2010. Capitol Bike Share's signature red bike, with playful yellow arrows in the shape of a devil's tail, now number around 2,500 bikes in about 300 docking stations in the district and nearby counties in Maryland and Virginia. The program was the first bike sharing scheme to turn a profit, helped by the large number of tourists who buy the pricier single or daily trips. Now some dozen American cities host bike-sharing programs with New York City's eight thousand shared bikes, the largest such program in the country.[46]

Bike sharing has much in common with the small, cool apartment aesthetic. Instead of a jumble of beat-up commuter bikes, a bike sharing docking station is a sleek grid of solid colors locked in place in perfect alignment, a simple urban sculpture whose look ebbs and flows as the wave of commuters fills up the metal structures with color and empties them out again. The pattern of dispersion and concentration varies throughout the day, and tracking software helps ensure that "rebalancers" go where they are needed to see that no docks are full or completely empty for very long. The aesthetic of the bikes and docks ties in with the symbolic identity of the city or the sponsor in that city, which can be a private company, a nonprofit, or city government. Washington DC's bikes match the dominant red of Washington DC's flag. Chicago's match their city's soft blue flag color. New York City's stronger blue matches its sponsor Citigroup's logo. Like swords converted to pruning hooks, the phalanx of colored bikes boasts of city regiments in native uniform. The riders wheeling the bikes out of their ranks can be seen as waging war against congestion, smog and $CO_2$ emissions.

Bike sharing can be liberating for people who already own a bike because a member can unlock a bike in less than five seconds and return it in less than three seconds. They can choose a one-way trip to avoid the uphill side of commuting, and can enjoy the freedom to change plans at the last minute, and during a change in the weather they can switch to the subway. In fact, the Capitol Bike Share had its greatest usage on August 23, 2011, the day that Washington DC experienced an earthquake, and car commuters overwhelmed local streets. "Roads were saturated and I was easily the fastest moving vehicle on Florida Avenue," recalled a bike share member.[47]

Earlier bike-sharing schemes were often ruined by theft, but Capitol Bike Share invested in bikes with a distinctive shape that evades concealment and disguise. Since the stations tend to be spaced at less than a half-mile interval and only the first twenty minutes are free, riders are deterred from venturing far afield. From the moment that users remove a bike from a docking station to the time that they return it, the activity is recorded through a wireless data link that connects the docking stations with a central bike-tracking office. Users wanting to be sure that their preferred docking station has enough bikes or empty spaces can check in real time using a smartphone app or the website. In the first few years of the program, the Capitol Bike Share recorded 3.6 million rides and only 25 lost bikes, of which 11 were recovered.[48] Users say that they have avoided, on average, 158 miles of driving annually by using the service. Not a huge total, but the direct savings in carbon dioxide—about 1,600 metric tons—may be the least of the advantages.[49] The program is a morale booster for the urban resident, proclaiming loudly that bikes are no longer the vehicles of the marginalized. In concert with the boldly painted bike lanes and paths, bike sharing becomes the transit of the insider and its neighborhoods enjoy the proof of walkability and car alternatives. The presence of the solid bike infrastructure makes the prospect of a complete low-carbon life in a smallish living space more attractive.

The street that starts at the White House and ends at the top corner of the District of Columbia, the central spine of L'Enfant's original design, is the focus of much of the city's bus-planning dialogue. Today, Sixteenth Street buses form an almost continuous line along a street that also bears heavy car traffic. On a recent trip, I noticed that the inside of the bus looked very different from the ridership I was used to seeing. Most of the riders in the packed bus appeared to be under thirty-five years of age, and almost everyone was staring at a smartphone and had an audio plug in their ear. Washington DC bans the use of hand-held devices while driving, a motivating factor for some commuters to use public transportation.

Aggressive parking enforcement has also played a part reducing car ownership and driving in the city by ensuring that car ownership, parking, and driving are not worry free. The city's parking enforcement shows little mercy for cars that are parked slightly too close to a corner, a driveway, or many other infractions. Revenue from parking tickets and moving violations are a big part of the city budget in Washington DC, as they are in other large American cities that are especially dense. In 2014 Washington DC took in $179 million for traffic and parking violations, more than twice the revenues from taxes that are more closely linked to an environmental agenda—the motor fuel and the motor vehicle excise taxes.[50] In New York City the revenue from vehicle-related fines and fees has seen a boost in recent years and in 2015 reached $1.9 billion, an amount equivalent to about 2.4 percent of the entire budget.[51] While the environmental goal of making car owners pay more of the real costs of driving has failed at the fuel pump, Washington DC and other cities have found other means for making driving less of a free ride.

In this part of the city—zip code 20009—with few garages, cars compete for space and when all the street parking is filled, the only option is parking in another zone and risking a parking ticket. These conditions have spurred a trend toward ever smaller, more fuel-efficient cars that can fit into remaining street spaces. You find mostly cars such as Civics, Priuses, and Smart Cars on the neighborhood streets; SUVs are rare. The scarcity of on-street parking has also helped the neighborhood to look favorably on alternatives to car owner-ship, such as car sharing. Many DC condo buildings now allow car-sharing companies to keep cars on their property.

The first car share program in Washington DC, Zipcar, launched in 2000, remains the largest car-sharing network in the country, and now claims nearly one million members worldwide.[52] Zipcar offers recent car models, appealing to the millennial generation, and charges by the hour. Another program, Car2go, uses two-passenger Smart Cars that can be left where the driver chooses, instead of in the original pick up spot. Conventional car rental companies, including Enter-prise and Hertz, now also offer hourly rentals of cars parked in pub-lic alleys and various sites scattered around the neighborhood, and the scheme works in a similar fashion as Zipcar. The newest trend in DC car sharing is peer-to-peer sharing, where private car owners who want to share their vehicles use a website to arrange a time and a rental rate with a would-be driver. The cost and convenience of using car sharing seems to be more of a draw than the environmen-tal benefits. Only a minority of Zipcar members (36 percent) sur-veyed agreed with the following statement: "I want to protect the environment so I drive less."[53]

The proliferation of car-sharing choices obviously reflects a con-cept that succeeds, at least in urban areas such as metropolitan Wash-ington DC and the growing number of American towns and cities that have a stable sharing program. Car sharing makes urban living more attractive to residents who might worry about the scarcity of on-street or garage parking or those who do not want to invest in the cost of owning a vehicle outright. Using car sharing, which I did for several years, delayed the day in which I invested in a private vehicle. Other households use car sharing instead of buying a second car. A further advantage is that a shared car means that fewer cars need to be manufactured. Since about 10 percent of a car's carbon dioxide emissions arise from making a car rather than driving one, those savings can be sizable.[54]

On average, people who use a car-sharing service such as Zipcar drive about one thousand miles a year—much less than the American average. Therefore, it can be disappointing to read surveys that inform us that car-share members are only saving about a half a ton of carbon dioxide annually.[55] But these surveys, such those from Berkeley's Transportation Sustainability Research Center, accept that for the respondents, a compact city lifestyle is a given and they would not be driving much regardless. A broader view recognizes that car-sharing options actually sweeten the deal for apartment living, because it makes city living less expensive. In turn, the presence of so many apartments in places like Kalorama Triangle ensures that the shared cars are well used and can be priced reasonably.

## Meat Alternatives

In the United States cattle production is the number-one source of methane emissions related to human activities. The animal rights organization People for the Ethical Treatment of Animals (PETA) has its headquarters near Dupont Circle in DC and makes the connection between meat-eating and climate change in bold writing on the side of a PETA van that frequently traverses the neighborhood. Like most American cities, a culinary effort to support vegetarianism is apparent in many locally owned DC restaurants, but perhaps the strongest showing are the row of vegetable-centered lunch spots near Dupont Circle including Beefsteak, which features a beet "burger," Bibibap, which offers a vegetable-heavy take on the Korean rice bowl, and Sweetgreen, a salad-centered lunch venue. Another fast-food restaurant, the Burger Joint, offers a bean, turkey, or chicken burger, as well as a beef patty. The largest restaurant group in zip code 20009 owns a series of cafes and restaurants including Tryst, the Diner, Open City, and the Coupe, as well as smaller cafes. They offer a new vegan entrée every season. "There's a huge community of people here who want something special in their vegetarian meals and they are willing to eat out of their comfort zone," explained the restaurant group's executive chef, Rob Theriot.

Therefore, it is surprising to look at national polling data and see that not many Americans are faithful vegetarians in the strict sense. According to the Vegetarian Research Group's most recent survey, only 5 percent of women and 3 percent of men are vegetarians or vegans who almost never eat meat. The younger generation surpasses the rest by only a hair: 5 percent of those aged eighteen to thirty-four years say they are vegetarian or vegan, compared with 4 percent of thirty-five-to fifty-four-year-olds. Hispanics stand out as the most vegetarian, at 8 percent.[56] On the other hand, many Americans eat a vegetarian diet most of the time even if they are not vegetarians in a strict sense. The proportion of Americans who say that more than half of their meals are vegetarian is about 22 percent. Slogans such as Meatless Monday and "Be a Flexitarian" give support to the concept that eating less meat helps. Nationwide, many beef meals are being replaced by chicken. In 2014 poultry slaughter totaled a record 51 billion pounds, compared with 44 billion pounds in 2003.[57] Many people see chicken as a healthier option than beef, and because poultry produces a lesser amount of greenhouse gases than beef and lamb, the dietary shift in favor of chickens has had some benefits for the atmosphere.[58] Many Americans are surpassing the modest goals of Meatless Monday and a new challenge may be in order that claims vegetarianism for more than one day of the week. In this space I'll offer to raise the bar a few notches with Meaty Monday, where one day a week is set aside for meat while the rest of the week is for vegetarian meals.

Among the DC families surveyed for this study, about one-third said that they rarely ate beef. If true, such a diet would cut out 1.0 to 1.5 metric tons of $CO_2$ equivalent from their footprints. American emissions related to diet are quite low at present only because we have policies that avoid importing meat from South American countries, where clearing for pasture means a huge loss of carbon from tropical soils and trees. The import ban has to do with health reasons—avoiding foot and mouth disease—not environmental considerations. If the disease concerns change and import bans are lifted, the result could be a tremendously increased environmental cost to American beef consumption. As a habit, less beef in the diet portends a buffer against a time when beef consumption will be even more destructive than it is today.

Cutting a ton of greenhouse gases from diet is in a sense more powerful than cutting a ton of greenhouse gases from another source, because reducing beef and lamb consumption frees up American cropland for better uses. Instead of using the land for corn and soybeans for cattle, it can be used to grow plant protein for human diet or to sustain grass and woodland ecosystems and nature preserves. These uses can feed people who have lost their food sources due to climate change–induced drought and can provide a reserve of woodlands or prairies with their biodiversity and carbon sequestration benefits.

### Almost There

The low-carbon culture that has evolved among many families in central Washington DC seems almost too good to be true. The many characteristics that support low driving rates are present, including location, good transit, and pleasant walking—characteristics that complement each other. Less directly, these factors make apartments, condos, and smaller houses more attractive than they might otherwise be because leafy, safe, and interesting neighborhoods can make up for size in some people's eyes. And the presence of compact living puts more people on the sidewalks and attracts new restaurants, a further draw for many people. Less obviously, the creative and educational offerings in the city, especially bilingual education, have flipped one of the past motivators for fleeing to suburbs—the schools. On top of all this, the DC bilingual families seem to eat much less meat than the average American.

These Washingtonians' car-light and meat-light living are knocking about 3.5 metric tons off the carbon footprint, and the apartment and condo dwellers were shedding another 1–10 metric tons compared with the house dwellers. If the story ended here, this slice of life in central Washington could be described as an unmitigated success story. But it is the case that most of the families I surveyed used airplanes a great deal, in fact so much that flight related emissions were more than double the car-related emissions. The families chalked up about 2.4 million air miles in one year. The greenhouse gas emissions from this flying reversed in carbon dioxide the peddling exertions of 7,380 members of Washington DC's bike-sharing program in one year. The lengthy and numerous flights are compounded by the nature of flying—a gallon of fuel burned aloft packs more than double the destructive power of a gallon burned on the ground, because the plane's contrails trap heat and the $NO_x$ puts new ozone in the wrong place. Part of the traveling among the middle school crowd was a weeklong school service trip to a developing country "to participate in environmental activities," an excursion involving more than four thousand miles of long-haul travel. So all the while that the city is improving its bike lanes and green infrastructure, it is also offering free and subsidized airfare for DC public school 8th-graders to take enrichment trips abroad.[59]

Air travel is the fastest growing area of transportation, but alternatives to fossil fuel-based aviation fuel will not be available for the foreseeable future.[60] Some forty years has passed since the airline industry was deregulated, making flying affordable to a wide swath of Americans. Low-cost airfare supported the increase in study-abroad programs for American college students during the 1970s. And in the late 1990s a range of new programs began catering to clients as young as middle school students.[61] Washington DC's international travel programs for public middle school students offer few lectures and museum visits in the foreign destination but appear to simulate the experience of a family vacation with activities that include short hikes and a cooking class that promises to teach an authentic cuisine. DC educators explain the program this way: "Study abroad helps ensure that our global citizens have access to global experiences, so that travel becomes the expectation rather than the exception."[62]

Teaching the concept that young teens are entitled to international travel is an interesting one for an urban culture that has turned its back on some of the carbon excesses of earlier eras. Few DC families live in the large houses introduced to America in the late nineteenth century or participate in the unconstrained car travel that began in the early twentieth century. Now, in the early twenty-first century, we are at the early stages of embracing an idea that short-stay, long-haul air travel is not a luxury but a necessity for all Americans, regardless of the cost to the rest of the world's inhabitants.

# CHAPTER FOUR

# The Greenest Suburb

## Berwyn, Illinois

At least 150 million Americans live in suburbs, places where you easily find a ten, twenty, or thirty-ton life. If we make serious cuts in our carbon footprint someday it's hard to imagine that a trend toward ever-larger houses and longer commutes will endure, but not all suburbs are created alike, and some have lower per-person energy use than the city nearby. The greenest suburbs in energy terms, if not appearance, are most likely the towns across the Hudson River from Manhattan. Twice as many people live in Union City, New Jersey, per square mile as live in New York City, and in Hoboken, about 50 percent more. Most American suburbs would not manage this level of density, and the places lack a typical suburban feature—single-family houses. Instead we turn to Chicago, which has many suburbs present in many configurations and the advantage of excellent community-level energy data.[1]

Oak Park, the most famous Chicago suburb due to its Frank Lloyd Wright houses and the quickest train commute to Chicago's Loop, seems like it may be a good place to start. It has more train stops than any other Chicago suburb except for Evanston, and about half the population live in apartments. Within a few blocks of the green-line L tracks, you can plug your electric car into a recharging station, park your car in a garage powered by solar energy, dispose of your trash in a receptacle topped with a solar panel, rent a bicycle, visit an eco-friendly dentist, and buy glass coffee jars and low–volatile organic compound (VOC) paint at the Green Living Center. At two

Fig. 10. Downtown Oak Park, Illinois, view of the L. Courtesy of the author.

of the transit stops, large murals of planet earth captioned "350" have been painted next to the viaducts. The meaning of the number (parts per million carbon dioxide) is not lost on many Oak Parkers, and the village hosts regional meetings for 350.org, a nonprofit that supports campaigns to divest from fossil fuels. Aside from its strong eco-culture, a high share of residents use transit to get to work, contributing to the fact that Oak Park has even lower per-capita greenhouse gas emissions than the city of Chicago.[2]

Another good prospect is the next town over, Forest Park, an historic suburb with a strong blue-collar past that evolved into a racially diverse, pedestrian-friendly place with a hodgepodge of housing. Its moniker, "Big City Access, Small Town Charm," also describes its scale—only fourteen thousand people live here, compared to Oak Park's fifty-two thousand. Unlike Oak Park, Forest Park has neither Frank Lloyd Wright houses nor throngs of tourists. A Potawatomi burial ground in what is now Forest Park gave settlers of European extraction the idea of burying their own dead there.[3] Cemeteries still cover most of the land area, and traditionally its main street, Madison Street, offered mourners a wide choice of restaurants and taverns. Madison Street remains the spine of Forest Park's successful commercial district. About 72 percent of Forest Park's homes consist of multi-units, surpassing the city of Chicago in this regard.[4] Forest Park's per-capita carbon dioxide emissions are about 20 percent lower than Oak Park's, but not the lowest.[5]

That would be the town just to the south of Oak Park, Berwyn, which bears the slogan "City of Homes." It has the lowest per-capita emissions from both homes and vehicles of any community in the dataset of communities in the Chicago region.[6] In fact, Berwyn's household emissions add up to only five metric tons $CO_2$ per person![7] Their commercial sector emissions are also well below the regional average. Berwyn, a former Czech community that is now majority Mexican-American, has proportionately fewer apartment dwellers than Forest Park and fewer transit commuters than Oak Park, but its homes support a lasting legacy of low energy use.

Berwyn may be one of the best in the Midwest in its energy use, but it shares characteristics with other streetcar neighborhoods that developed in step with public transportation more than a century ago. Counterparts can be found in row housing in Baltimore and Philadelphia and the duplexes found in the older suburbs around Boston, such as Somerville and Medford, and the older bungalow neighborhoods of Atlanta and other cities. The suburbs surrounding Berwyn are also older streetcar suburbs but have more eclectic housing. Forest Park, with it apartments and converted houses, boasts the greatest compactness, walkability, and investment in apartment living. It has achieved its low carbon dioxide emissions without major planning interventions and its great transit and community loyalty has served its business district well. Oak Park is not far behind due to its excellent century-old apartment buildings, apartment residences that offset some of the high $CO_2$ emissions related to Oak Park's mansions.

Berwyn and its neighbors Forest Park and Oak Park have vastly different images and looks from each other but as a group show a diversity of low-carbon American middle class lifestyles. Middle class suburbs in the middle of the Chicago metropolitan area of middle America, where we can find smallish brick buildings and houses with some of their local shopping intact—not an image that conjures up a futuristic vision of the advanced, smart city. But these towns deliver on the carbon outcomes that make up the dreams of planners and environmental engineers throughout the nation. For many Americans who have never lived here or even visited, there is something familiar in these places, a reason why several family movies have been filmed here and why a good many family TV shows depict the exterior of a modest Oak Park house while all the actors play out their roles in a Hollywood studio.

Berwyn's household income ranks in roughly the 50th percentile for American income, whereas Oak Park's approaches the top 33rd percentile nationally. The wealthiest suburb in the greenhouse gas emissions data set, Highland Park, at about $115,000 per household has much higher income than Berwyn but emits carbon dioxide at about double Berwyn's rate. But lower incomes do not necessarily translate into lower $CO_2$ emissions. Suburbs further west, Bellwood and Maywood, have higher poverty rates than Berwyn but also higher $CO_2$ emissions.

### Berwyn Bungalows

In the Chicago area one house type dominates the rest—the American bungalow. Charming, rinky-dink, or cozy, about one-third of all houses in the city are a 1.5 story, brick bungalow built between 1910 and 1945. The bungalows are small, ranging from about 900 to 1,500 square feet, and are in fact smaller than 75 percent of new American housing stock. Ubiquitous in blue-collar neighborhoods of Chicago's southwest side and in some of the blighted sections of the West Side, the bungalow can also be found in tonier Chi-

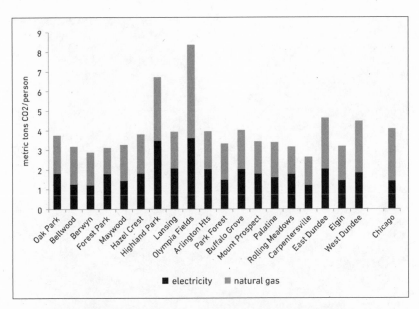

Fig. 11. Suburban Chicago $CO_2$ emissions from residences compared. Data from Center for Neighborhood Technology for 2007 as published in CMAP, *Homes for a Changing Region*, 2012, 2013, 2014.

cago neighborhoods such as Ravenswood and Jefferson Park. The compact bungalow can be seen in Forest Park, parts of Oak Park, and in Maywood, but nowhere in America can you find such a large concentration of bungalows as remain today in the suburb of Berwyn. The small houses of Berwyn sit on small, narrow lots, not interrupted by driveway cutouts, making for a compact urban form. At almost fifteen thousand people per square mile, Berwyn is almost 30 percent denser than the city of Chicago and it is the dominance of the bungalow as a residence that underlies Berwyn's lower $CO_2$ emissions.

When the original developers of the land that became known as Berwyn sought to sell land parcels during the building boom of the 1880s, they had in mind a different type of community, a town with large houses and generous tracts that would attract upper-middle-class families. But to their disappointment, these families chose to

Fig. 12. Classic bungalows such as these make up the largest share of housing in Berwyn. Courtesy of the author.

settle on the higher ground north of Berwyn, in Oak Park or in Riverside, the Frederick Law Olmstead designed suburb, located along a bucolic bend of the Des Plaines river. Parts of Berwyn were swampy and remained vacant for decades.[8] When the town finally started to develop in the early twentieth century, the construction boom was one of the most rapid in the country. Berwyn had fewer than six thousand people in 1910, but by 1930 its population had swelled to over forty-seven thousand people. Strict housing codes led to a uniformity of construction, with bungalows and two- and three-flat brick buildings making up almost the entirety of Berwyn housing.

Many of Berwyn's new residents were of Czech descent, first- or second-generation immigrants who had been living in Chicago's Pilsen neighborhood. The Western Electric Hawthorne Works, which manufactured the telephones for the Bell system, employed thousands of Berwynites, earning the name "Bohemian University."[9] A local banking industry that grew up along Cermak Road was large by suburban standards. Even in the 1980s you could find Bohemian restaurants that served simple, inexpensive dinners of meat and potatoes and boiled vegetables served in small, plain rooms. Delis offered authentic apple strudel and old-world salamis, items unavailable in the suburban melting pot of Oak Park. But during the 1960s, the Czech population started to leave, and the flight was almost complete by the 1980s, with the residents dispersing as rapidly as they had coalesced in the 1920s. Berwyn's stores and restaurants became more diverse and a music venue called Fitzgerald's attracted people from all over the western suburbs. Many Italian-Americans moved into the houses and stayed for about two decades, but in the early twenty-first century, the population profile changed once again. Now Hispanics make up about 60 percent of all residents, with a majority of residents speaking Spanish in the home. The largely Mexican-American population carries on the Berwyn tradition that has found the town affordable to a succession of immigrants and first-generation descendants. Along with this group, artists, DINKS (dual income no kids) and others have added to the demographic.

Berwyn houses sit on small narrow lots of 0.10 acres, more diminutive than the smallest suburban lots found near Washington DC, the 0.25 acre lot being the median size in Montgomery and Prince Georges counties and not much larger than the typical Chicago lot of 0.07 acres. In Berwyn, strict building codes helped ensure that homeowners do not attempt to enlarge their houses. The uniformly narrow lot shape also supported a uniformity of building width. Choosing large houses to keep up with the Joneses seemed to be less of a factor in historic communities such as Berwyn and Forest Park.

Like Berwyn, during the Victorian era few Forest Park residents built Victorian houses, but one such house attracts curiosity because it is rumored to be haunted and because it is the only Victorian house remaining in Forest Park.[10] In the late nineteenth century, Victorian houses were built in nearby Oak Park, and many of the more recent buildings were sited on similarly large lots, which endured as invitations to expand the smaller houses. With its narrow frontage and long lot configuration, the Berwyn bungalow effectively put a curb on the prospect of building large houses.

The bungalow has long appealed to people who want something solid and private at a moderate cost. The narrow but significant backyard can take on highly individualized interests, such as a bungalow on the north side of Chicago where you can see a sign, "Welcome to Martin's Farm," and the presence of a vegetable garden, a chicken coop, and a koi pond with frogs. "To me bungalows were always well grounded close to the earth—almost sprouted from the earth," explained bungalow owner, Beth Berger Martin in *American Bungalow* magazine. "Having victory gardens and keeping chickens seemed right."[11] In Berwyn, classic bungalows can be bought for only $150,000–$200,000, and in Oak Park similar bungalows fetch $300,000–$400,000.

Next to the cool apartment and the tiny house, the bungalow may not seem very fashionable, and style conscious Chicagoans have traditionally chosen converted industrial buildings and renovated brownstone row houses. But in an emergence of a perspective that values the particular details, the tile and brickwork, as well as the floor plan of the Chicago Bungalow, style-conscious singles and families have been buying them. Some of the Berwyn house owners have contributed photos of their homes to the design blog apartmenttherapy.com, revealing an uncluttered contemporary style. A group of local designers, Prairie Mod, makes home furnishings that seek to combine Frank Lloyd Wright features with the scale and details of the bungalow house in mind. The style recalls the early twentieth century, when bungalow owners were choosing mission or Arts and Crafts-style furnishings instead of ornate, mass-produced Victorian furniture.[12] From afar the houses may display a uniform look, but experts on this architectural form have found forty variations of the bungalow vernacular in Berwyn.[13] Close up, individualized brick work, porches, and decorative window glass help to give the Berwyn streets a "syncopated rhythm," in the words of *American Bungalow* magazine contributor Mike Williams. In his article, "Berwyn: Chicagoland's Hidden Treasure," Williams describes the rare craftsmanship he found in Berwyn's homes. "Face bricks are laid not just in simple rows but in complex, dizzying patterns, embellished with beautifully carved limestone ornaments."[14] The bungalows attract their own house walk tour that is now in its eleventh year in Berwyn.[15]

The bungalow's design makes it easier to improve the energy efficiency of these homes wholesale. The Historic Chicago Bungalow Association, a non-profit that works with city agencies, has helped more than three thousand bungalow owners to improve energy use in their homes. The Chicago program offers free attic insulation, air sealing and other conservation measures for middle- and low-income owners, projects that erased about 1.5 million metric tons of carbon dioxide related to the buildings. Similar improvements may be in store in Berwyn now that much of the town lies in the new "Central Berwyn Bungalow Historic District," a national landmark designation that provides tax breaks for some rehab projects such as improved energy conservation.[16]

If the bungalows look so great and cost so little to buy and maintain, why aren't more people building such houses? In many parts of the country the absence of small house choices is more a problem of lack of supply than lack of demand. Anecdotally, realtors often mention that younger people are frustrated in their search for small, well-built houses. Rather than waiting for such houses to get on the market, however, many Americans now take matters into their own hands and build a small house themselves. Small house designs can be chosen from a growing selection of blueprints for compact homes.[17] Currently, more than one in five of the houses that owners build themselves are small (<1,400 square feet), whereas only about one in ten of the houses that contractors build are of this small size.[18] The owner-built share of small houses has been increasing somewhat, showing a tangible demand for houses that are on the scale of the Berwyn bungalow.

Bungalows are small, but the size of the houses alone does not explain all of Berwyn's high density and its low carbon dioxide emissions. Some of the taller structures that look like elongated bungalows are actually three- or four-unit buildings that were built as multi-units. These residences make up about 14 percent of the town's housing stock, but were built for this purpose rather than converted. If you look closely at some of the houses of typical size you will see a second doorbell and perhaps a second door because many of the small houses in Berwyn, about 17 percent, are two-flats. Since more than 80 percent of the residential land area in Berwyn is zoned for single-family houses, conversions have been the best chance for the town to achieve greater density, a lesson that holds promise for much of America's suburbs.

Many people find a converted house appealing because they offer private or semi-private yard space and the outward appearance of a single-family house. Two-unit buildings are relatively rare in the country as a whole—only about 4 percent of American households live in such buildings, but they are over-represented in these lower-carbon communities in the Chicago area. In Forest Park about 22 percent of the building stock has two to four units, and many of these buildings began as single-family houses. Local historian and newspaper columnist John Rice attributes some of Forest Park's conversions to the large number of German immigrants who lived there during its early years, following a tradition of building a *Daudy Haus* or an apartment into their house for the older generation. Later, during the housing shortage that followed World War II, Forest Park was particularly welcoming to veterans and allowed additional single-family houses to be converted to duplexes, a housing form sought after by veterans with young families. "If you visit Forest Park during Memorial Day, you'll see flags everywhere here," offered Rice, who holds that this part of Forest Park has changed little.

Unlike Berwyn and Forest Park, few of Oak Park's houses have been converted to multi-units although the town has historically been tolerant of such conversions. In the late nineteenth century many large Victorian houses sprang up in Oak Park and remain in a spectacular state of preservation in and around the Frank Lloyd Wright historic district, objects of curiosity to the thousands of European visitors who attend the Prairie School walking tours. Some of the wooden houses are enormous, on the scale of the great houses of a European aristocracy, and the town has enough Victorians to justify a Painted Lady tour. When social life in Oak Park changed in the 1890s with the growing popularity of clubs like the Nineteenth Century Club for discussing history and the Oak Park Club for bicycle excursions, some of the social purpose of the large houses was made redundant. The social forces that pulled residents away from mansion living in central Washington DC were also at play in affluent Midwestern suburbs like Oak Park. Fewer residents were interested in the large houses, and developers bought land in central Oak Park to build apartment houses. Some of the Victorians were converted to two, three, or four flats. Today about 6 percent of Oak Park housing can be described as two-unit dwellings and 5 percent are three- or four-unit buildings. Oak Park's built environment remains significantly more carbon intensive than Berwyn's, and its community-level $CO_2$ data belies the fact that many Oak Park residents own second homes in places like the lakefront in Michigan and Wisconsin and bear a higher carbon footprint than revealed in the data discussed here.

In the past in Berwyn and Forest Park, if someone wanted to convert their house to a two-unit it was nobody else's business. Today if a homeowner wants to sell their converted house they can face spools of red tape. In Berwyn an ordinance requires some multifamily houses to de-convert before they are sold if they were not taxed as multi-units. Converted houses became a bogeyman, taking the blame for house foreclosures and other problems despite the obvious point that owners of converted houses pay off their mortgages more easily because they have rental income. In Forest Park a similar rule makes it hard to sell a converted house if the room ceilings are lower than a specific height. A local resident fought back in a guest editorial where she claimed that "Our village council/plan commission talk ... renters are bad for civilization, renters have 'no skin in the game.'" Explaining that her two flat helps her ailing family members, she concluded that the de-conversion proponents were "a crew of smug, lazy brand-bashing bloviaths."[19]

In an era when racially based attitudes take a more muted form, generalized fears seem to have shifted to house shape with claims that converted houses have been tied to a range of social ills, including Berwyn's lackluster school test scores. The conversions have been linked to charges of school crowding despite the fact that average household size in Berwyn today is below what it was during its early and mid-century boom, the era when the schools were built and filled with the families of the original Czech settlers. Perceptions about schools are one reason why a classic bungalow for sale in Oak Park will fetch at least double the price as the same bungalow design in Berwyn. The Berwyn schools, which mainly educate native Spanish speakers, tend to put off many English-dominant families who, unlike their Washington DC counterparts, do not seem to view a concentration of Spanish speakers as a wonderful opportunity for their children to become bilingual. Anonymous online community forums for the town of Berwyn air the views of environmentally conscious parents who self-consciously decide to choose to live in a sprawling suburb because they think that it is better for their children.

The discussion over conversions has been dominated not by organizations looking after the broader interest, but by house owners worried about property values. As is the case in Washington DC, the conversions are not recognized as an environmental and affordability strategy, though they dovetail with the goals of both types of advocates. Even sustainability interests at the U.S. Housing and Urban Development Department (HUD) that have funded local smart-growth studies for Berwyn and nearby suburbs have jumped on the anti-conversion bandwagon, suggesting that community development block grant funding might be used to help homeowners subsidize the cost of de-conversions.[20] These comments about reducing housing density can be found in recent planning studies that lay out blueprints for reducing carbon dioxide—from driving, no less! Despite its lack of allies, the converted house seems to enjoy a degree of longevity in Berwyn and Forest Park. People who want to live in them or sell them as multi-flats seem to be holding their ground, especially in Berwyn. Some converted houses are still finding their way to market, backed with assurances that their sale has been cleared by the city.

## Suburban Evolution

Berwyn's official motto, "City of Homes," generally evokes its actual built environment. The town has few large apartment buildings, and the more interesting examples of larger multi-units must be found elsewhere, especially in Oak Park. Oak Park's examples stand out because many of its original apartment houses date from the early twentieth century and show both exterior style and interior house features. In the older neighborhoods, you can find courtyard apartments dating from the 1920s where the properties are cut deeply with narrow, long gardens, bringing some measure of green space and quiet into the depths of the tracts. Some of the apartments contain working fireplaces and offer light from more than one aspect. Most of the lots lack outdoor play space but sit across the street from public parks, including Scoville Park, Mills Park, and Austin Gardens. When Oak Park's population expanded in the 1920s and 1930s, many of the newcomers moved to Washington Boulevard, where vintage apartments and condos are solid along most of its 1.5-mile length. Many of the street's apartment dwellers use the Washington Boulevard rapid commuter bus to downtown Chicago.

A medium-sized apartment building, the Salem Munyer apartments, now known as the Linden Apartments, sits on a quiet street in the middle of Oak Park, "Arguably the greatest Prairie School apartment building ever designed," wrote local historian Martin Hackl in his book about its architect, John Van Bergen.[21] As a young man Van Bergen had worked for Frank Lloyd Wright, but unlike his employer he took a strong interest in designing for moderate-income clients. When the Munyer building was completed in 1916, Van Bergen offered that it was a "new kind of apartment building. . . . It differs markedly in type from the ordinary apartment building and has been arranged to give of the maximum of light and air to each apartment."[22] I know the building well because I grew up there, and I happen to agree with Van Bergen's description.

Along with abundant light and air, the three-story, eighteen-unit building solves some of the problems with apartments that tend to keep families from viewing them as a first choice. The layout of the grounds maximizes play space because while the front is landscaped, a generous grass playfield covers most of the back. "The front and back steps and the large communal yard were unending sources of places to play and run as a child," recalled former resident Annette Frost-Jensen. "Later, when we moved into a house, I missed the apartments."[23]

Remarkably, every unit in the building has at least three exposures, and most have four, a feat the architect achieved by adding a sunporch and doing away with a central corridor. At any given time, residents can choose between sunny rooms and shaded ones and maintain a cross-breeze during the warm weather months. The privacy and extra light and air circulation are enabled by a layout organized into tiers instead of hallways, and the floors are accessed through stairs, not elevators. The stairwells separate units and insulate against noise. Over the years many families have made the Linden apartments home despite the fact that the larger units are comparable in price to a single-family house.

The Linden apartment building sits on land now zoned for single-family houses and is surrounded by houses. But it is an historic example of how denser development can fit in and enhance an upper-middle-class suburban neighborhood. Compared to the more ornate styles of apartment buildings imported from Europe, the elegant simplicity of this unique Prairie School design provides more visual continuity with the neighboring houses. Eventually, the Linden apartment building won landmark status due to its architectural merit, adding prestige to a street with otherwise undistinguished buildings.

In contemporary times, Oak Park is embracing new large multi-unit projects near its historic downtown. The first mixed-use building went up in 2010 near Lake Street, consisting of a Trader Joes on the ground level and two hundred apartments above, including a green roof, Wi-Fi and other amenities geared to appeal to millennials. Village officials viewed it as successful enough to approve three more such projects in downtown Oak Park totaling 750 new apartment units. One of these will be built on the site of the parking lot that now interrupts the Lake Street storefronts. With heights of ten to twenty-one stories, the buildings will tower over much of the neighborhood and will slow Oak Park's trend toward declining population and lower density. (Oak Park has about 20 percent fewer residents compared to its 1970s population peak.) All of the buildings will be within three blocks of the train station, a significant investment in smart growth. Perhaps Oak Park will move into first place as the lowest carbon footprint suburb, but only time and actual utility and vehicular data will reveal the answer and in the meantime, that distinction remains with Berwyn, City of Homes, where the small house, converted house combination still trumps the larger lots coupled with apartments.

## Renewable Credits

The Chicago area tends to rely on natural gas for heating, and Berwyn is no exception. About 95 percent of Berwyn households use natural gas to heat their homes. In many parts of the country using natural gas for heating is a no-brainer (environmentally speaking) because the alternative is to use electricity generated from coal. When the coal is used to generate electricity, about two-thirds of the primary energy is lost, and burning coal emits more $CO_2$ than burning natural gas. Berwyn's investment in natural gas, which surpasses Chicago and Oak Park's rates of 84 percent, is optimal compared with a coal alternative.

But Illinois generates much more nuclear energy than any other state. About half of the electricity the state generates comes from nuclear power, and Illinois is planning to keep its older nuclear plants going for at least another decade. Wind energy has been making gains and in 2015 stood at about 6 percent of the electricity generated.[24] But for now, Illinois's electricity carbon footprint is lower because of its large nuclear plants. In 2015, the carbon intensity of Illinois electricity was only 956 pounds $CO_2$ per mwh, comparing favorably to other Midwestern states like Ohio that use more coal and have a much higher carbon intensity at 1,511 pounds $CO_2$ per mwh.[25] Whether Illinois' carbon intensity will remain low depends upon whether the state will continue to keep its nuclear plants running, or whether wind will take up an increasing share of the electricity load.

A recent deal in Oak Park put into sharp relief the gap between a broad motivation to use more renewable energy and the practical challenge of sustaining a village-wide decision. Census data from 2010 reveals that Oak Park's solar added up to no more than 0.1 percent of the village's residential heating use. But recently many Oak Parkers were heartened with the idea that they could make a village-wide switch to renewables. In 2012 and 2013 Oak Park bought renewable energy credits from a broker while bundling, or aggregating, Oak

Park's residential energy accounts. The town's decision to contribute to renewable investment dovetailed with investments that Chicago area utilities are obliged to fulfill, but the deal won a green power award from the EPA and was very well received by many Oak Park residents.[26] Oak Parkers paid slightly more for their electricity as a result of the deal, but local government officials offered that Oak Park was the first suburb in America that could say that 100 percent of its electricity comes from renewable sources. "The fact that electricity generated by coal power is being used in Oak Park, Illinois, doesn't change the fact that our wind-generated electricity is responsible for getting the total amount of electricity we use added to the grid from renewable sources," announced former Oak Park village president David Pope in a somewhat cryptic description of the transaction.[27]

When the agreement to buy renewable-energy credits expired two years later, however, Oak Park village officials decided to return to "brown energy" (fossil-fuel energy) because it was slightly cheaper. Many Oak Parkers were outraged about the change, not understanding in the first place that the agreement was not for green energy supply, but for green energy credits. The wind turbines were several hundred miles away, and their own electricity had all along come primarily from nuclear power and coal.[28] Many other Chicago suburbs subsequently brokered deals similar to Oak Park's original renewable energy purchase. And many Oak Park residents, about 15 percent, opted to pay more for their electricity to share a renewable energy credit once the village was no longer in the game.[29] A broader and more relevant question is how Oak Park's and Berwyn's consumption of energy is going. These questions are easily lost in the glamor of buying renewable energy credits.

## Walkability and Mobility

Berwyn's most famous landmark, the Spindle, impales eight cars on a metal stake in a giant parking lot. The sculpture (now demolished) is a fitting image for a town that encompasses the original Highway

66 on Ogden Road. Monuments from the early days of the Interstate Highway system, including one of the original White Castle fast food restaurants, remain in Berwyn. These vestiges of King Highway and King Car provide little clue that Berwyn's car-related carbon dioxide emissions are far lower than the national average and one of the lowest in the region. Berwyn's per-capita carbon dioxide emissions from cars are only 2.1 metric tons compared with 2.4 metric tons in Chicago. Some of Berwyn's lower driving rate compared to the city can be tied to slightly larger household size.[30] But fewer drivers per household in Berwyn does not explain all the difference.

Berwyn has some good transit options and some characteristics that make frequent and long car trips unnecessary, though it lacks some of the features that are thought to support walkability. Smart growth advocates suggest that walking is enhanced by views of interesting housing of varying size.[31] The cookie-cutter houses of Berwyn are not recognizable as a New Urbanist plan, stretch as they do with monotonous size and spacing. In fact, Berwyn's walk score, determined by modeling many factors including the location of amenities, proximity to transit, and presence of sidewalks, suggests that Berwyn is not among the handful of Chicago area towns that walk score describes as highly walkable. This select group includes only four towns in the entire Midwest—Chicago, Forest Park, Evanston, and Oak Park. A score of 70 rates a neighborhood as highly walkable, and Berwyn just misses it at 69.[32]

Walkability, however, is more about a place's potential for walking than a measure of what is actually taking place there. In Oak Park, you can find the highest walk score in the area surrounding the downtown business district, which gets a walk score of 92—a "walker's paradise." One of the village's PR photos shows an intersection in this neighborhood with several pedestrians of different skin color happily crossing the street.[33] But how pedestrianized is this neighborhood really? My father happens to have an opinion about that because for years he exercised in a gym a half-block from this intersection and, while sitting on a stationary bike, he had the habit of counting the passing cars and pedestrians. His tally after several weeks was cars: 1737, pedestrians: 394. This works out to 82 percent of trips near Oak Park's main commercial area being by vehicle. Better than most suburbs, no doubt, but not what you'd hope to see in one of the most walkable neighborhoods in the Midwest.

In the case of Berwyn, despite the lower walk score, Berwyn sidewalks often have people visibly walking on them. Like much of the Chicago area, Berwyn has sidewalks fronting all of its housing, and the sidewalks are not interrupted by driveway cutouts. Most automobiles are parked in garages in the alleys, making for a safer walking and playing area in the front of the properties. Garbage cans and recycling bins are also relegated to the alleys rather than the street curbs. The long, narrow lots and the street-facing porches help to put neighbors in proximity with each other, though the blocks tend to be too long for ideal walking conditions.

In Berwyn you can find long stretches of bungalows that seem to be far from the main commercial streets, but the town actually has several local neighborhood stores amongst the houses that would be a short stroll away. No single amenity seems to encourage people to walk more than the nearness of a grocery store, according to models that analyze and predict how walkable a given location may be. In Berwyn all homes are two-thirds of a mile or less from a grocery store, whereas in Oak Park this distance can surpass a mile and a half. Some of Berwyn's food shops have been around for generations, as I learned while chatting about Berwyn with a cab driver who grew up there. The young man could reel off names of small corner stores that are still around and selling homemade food.

Aside from the community ties grocery stores can foster, child health advocates including the Centers for Disease Control and Prevention see them as part of their arsenal against child obesity because they tend to stock healthier foods than convenience stores and fast food outlets.[34] Bringing the grocery store back would require adjustments to the zoning code and possibly adjustments to the market conditions where small groceries face much higher unit costs. The city of Washington DC recently overcame considerable opposition when it rewrote the zoning code to affirm a place for the small corner grocery in residential neighborhoods.

Over in Oak Park small independent grocery stores were an important part of neighborhood life during the mid-twentieth century, but their decline was rapid in the 1960s. In 1957, Oak Park had at least forty-seven grocery stores and food shops, but in about one decade the number was down to about one dozen.[35] The grocery stores could not keep up with high taxes as well as higher unit costs and a dwindling customer base that was drifting to the supermarkets.[36] A range of incentives including tax breaks or credits, loans, and grants would make the small grocery proposition more practical. Although today some corner houses in Oak Park have the telltale appearance of a former shop, current plans to rezone parts of Oak Park do not put the local store back into the scene.[37]

Although Berwyn is relatively well served by small food stores, it has fewer parks than Oak Park. Its largest greenspace, Proksa Park, is beloved by generations of residents who find repose and recreation in its fifteen acres. "One of the prettiest parks in the Midwest," enthused a local journalist who happens to live in Oak Park.[38] It offers garden plots and amenities like tennis courts and children's playgrounds, but more unusually, the park includes a running creek and two ponds. "When my kids were small, we visited Proksa three or four times a week," recalled longtime resident Nadine Brockman.

Then there is the obvious point that good sidewalks and street crossings encourage walking. Narrowing the streets—"road diets"—can bring out pedestrians by adding width to sidewalks and making space for sidewalk cafes, benches, and the like. In this regard Berwyn is nothing special; the intersections and sidewalks look much the way they appeared decades ago. Berwyn lacks the street furniture and pedestrian-friendly curb design and intersections that harbor respect for the pedestrian.

But Forest Park is an altogether different story. The Edward Hines, Jr. Veterans Administration Hospital has a program to help people who have recently lost their sight to become more independent and mobile again. "They take them here to Forest Park to practice on our sidewalks," explained John Rice. They are learning new walking skills on some of the most carefully laid out, pleasant sidewalks of any suburb in America. Starting with quiet residential streets, you will likely find at many intersections bulging corners that jut into the street, shortening the distance between curbs and occasionally a bench next to a newly planted tree. The walking lane from one curb to the next tends to be slightly raised and textured so that feet know they are in the right place and won't easily slip. Near some of the busier intersections the sidewalk scape even includes three-feet-high poles that can help orient a cane user to the presence of a crossing lane.

Forest Park's streets and sidewalks fit a community that has long been hospitable to veterans, but the specific features have not hurt Forest Park's walkability in general. It has earned the highest walk score of any town or city in the Midwest. At the Forest Park Starbucks on a weekend morning in early summer, I chatted with clients ranging from recent college graduates to retirees who had all arrived there on foot or by bike. One young lady told me how she loved living in Forest Park because it was so easy to get to downtown on the L and walk around. A downside was how easy it was to get a parking ticket by parking the car in the wrong place, she added in an observation that seemed to support her earlier praise.

Lacking Forest Park's streetscape and sidewalk planning, Berwyn's low car usage rate is doubly remarkable because its transit options are limited. It has three stations on the Burlington–Santa Fe commuter line, but unlike Oak Park and Forest Park, it has no CTA (Chicago Transit Authority) stations within its borders. Oak Park has more train transit with four green-line CTA stops, three blue line stations, and a commuter train station, all offering a zippy ride into Chicago's loop within twenty-five minutes. A peculiar feature of the CTA lines run-

Fig. 13. Madison Street, Forest Park's main street, offers many solid blocks of walker-friendly shopping and dining that includes bike racks and crosswalk posts for blind pedestrians. Courtesy of the author.

ning through Oak Park is that the stops are more closely spaced in the village than they are in the miles of Chicago between the Loop and Oak Park. Over the years some of the West Side Chicago neighborhoods have lost a stop or two, but the western suburbs have held on fiercely to their access. The Blue Line runs between two lanes in the Eisenhower Expressway through Oak Park and ends in Forest Park. It is one of only a handful of transit lines in the country that runs all night long seven days a week. The presence of Oak Park's excellent historic trains shows up in the data, and many Oak Park residents take transit to work—about 21 percent, compared with the state average of 9 percent. In Oak Park, "only" 58 percent of residents commute alone in a car, but this is one of the best rates in Illinois, where 74 percent drive alone to work on average. Forest Park, a smaller town than the others, has good coverage through two blue line stops and a shared green line stop and commuter stop, but the residents commuting alone to work is higher than in Oak Park or Berwyn. Oak Park, Forest Park, and Maywood all share Berwyn's low driving rate, and the vehicle miles traveled per person is lower than Chicago's.

A reason why many west suburbanites take the trains instead of driving is that the Eisenhower Expressway cuts through Oak Park and Forest Park and is notoriously slow. On a cold winter day the scene might recall a Derek Walcott poem about Chicago after a snowstorm, "Cars like dead horses, their muzzles foaming with ice."[39] Passengers on the Blue Line train that runs along the middle of "the Ike" have an up-close view of the crawling traffic. The city approved the typical solution posed to speed up traffic—widen the expressway—more than a decade ago, but the planners at Chicago's Department of Transportation underestimated the power of Oak Park residents to get something done, or in this case, to keep something from happening. A group of Oak Parkers led by transportation planner Rick Kuner asked how widening an expressway will improve life in Oak Park, and more specifically why village residents would want the extra, faster-moving traffic in their neighborhood. The group, Citizens for Appropriate Transportation, advocated improving the track for the blue line train and extending the blue line further west. They asked the broader question raised by smart growth advocates: Why widen a road when the extra cars will just lead to more congestion? The argument that road construction actually induces additional traffic has been demonstrated in Atlanta and other American cities. Increased traffic capacity often means that people will choose homes further from their workplace, thereby eroding the effects of the original road widening.[40]

To get to work, Berwyn residents use cars a great deal compared with Oak Parkers. About 70 percent drive alone, and only 12 percent take transit. These statistics cast a question over Berwyn's low overall car use, but compared to Oak Park, Berwyn has the edge in other characteristics that feed into lower transportation emissions. About half of Berwyn residents work in Chicago or in Berwyn itself. About half of Berwynites work in health care and social assistance, and the MacNeal Hospital in south Berwyn is a large employer.[41] The majority of Oak Park workers, on the other hand, are more broadly dispersed to employment in other suburbs and towns, facing a potentially longer commute. And although Berwyn has fewer transit stops, residents have partly made up the difference by carpooling. About 11 percent of Berwyn households share rides to get to work compared with 6 percent in Oak Park and 4 percent in Highland Park.[42] While Berwyn has fewer rail options than the wealthier suburbs nearby, they have partly made up for it through strong community connections.

A vision of a car-unfriendly suburb where people mainly use bikes and commuter trains may sound like an unrealistic utopia, but this describes what Oak Park was like for decades before car ownership became widespread. In the late nineteenth century, before cars were available, Oak Park's homes were concentrated in a half-mile area on either side of Lake Street, and grocery stores and other amenities were within a few blocks of all the residential tracts. When Frank Lloyd Wright moved to Oak Park in 1889 and developed the Prairie style in the 1890s, biking was an important part of local transportation. Bicycle design had recently evolved from the oversized front wheel to something like its present shape and although Oak Park was a culturally conservative place that banned the sale of alcohol and frowned on theater attendance, Oak Park women donned bloomers and took to the bicycle. Oak Park's largest social club, known in the late twentieth century as the Oak Park Club, began as the Oak Park Cycling Club a century earlier.[43] Local historian May Estelle Cook recalled the camaraderie of Oak Park bike clubs: "The auto was still in its infancy and often was more trouble than it was worth ... [and] required a gallon of soft water every mile, usually made twelve miles an hour."[44]

By 1920, when Oak Park's population reached forty thousand residents and Berwyn's population reached twelve thousand, car ownership in America was still a rarity and fewer than 10 percent of the population owned cars.[45] Most residents were using street cars, commuter trains, and bikes. Today about 1 percent of Oak Park residents commute to work using bikes or roller skates, which represents more bike commuters than found in Berwyn or Forest Park. Oak Park officials have recently approved designated bike routes that aim to support safer cycling. But Oak Park residents sometimes wonder aloud whether the village is really committed to bicycles. Longtime resident Bob Stigger recently posed this question in Oak Park's weekly paper: "Also, somebody please explain to me why not one employee of a supposedly eco-leadership municipality is able to bicycle around town now and then on village business."[46]

In the commercial areas, a blind person walking along the sidewalks of the uptown or downtown neighborhoods in Oak Park could be forced to stumble upon any number of signs that sit directly on the sidewalk and proclaim, "No Bike Riding Roller Blading Skateboarding on Sidewalk." To top it off, bike racks are a rarity. The worries about errant bicycle riders may be hard to fathom except for a long-standing local idea that bike riders ruined Oak Park's downtown shopping in years past. In the early 1970s when Lake Street became pedestrianized, a local columnist for Oak Park's weekly paper named Harriet Vrba wrote in detail about her peeves with youthful bicyclists on sidewalks.[47] Her attention coincided with flagging retail sales in Oak Park as local shoppers took to the new malls built further west, but Vrba was quick to suggest that bikes were partly to blame.

In the respect accorded to bicyclists in Oak Park's shopping districts, and Berwyn and Forest Park's streetscape, these suburbs differ from a city like Washington DC where planners have changed many street configurations and added lane dividers to give room to bicycle commuters. In DC about 5 percent of all residents commute to work on a bike, and about 30,000 people in the region are members of Capitol Bike Share. DC's bike use is aided by a bike-friendly transit system and a level of density that is double that of Chicago's. The neighborhoods of 20009 DC are also twice as dense as Berwyn and have the advantage of being close to employment compared with close-in suburbs such as described in this chapter.

A long-distance bike path, the Prairie Path, starts at the edge of Forest Park and heads west sixty-one miles through Maywood and other suburbs. It dates from the earliest days of rail-to-trail conversions and sits on the site of a former commuter train line that disappeared when the Eisenhower Expressway was completed in the 1950s. Here and there along the bike trail the remnants of brick commercial buildings bearing the fanciful details of Gothic architecture circa 1900 recall the neighborhood's past glory. But now Maywood is one of the poorest suburbs in Illinois, and for many miles the almost-empty bike trail passes by run-down houses and boarded storefronts. Losing the commuter line was a poor deal for Maywood, which now has only one commuter rail station on the northern edge of town. The commercial buildings that benefited from the rail traffic are now mostly shuttered, and Maywood's unemployment rate is over 11 percent, higher than neighboring suburbs.[48] Despite the low income, Maywood has slightly higher per-capita greenhouse gas emissions than Oak Park, revealing opportunities for both emissions reductions and economic improvement.[49] A scenario that includes extending transit into the town, new commercial investment, apartment construction, and possibly house conversions, would see a change to higher income and lower $CO_2$ emissions.

## Main Streets and Strip Malls

The urban structures discussed so far—transit options and housing structures—have a clear link with $CO_2$ emissions. The smaller houses and the house/apartment combinations found in these suburbs have

enabled a lower carbon footprint. Similarly, very good transit combined with congested highways has contributed to these suburbs'
low vehicle miles traveled. Residents of these suburbs drive about
one-third less than the Illinois average. More difficult to untangle
is the relationship between these suburbs' overall carbon footprints
and their commercial districts. Does the presence of a local strip
mall mean that people are driving to a destination that could have
been set up as a small, local walking destination? Or does it mean
that people are driving to a local strip mall instead of wasting fuel
driving to a mall in a distant suburb? The latter argument offers an
environmental justification for inducing local driving. Is a large local
restaurant scene a good thing? Or would it be better if more people
ate at home, so we would save on the heating and cooling of par-
tially full restaurants? A striking feature of Berwyn is that the energy
used in its commercial buildings is modest as well, and considering
these buildings, Berwyn's per-capita emissions are about one-third
below the average for Cook County.[50]

Berwyn's main commercial district is the 30-acre Cermak Plaza, a
1950s development that sits alongside of a massive parking lot that
has lost some of its customer base to newer malls further west. Cermak Road was once a banking center known in the early twentieth century as the Bohemian Wall Street due to its large number of
Czech-American clients. Aside from Cermak Plaza, the road now has
an eclectic mix of fast food restaurants and other stores including
the "World's Largest Laundry Mat." The town's other commercial
streets are also car-oriented, but the small parcel size found throughout Berwyn cannot accommodate large national and regional chain
stores.[51] The exception to the car-oriented commerce is Berwyn's
Depot District where small, pre-war commercial buildings line the
road near the commuter line's Berwyn station. Marketing its transit
access and walkability, the town's first large mixed-use condo building was completed in the Depot District about a decade ago, offering units that are more expensive than the Berwyn bungalows that

typically sell for less than $200,000. Berwyn developers are hoping that the area, with its early twentieth-century glass storefronts, will evolve into a thriving shopping area, but the Depot District still has a quiet, residential feel.

While most of Berwyn's commercial areas have little of the look of sustainability, in this respect Forest Park could not be more different. Most of its car-oriented shopping has been a major flop, while its old main street is the envy of its neighbors. Its enclosed mall, the Forest Park Mall, became one of the nation's "dead malls" before it was sold—all four hundred thousand square feet of it—to a mega-church. The site seems fitting for a social phenomenon that has found membership in widely dispersed American suburbs in contrast to the smaller houses of worship rooted in a particular place.[52] Forest Park's successful main street, Madison Street, in contrast, is less than hospitable to cars. It was laid out to be a wide avenue like Oak Park's Lake Street, but it has received a tuck here and there as it narrows to accommodate patio space for restaurants. The bump-outs, along with historic lampposts and planters, provide a slower car journey but reveal a lively scene with local spots that seem to be from a bygone era—an archery store with a target range, an army-navy surplus store, and bars with much of their original century-old rooms intact. Spanning the width of Forest Park, a half mile from the L and commuter station and next to the neighborhood zoned for apartments, Madison Street presents a spectacular example of a pedestrian-oriented, thriving commercial district.

For most of its history, Madison Street in Forest Park was not particularly prosperous. It did not attract large department stores or the smaller chains like Woolworths and Walgreens that were once so important to towns until the mid-twentieth century. These larger stores chose to locate in Oak Park. Today Forest Park's downtown thrives in part because historically the main street was lined with an eclectic mix of small shops, bars and restaurants. There were few large lots capable of hosting big box stores. Although the Forest Park business district suffered high vacancies during the 1970s, business picked up over the decades as loyal local residents frequented Madison Street. Over the years, community cohesion in Forest Park has helped to maintain the strength of Madison Street. "It's easy to set up a business here," remarked Jayne Ertel, the co-owner of a Madison street coffee shop named Counter Coffee who happens to have converted her business van to run on used cooking oil from local restaurants.

Oak Park, with its persistent problems of turnover and high vacancies, looks with envy at the success of Forest Park's Madison Street. In Oak Park near Harlem Avenue, cars move briskly along the main street, Lake Street, past big box stores like Old Navy and the Gap. Until the 1970s, this neighborhood was a thriving shopping district with two large department stores and solid blocks of retail but new enclosed malls, such as the toney Oakbrook Center, lured away many of Oak Park's shoppers. In an effort to keep shoppers home, Oak Park did what several hundred towns undertook during this decade— they converted their main street to a pedestrian mall. The transformation, completed in 1973, brought grass, small fountains, and new trees over an area that had been asphalt. But over the next years the street was beset with vacancies. Marshall Field's, the department store that had been the cornerstone of Oak Park's downtown since the 1920s, closed in the 1980s and the building proved hard to rent.

Finally in 1988 the village tore up Lake Street's pedestrian mall and repaved the road. Erasing the pedestrian mall had its parallels throughout the United States as the pedestrianized streets disappeared almost everywhere except in college towns.[53] In Oak Park the new road project justified itself as an environmental innovation that would keep Oak Park shoppers driving locally instead of driving to more distant shopping. The repaving won an environmental award, but two decades after Lake Street's landscaped mall disappeared, business is still slow in downtown Oak Park. These examples support the smart growth edicts that small, walkable commercial areas pay long-term dividends through a loyal proximate customer base. Forest Park's main street attracts many customers from Oak Park and nearby suburbs and sustains many family-owned businesses that have deep roots in Forest Park. From a greenhouse gas standpoint, however, the success of the beautiful, walkable, commercial areas of Forest Park opens up a host of questions and the conundrum that a large amount of energy is consumed in Forest Park's commercial areas.[54]

## None of the Above

Berwyn and the other suburbs visited in this chapter can all claim relatively low $CO_2$ emissions levels. A suburb south of Chicago, however, shows in stark relief how high carbon dioxide can go in the absence of these features. This suburb, Olympia Fields, is a small community that took shape on the grounds of a golf course in the mid-twentieth century. It has few small tracts and few apartment buildings to offset the impact of its large lot houses. Olympia Fields's per-capita $CO_2$ emissions tower over the others, more than doubling the emissions rate seen in Berwyn (see figure). The runner-up is Highland Park, an affluent suburb north of Chicago that was the location for the movie *Home Alone*. It might have been the highest emitter were it not for the apartment buildings that make up about 20 percent of the housing stock.

Today, Olympia Fields's eight thousand residents are served by one commuter rail station, and only about 18 percent of residents take transit to work. Residents of Olympia Fields drive more than twenty-two thousand miles each year compared with an average of about fourteen thousand in Cook County, which encompasses Chicago and nearby suburbs.[55] Almost all the homes in Olympia Fields are detached single-family houses, and about 72 percent of all residences have at least seven rooms. With a median household income of $85,917, Olympia Fields is much more affluent than Berwyn, but many of its residents have been underwater in their large houses.[56] An aging population—about two-thirds of the population is at least

50—the lack of age diversity is a community concern.[57] The town hopes that a new mixed-use development next to the commuter train station will help improve the picture.

The carbon profile for Olympia Fields would surprise few adherents from the smart growth and New Urbanist crowds. A post-World War II suburb with large lots, large houses, and transit that is mainly unavailable, Olympia Fields is a textbook example of a sprawling outer suburb. Smart-growth advocates like Arthur C. Nelson predict that hundreds of thousands of houses in similar suburbs will go unsold in America during the next two decades.[58] The reasons are partly demographic—smaller households for the younger generation and the growing population of retirees who do not need large floor plans. But also, there is a real shift in what the youngest generation of adults—the millennials—say they want. Recent surveys say that a majority of this group—according to RCLCO Consumer Research, as many as 77 percent—want to live in an urban core, which could mean an urbanized suburb, but definitely not the kind of houses that now exist in Olympia Fields.[59]

## A Berwyn Future

But as an alternative to large-lot suburbia, is Berwyn the answer? Will many people want to live in small houses on long, narrow lots? Even Berwyn is not sure and, wanting to attract more millennials, the town invested in an ad campaign called "Nothing Like a Suburb."[60] To project the idea that Berwyn is an interesting place and its housing is not as homogenous as it seems, the campaign aired slogans like, "Live Culture Shouldn't Only be Found in Yogurt" and "Cookie Cutters are for Cookies." Underlying Berwyn's interest in attracting residents who want to live in dynamic urban neighborhoods, the town has adopted a new comprehensive plan that lays out land use, transportation and park improvements. Unlike the many suburbs that remain zoned for single-family houses and are hostile to new multi-unit projects, Berwyn's plan forges a different path. The new plan, adopted in 2012, defines a large area in the center of town as eligible for multi-unit housing. Two- and three-flat buildings are now present in this neighborhood, but multi-units may now be built in the entire eighty-block area, and along the commercial thoroughfare of Ogden Road and the Depot District.

If developments go as planned, Berwyn will be a mecca for even more compact residences. The plan also designates new "greening" projects, including a pedestrian/bike path to connect the town to the forest preserves that lie to the west, as well as plans to expand Berwyn's neighborhood parks and to design "complete streets" that would make walking more pleasant and local shopping more attractive. Ironically, the only thing lacking in the plan to improve walkability would be the presence of some large houses to add more variety to the streetscape. This is a form of variety, however, that has not been a part of Berwyn's culture. And with its small lots and architecturally notable bungalows it looks to remain that way. Building larger houses amidst the small ones might make for more rewarding walking, but it would not help the cause of reducing per-capita energy use, and in Berwyn the diverse housing expected in the future will be the low-carbon-footprint kind. The rare suburb of five-ton lives, through its new plans, Berwyn looks to do even better. From its unlikely origins as a working suburb with little interest in environmental organizations and prestige, Berwyn is leading the country in that regard.

# CHAPTER FIVE

# College, Commercial Carbon

## The New School, New York City

Holding a stack of energy questionnaires, I walked along a park near Georgetown University and paused in front of a young woman, intent on her laptop. She looked to be an unlikely respondent—too stylish and absorbed—but she agreed to be interviewed. When I came to the question, "If we approached a planetary emergency, what will you be willing to give up?" it turned out that she had already done it all. Her life was carless and meatless and her apartment was tiny, she said, and she liked it that way. Beaming, she added that she had just changed the power plan on her laptop, so her energy use was lower still. With her confidence and apparent personal independence from fossil fuels, she was not a person I would easily forget. The next generation will be known for this attitude, perhaps.

The carbon output of her university, Georgetown, at about 8 metric tons $CO_2$ per student, matches the American campus average almost exactly.[1] Despite installing solar panels on a half-dozen charming, two-hundred-year-old row houses recently and announcing that it was on course to become the greenest campus in America, the renewable share of Georgetown's campus electricity remained at about 0.1 percent, also typical for an American university. Arizona State University boasts the largest campus solar array, and because they need little heating fuel, their solar has made a dent in their overall energy use, lowering their carbon footprint by about 7 percent.[2] In northern climates, energy used for heating surpasses energy used in air conditioning by a long shot.[3] In chilly New Jersey, Rutgers University's solar installations reduce their greenhouse gas footprint by about 3 percent, the best result to date for an American campus that experiences cold winters, but of course a minor improvement for the atmosphere.[4]

The American university with the lowest carbon footprint is a place that does not generate any renewable energy of any kind, a place that's often overlooked when the latest green awards are announced. The Sierra Club's 2014 edition of their Cool Schools ranking of the 173 greenest colleges omitted them altogether.[5] But the New School in lower Manhattan, with emissions at about one metric ton per student, stands head and shoulders above other American universities in its carbon dioxide profile. Like the runner-up, DePaul University in Chicago, the New School's compact campus reflects a purposeful use of space, as well as innovation in how it uses conventional energy. Cars are not a part of the campus scene, and the university offers no place to park them.

The New School and other lower-emitting universities have remained unfashionably compact, running against the tide of America's academic building boom. The total square footage of all commercial buildings, which includes all education buildings, in America has increased by about 20 percent over the last decade, part of a longer-term construction trend.[6] While the U.S. population grew by 40 percent between 1979 and 2012, the square footage of U.S. commercial buildings expanded by about 70 percent during this time.[7] Greenhouse gas emissions from this sector has grown to about 3 metric tons per American, a number that rivals emissions from American homes, revealing that not only are American homes larger, but so are offices and classrooms. In Canada, for instance, per-person emissions related to commercial buildings is about one-third as much as American emissions. In Europe, these emissions are about half as much as America's.

Despite students' genuine interest in greening campuses and university administrators' professional commitments to reduce energy use, signs point toward an increase in energy use during these years of climate commitments and targets. When the University of New Hampshire looked at 267 campuses that had at least five years of energy consumption data, they found that over the years 2007 to 2014 the greenhouse gas emissions had declined because the electricity they purchased was increasingly generated from natural gas, not coal. During this time, the campuses had actually increased their energy use by 3 percent.[8] The increase was slight, but many of these particular institutions had made bold climate pledges. Students, of course, are paying for the high energy usage through tuition, which comes out to $800–$900 annually in the United States, more than double what Canadian university students are typically paying for utilities.[9]

The New School campus, with a student body of more than nine thousand and seven separate colleges or divisions, consists of a total of only twenty-one buildings, fewer than might be found at a small liberal arts college. The student life office does not pretend to offer many recreational amenities. Under a picture of four undergraduates sitting contentedly on a sidewalk the text reads, "On the weekends, when many clubs stay open well past dawn, your marathon nights might run all the way to the next afternoon." I spoke with an undergraduate who had no problem with it. "The city *is* the campus," offered current undergraduate Lauren Eckersley. "We hang out in Union Park and Washington Square and up on the High Line—we can be there in fifteen minutes. I haven't noticed if there's a gym or not."

The University was founded nearly a century ago by a group of Columbia University faculty protesting America's involvement in World War I, and when they moved downtown to Greenwich Village they did not try to imitate the large neoclassical style popular in commercial and academic buildings of the time. The university expanded rapidly after 1933, creating the University in Exile as a distinct program that welcomed to its faculty outstanding European academics seeking refuge from Nazism. Marlon Brando attended the acting school during the 1940s and said of it, "[The faculty] were enriching the city's intellectual life with an intensity that has probably never been equaled anywhere." Several decades later, when urban centers were not considered safe and the middle class had completed its retreat to the suburbs, the New School remained in its Greenwich Village location. In the 1970s while many urban campuses, such as DePaul University, were establishing satellite campuses in the suburbs, the New School instead expanded its programs in the city. They merged with Parsons, New York's eminent design school and established an undergraduate program, the Eugene Lang College, and later Mannes, a renowned school for jazz and contemporary music.

Greenwich Village, with its narrow streets and leafy sidewalks may not be Manhattan's densest neighborhood, but with its small apartment buildings, brownstones and medium sized office buildings, it is much denser than most American neighborhoods. New School buildings blend in at the street level and rise higher than the surrounding buildings in a few sites, especially the new University Center on 5th Avenue. But the campus buildings cannot be described as skyscrapers and most of the New School's buildings are less than 15 stories in height. The New School's location in New York City harkens back to the time when most American colleges were founded in the colonies' most important towns such Boston, New York, Philadelphia, and Williamsburg. An exception, Dartmouth, founded in the hinterlands of northern New Hampshire in the 1760s, had the mission of educating American Indians. The small colleges that opened in the rural Midwest in the early nineteenth century, such as Oberlin and Grinnell College, were the ideas of churchmen who wanted to bring Christianity and learning to the "wild" western lands. Suburbs and smaller towns only became common sites for higher education with the legislation in the 1860s that founded land-grant universities in every state, with a partial mission to improve agriculture. Providing students with a rural idyll and recreational amenities was not part of American higher education's original mission, although these features pad the carbon profile of many universities today.

In a quiet part of Eleventh Street the New School houses Eugene Lang College, and the small entrance opens on to a café with about twenty tables. Except for the closely spaced arrangement of tables and chairs, little distinguishes the room from any number of New York City cafés, but almost every seat was taken, and no one was waiting for a table when I visited one winter afternoon. Elsewhere in the university the New School has invested in student-use and circulation studies and has applied this data to repurpose existing space rather than building or leasing new facilities.[10] A similar principle seemed to be at work here, and when the café filled up at lunchtime a group of students reconvened outside despite the chill of a mild January day.

Inside I chatted with students from Los Angeles, Richmond, and Beverly, Massachusetts—all places with a great deal more sprawl and living space than their Manhattan dorms and apartments, space that they expressed no regret in losing. Not surprisingly, none of the students were aware of the New School's energy-use statistics and their outstanding nature. I looked around thinking that somewhere in this room or not far away was the greenest college student in America, but like the rest of America, the individuals in this room had little idea of how their utility bills related to their carbon footprint and how this compared with anyone else's. "About average," offered a young man who was working on a degree in history. "My appliances are pretty old."

The New School's one-metric-ton $CO_2$ footprint is a tidy outcome considering that the average for American buildings—commercial plus residences—adds up to more than six tons per person.[11] The comparison may not be entirely fair, because we would expect the non-campus buildings to have higher emissions. We would expect a college's per-student emissions to be lower than the wider world because dorm rooms are smaller than apartments and houses, and because higher education's functions are more limited than that of the commercial sector at large. The world of commercial buildings outside of academia expands into many kinds of functions and includes government buildings such as fire stations, town halls, and K-12 schools, as well as office buildings, restaurants, and wholesale and retail outlets, warehouses, and many other types of buildings. In this respect, it is not surprising that the New School's per-capita emissions of about one ton are much lower than typical for the U.S. commercial sector, even when emissions from the university's residential halls are considered as well. What may be surprising is that American academic emissions typically surpass the commercial and residential sector combined. Over the period 2005–2009, the U.S. commercial and residential sector averaged 6.8 metric tons per person, and higher-education emissions averaged 8.6 metric tons per student, about 25 percent higher than the national metric.[12] Higher Education has shied away from making comparisons, but the selective colleges, which average about 15 metric tons $CO_2$, tower over the already-hefty average emissions from American colleges and universities, which surpass U.S. commercial and residential sectors combined, dwarfing comparable emissions from Canada (see Figure 14).

Outwardly, American academia seems to have embraced green culture on many levels, and the car-free, dorm-residing American college student may seem to be our best example of a lower-energy-consuming individual. David Owen makes that case in his book, *The Conundrum*, which explores how behavioral adjustments can sabotage technological improvements in energy use. "College students usually live even more compactly than Manhattanites or Hong Kong residents ... and favor inherently low carbon forms of recreation (sleeping late, engaging in pointless but environmentally non-destructive philosophical speculations; having sex)."[13] But although dorm rooms tend to be much smaller than apartments and houses, as Owen points out, the rest of the campus has invested in the equivalent of the corner office and the all-inclusive resort.

Like the boom in commercial construction, construction in higher education has outpaced the growth in student enrollment.[14] The current spending of about $11 billion per year doubles the spending level

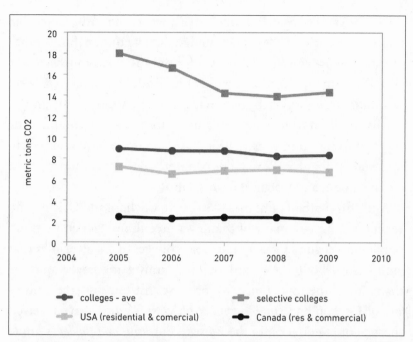

Fig. 14. Higher-education per student emissions compared with commercial and Canadian per capita $CO_2$. Compiled by the author from Sustainable Endowments Institute reports and U.S. EPA's *Inventory of U.S. Greenhouse Gas Emissions and Sinks: 1990–2014.* "Selective colleges" accept fewer than 30 percent of applicants.

of twenty years ago.[15] Construction slowed after the 2008 recession but picked up sharply again after 2012. The construction boom has led to compounded expenses as colleges pay for more janitors, facility managers, replacement materials and upkeep for the new buildings, which accrue these expenses indefinitely. It is not entirely coincidental that student indebtedness rose rapidly during the construction boom. Earnings of recent graduates have not kept pace with their debt loads. By 2010, the average student debt/income ratio was twice as high as it had been one decade earlier.[16]

Students at the New School have not been immune from rising tuition costs and indebtedness, but the bottom line is less onerous than at nearby schools. Current tuition for undergraduates at the New School stands at $40,550 annually—higher than the national average for private colleges, but substantially less than nearby Columbia University, which asks $55,356 for undergraduate tuition. But another statistic is pertinent here: The New School sustains a much smaller class size than typical at 9:1, a student-to-faculty ratio that *U.S. News and World Report* says is the best in the country. Although the university has received little if any recognition for its carbon footprint, its restraint in building construction has freed up resources for teaching. And although college guides do not yet count carbon, they do count student and teaching faculty ratios.

Aside from urban campuses like the New School and DePaul University in Chicago, many of the lower greenhouse gas emitters are public universities. Of sixty four-year colleges and universities that emit at a level of five tons or less, public universities make up more than half of the total. Only two of these institutions—the University of Oregon and the University of Washington—have received special commendation in the most recent *Princeton Review*'s guide to green colleges.[17] Many of the lower-emitting colleges are located in the milder regions of the South and West, but over half are in the colder climate regions, showing that low emissions can be achieved anywhere.[18] The presence of so many public universities on the list reveals that students who live lower-emissions lives and those who pay less tuition are often one and the same.

### The Amenity Race

But on the whole, an edifice complex has pervaded higher education's public and private campuses and its reach includes athletic, dormitory, and arts facilities alike.[19] The trend in college athletics and non-varsity sports has been to increase traveling opportunities, enlarge buildings, and provide all-season training fields, rinks, and pools. None of these trends, of course, serve the goal of carbon neutrality! Particularly controversial are projects that cater to the comfort and training of a small slice of the student body: the elite athletes who play football or basketball for major teams. The emissions related to intercollegiate sports programs can be hard to pin down because the facilities usually do not report energy use and many of the power league football campuses do not even release campus-wide greenhouse gas inventories. A student writer for the University of Arkansas's *Razorback Reporter* provides some insight, revealing that the university spends three times more on energy for the football stadium than for the student union building that serves all the students. The annual carbon footprint for the stadium came out to 6,973 metric tons of $CO_2$, according to the reporter's investigation. This figure might seem impossibly high if not for the stadium's accessory functions, including remedial classrooms for athletes, the standard whirlpool baths, kitchens for catering athletic events, and machinery storage for turf maintenance.[20]

Arkansas's spa-like amenities for football players are not unusual, and when *Washington Post* reporters William Hobson and Steven Rich looked at financial records for forty-eight public universities in the Power Five football conference, they found that spending for buildings and operations had jumped nearly 90 percent between 2004 and 2014 (with adjustment for inflation), and had reached $0.77 billion in 2014.[21] Some of the schools raise enough money from tickets and ads, but many do not, and in 2014 students from these schools paid some $114 million in required athletic fees, regardless of whether they attended sports events or had any desire to support them. "It's a never-ending arms race to build shiny objects that appeal to 17-year-olds," commented a Colorado Board of Regents member to the *Washington Post*.[22]

Some of these facilities—like indoor football fields—were considered unnecessary in an earlier era when more sports were enjoyed in the great outdoors during less-than-ideal weather. Even practice sessions for competitive football were held outdoors, but now many universities in mild climates regard indoor football training facilities as necessities. The University of Virginia claims that their recently completed seventy-eight-thousand-square-foot indoor practice facility is "one of the finest" in the country, a distinction that has not impressed UVA students who charge that the mandatory athletics fee of $657 is excessive and unfair.[23] Perhaps the country's largest such all-season facility is now in the works at the University of Maryland, part of a $155 million renovation of the university's original field house. As in Virginia, Maryland plans to dip heavily into funds raised by mandatory athletic fees levied on all students.[24]

Other large energy consumers on campus—new indoor swimming pools and all-season skating rinks—represent luxury items that are becoming more common at the high school and community level as well. Many of the new buildings use a great deal of energy because they require heating, cooling, and ventilation simultaneously. Indoor pools, or natatoriums, typically consume about five times more energy than a commercial building of similar size, and of course, far more energy than a similar-sized pool located outside. An Olympic-sized indoor pool may consume about ten times more energy than an outdoor pool of the same size.[25] Colleges and universities are increasingly building natatoriums that offer water park features, such as lazy rivers and underwater lounges, in addition to lap lanes. A recent college ranking site offered a listing of the "30 Best College Pools" and put in first place the facility at Pensacola Christian College that offers an indoor water park and simulated surfing, including the "million-dollar wave ride, FlowRider."[26]

Indoor ice rinks tend to be extremely energy intensive as well, because the HVAC systems simultaneously maintain the ice, circulate the air, and provide a comfortable sitting temperature. At a minimum a standard-size ice hockey rink will emit at least five hundred metric tons of $CO_2$ each year and usually twice that amount.[27] The average ice hockey arena is thirty-four thousand square feet, but even some smaller colleges now require larger arenas. At Bowdoin College the indoor hockey arena completed in 2009 is a LEED certified project despite its 70,520-square-foot size. Although the facility did not earn the higher tier of Silver, Gold, or Platinum, its LEED certification is meant to connote superior resource use and energy efficiency. Given the size of the small liberal arts college, the $20 million cost of the arena represents $10,000 per current student.[28]

Universities with more of an academic than athletic emphasis have directed much new construction to the arts. In the Ivy League recent expansions have accrued costs in the multi-billions as some of America's oldest universities eye each other's exhibit spaces and pedigree architects. Yale University spent $135 million to remodel its art gallery and expand its exhibit space to encompass 69,975 square feet, which falls short of Stanford's newer 96,000-square-foot arts complex. The Harvard Art Museums renovations cost $400 million, and Princeton spent a similar amount for their arts center development although its director, Stanley Katz, voiced his lack of enthusiasm to the *New York Times*: "So far as I can tell, the expansion contributes in only modest ways to the intellectual mission of the university."[29]

Continuous lighting on exhibits means art museum electricity use is considerable whether or not visitors are present. And increasingly, visitors are not present, with a steady downward trend in art museum visitors throughout the nation. In 2012 only about one in five Americans reported visiting an art museum in the past 12 months, and attendance for 18–24-year-olds is slightly lower and has dropped by about 25 percent over the past decade.[30] College-age Americans and young adults also have been attending fewer plays, classical and jazz concerts, musicals, poetry readings, and similar events.[31] Despite the low level of interest, universities and colleges have been investing widely in new buildings to house art collections and to encourage collaboration among art programs. At the New School, the art gallery displays primarily student and faculty art and perhaps qualifies as a museum in that it displays the works of outside artists as well. But totaling four thousand square feet, the space is certainly diminutive in the context of a growing trend of campus art museum investment.

An unusual feature of the New School's building entrances is how unremarkable they are. For some buildings, you need to know the address to find the revolving door, and a security desk fronts a small lobby or foyer. If you arrive instead at one of the new buildings at Duke, MIT, Yale, Tulane, or any number of campuses, the architectural forms convey that you have arrived at an important place, and the soaring ceiling height of the ubiquitous atria or courtyard recalls no other function so much as the terminal of an airport. For instance, the new building for the Yale School of Management encompasses an astonishing 242,000 square feet at a cost of $130 million. Students using the library have an enticing view of the outside as the long, narrow room is lined on both sides with an expanse of glass. The new building is a far cry from Yale's main library, built in the 1930s with much smaller windows—a style that tends to use half as much energy per square foot as modernist glass libraries, and a form that presumes that students are there to study.[32] Designed by the British architect Norman Foster, who built London's Stansted Airport, the building was opened to great fanfare in 2014 despite a small picket line manned by more neighbors than students. "It is out of perspective, it is gross and it belongs somewhere else," said Nancy Ahern, a former neighborhood representative.[33]

Airport entrances and exits loom large out of consideration for visitors who have not been there before, are travel weary, and do not know the local language. The New School's lobbies, in features shared by DePaul's downtown campus, presume that students do not need these cues, and the functional entrances and lobbies are factors in the schools' low carbon intensity. DePaul recently acquired an historic building in downtown Chicago; but with its compact use of space it has little in common with the monumental designs that predominate in contemporary academic architecture.

## Car Culture

In his book *The Uses of the University* the late Clark Kerr, chancellor of Berkeley, summed it up as follows: "The Three Purposes of the University? To provide sex for the students, sports for the alumni

Fig. 15. Yale School of Management building, designed by Norman Foster, completed in 2014. Photo, "Front facade of Edward P. Evans Hall shortly after completion," by Nick Allen, distributed under a CC-BY-SA-3.0 license, Wikimedia Commons.

and parking for the faculty." The New School, which does not own parking garages or even provide discounts for nearby garages, utterly fails Kerr's tenets in this respect. "If you live on campus you basically need your feet," advises a New School student. Other Manhattan universities subsidize a larger footprint. NYU students and staff receive discounts at downtown garages, as do Columbia students, who also can access free parking when they visit the medical school campus.

Cheap parking in academia has come with a cultural shift that discards any notion that many students cannot afford to drive. In an earlier generation, it was not unusual for a college such as Carleton College in Northfield, Minnesota, to deny parking permits to students who received financial aid, the logic being that a student who could afford the luxury of a car shouldn't be asking for tuition assistance. But now such places tend to offer parking to students regardless of financial aid package. At Oberlin an annual parking permit costs only $150. Reed College "encourages students to use public transportation," but if you have a car, parking is free and "the community safety office will jump-start your vehicle, open vehicles when the keys are locked outside, and escort you to or from your vehicle after dark."[34] Little wonder that more Reed students have cars and the parking lots have grown to surpass the ground floor space of dorms. In previous decades MIT sent a letter to new students telling them that if they have a car they should not bring it to Cambridge, because it is not needed and there is no parking. In recent years MIT has invested in underground parking, including a 290,000-square-foot heated garage beneath the Silver-level LEED-certified STATA Center at MIT designed by Frank Gehry.[35]

An alternative to heavy parking subsidies is to offer discounted or free passes for public transportation. DePaul University does this, and the 1.5 million free CTA trips their students have taken explains why their commuting and travel carbon footprint, at about half a ton $CO_2$ per student, is extremely low. A similar program is offered at some 130-plus American colleges and universities through the Universal Access Transit Pass, or U-pass. In the program, student fees or tuition are used to purchase access to local transit, spreading the cost among car commuters, walkers, and transit users alike.[36] Student participation is usually mandatory, but not surprisingly, faculty and staff can usually opt out.

Historically, opposing parking lots has not been a focus of campus environmental activism, but a former student from Valdosta State University in southern Georgia named Hayden Barnes fought this battle on his own and won a succession of legal and personal victories. His fight began in 2007 when as a sophomore Barnes spoke out against a planned $30 million investment in parking garages. "Have there been any alternatives explored to building two large, expensive and ugly parking decks on campus? . . . I think the decision to build these parking decks is going to be looked down upon by future generations who are going [to] recognize them for what they are, a bad investment, a short-term solution to a long-term problem."[37]

The young man, who sported a reddish beard trimmed low on his chin in the tradition of Henry David Thoreau, reached out to a student environmental organization, but they showed little interest in his cause. Undeterred, he put together a poster with images of a bulldozer, urban smog, and an asthma inhaler with the title "Zaccari Memorial Parking Garage," referring to the college president who had been a booster of the garage.[38] Ronald Zaccari was not amused, and almost overnight, Barnes found himself expelled in a unilateral action by President Zaccari.

Barnes was not the first student in the United States to oppose a parking construction project. In 2005 Cornell University students tied themselves to tree canopy platforms in a small woodland slated to be cleared for a new parking lot. The protesters quit the tree platforms but succeeded in negotiating better alternative transportation. At Washtenaw Community College in Michigan in 2010, students made a rare connection between a proposed parking garage and energy use. "It does not promote climate leadership, model ways to minimize global warming emissions, and does not help educate our student body on how to achieve climate neutrality," argued Washtenaw student Beth Jakubowski for the *Washtenaw Voice*.[39]

Unlike the other cases, though, Barnes was the victim of a public reprisal that had nothing to do with his educational performance, but as Valdosta State's president and board would discover, Barnes was a particularly tenacious person. Through the help of the legal defense group the Foundation for Individual Rights in Education (FIRE) and ten other organizations, Barnes launched a charge that Zacarri and the university had violated his civil rights. A verdict came down in 2010 that held president Zaccari personally and financially liable for violating the student's civil liberties.[40] Valdosta State appealed various charges but dug a deeper hole for themselves when a court awarded Barnes an additional $900,000 in 2015.[41]

In the Barnes case a brave student pushed a logical point: Why should students, including students without cars, pay for parking garage construction? Unfortunately, all of his supporters were civil liberties groups—not environmental litigators such as Earthjustice or the Natural Resources Defense Council—and his profound questions fell by the wayside. But the Barnes case confirmed the essential powers of students to raise unpopular opinions, and to affirm values of conservation and thrift. He was so thoroughly vindicated that future students may be encouraged to take a similar stand against university investments that are counter to their long-term interests.

## Higher Flying

The New School's Achilles heel when it comes to carbon dioxide ties in with its perceived strength, its geographical diversity. One in four undergraduates hail from another country and their jet travel overwhelms their other sources of greenhouse gases. The New School does not publish their jet travel emissions but other colleges that do report that air travel may average many tons $CO_2$ per student. Among the schools that keep track, Emory University reports a whopping eight metric tons per student for this kind of travel combined with daily commutes and special trips. Duke University, with its professional-level athletics, is not far behind at six tons. And since carbon dioxide has a more potent impact higher in the atmosphere than at the surface, the actual global warming impact of the air travel will be higher still.

The enormous difference between Emory and a regional university like DePaul arises from the large number of students who travel from out of state to attend. In Emory's case, out-of-state students make up about 70 percent of the student body. For most of the Ivy League, at least 80 percent of undergraduates are from out of state, a fact that does not necessarily entail much extra $CO_2$ from those able to take a train or bus. But highly selective colleges strive for inter-coastal diversity and admit many students who may not have a chance to attend a similarly selective college closer to home. The students who commit to geographically distant schools are of course accruing a huge number of air miles, as are their visiting family members.

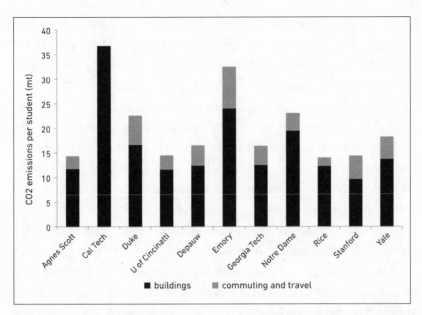

Fig. 16. Highest-emitting U.S. universities. Created by author from Sustainable Endowments Institute, detailed reports circa 2009.

In many cases the private colleges draw from a more dispersed pool of applicants and have far higher transport emissions than the public universities nearby. For instance, per-person transportation emissions from Colorado College are four times higher than comparable emissions at the University of Colorado Boulder. Stanford's transportation emissions are five times higher than Berkeley's, a difference of four metric tons $CO_2$ per student. If selective colleges and universities instead gave preference to students from within their own time zone, they could achieve a degree of geographical diversity while cutting down on the long-haul flights, given that U.S. train and bus lines are well served on a north-south gradient. The highly selective colleges that aim for geographical diversity already can work from a vast applicant pool and can select from many other criteria, including academic, extracurricular, social, economic, and racial. A school's desire for geographic diversity may have some justification, but compared to the other criteria it bears the highest environmental cost.

For research universities one would expect faculty travel to add a great deal to the overall emissions. For instance at Duke such travel (combined with air travel for sports teams) makes up about 20 percent of overall campus emissions; at Colgate University in New York State it makes up 25 percent. A closer look through the lens of Colgate data, however, reveals that although faculty air travel is high, college athletics contributes nearly as much to airplane emissions—certainly an interesting result, and one that is probably not unique to Colgate.[42] Perhaps the greatest evocation of the privilege of elite players are the private jets that some universities, such as Duke, maintain for their teams, or the wide-bodied jets that some universities lease from commercial carriers. Air travel related to title games can mean flights for several hundred members of university staff and their spouses.[43] Duke University happens to be one of the few members of the Atlantic Coast Conference (ACC) for college football that has released a greenhouse gas inventory, and if they are typical, air travel constitutes a very large portion of emissions. Duke's per-student air-travel emissions increased by 13 percent between 2009 and 2014, from 3.3 metric tons per student to 3.7 metric tons.[44]

The carbon footprint of the 1 percent in Division I sports is undoubtedly enormous, but the growth in less-competitive club sports drives the larger part of college students' high mobility. Nation-wide, five times more students participate in sports clubs than in NCAA and NAIA sports.[45] Club sports cover the gamut, including quidditch (a broomstick-wielding contact sport), table tennis, and many types of martial arts. The explosive growth in team travel, compared with a generation ago, reflects a cultural shift from the time when many college teams were satisfied with competing locally, even if that meant playing against high school teams or the B league at the local tennis club.

Today even universities that are not known for an athletic emphasis often sponsor many traveling teams. For instance, the University of Colorado at Boulder spends about $300,000 each year for 110 trips for club sports. Mindful of the carbon implications of the program, they issued a handbook called *Pledge to Travel Green: Club Sports at University of Colorado Boulder, 2014.* The handbook recommends using US Airways because it is the "only airline with a LEED Gold certified corporate headquarters and a LEED certified operations control center." The handbook also notes that Delta Air Lines may be a good choice because of its green actions, including the airline's support for solar panels in a Nike retail store in the Portland airport. The fact that the name of LEED and solar power are being used to justify airplane travel—which involves neither buildings nor solar panels—exposes the long arm of green PR in academia.

Colgate, Duke, and many other universities buy carbon offsets to "neutralize" their emissions from air travel. Offsets are credits for reducing carbon elsewhere by, for example, paying for an organization to plant trees abroad. Because they are hard to authenticate and do little to reduce consumption, they have fallen out of favor in many environmental circles. They are also less than popular with indigenous rights groups who have observed "carbon cowboys" pushing traditional communities away from forests with false promises of offset money.[46] Kevin Anderson, the deputy director of Europe's preeminent climate research network, the Tyndall Centre, had this to say about it: "[Offsets] militate against market signals to improve low-carbon travel and video-conference technology."[47] The Tyndall Centre fielded a survey that reported that 80 percent of the academic respondents said they would support an organization-wide policy to reduce flying so long as the flightless were not put at a disadvantage.[48] A new app, the Tyndall Travel Tracker, helps researchers to project air miles and decide which meetings may be inessential. Anderson himself has made a pledge not to fly, and when he decided to attend a conference in Shanghai recently he traveled by train from his home in Manchester, UK. "The train's ability to reverse many of the choices that clutter my daily life gave me the seclusion and concentration I needed," recalled Anderson. "By the time Moscow arrived, I had completed 75 percent of the writing. This would have taken another six months had I flown to Shanghai."[49] A growing number of academics in the United States are making public pledges to reduce flying by lending their names to a blog by Parke Wilde called "Flying Less: Reducing America's Carbon Footprint."[50]

In the United States, meteorologist and writer Eric Holthaus vowed after reading an Intergovernmental Panel on Climate Change (IPCC) report in 2013 that he would go cold turkey on airplane travel. His statement appeared in the press with the headline, "Meteorologist Breaks Down in Tears after Climate Change Report, Says He Will Never Fly Again."[51] But whether such individual pledges are influencing the wider culture is uncertain. National-level data suggest that passenger flights, or "enplanements," continue to grow in the United States. In 2014, these were at 762 million passengers, up from 740 million in 2013.[52] Carbon dioxide emissions from international flights departing from or arriving in the United States has more than doubled since 1990.[53] Air ticket prices have held stable, and many Americans have expanded their reasons for flying, just as higher education has found new reasons to use airplanes, including "alternative" (sober) spring break trips and intercollegiate athletics. American academe still lacks a strong voice on the serious question of the climate impact of flying, and the American College and University Presidents Climate Commitment, which calls for the purchase of carbon offsets for faculty travel, falls short of the Tyndall Centre's example.

### New "Green" Buildings

In 2014 the University of Massachusetts at Amherst won a national climate leadership award, an honor bestowed by the American College and University Presidents Climate Commitment (ACUPCC) network. The award site notes that UMASS has pledged to procure at least 20 percent of its food from local sources, and that all freshmen will be encouraged to read a book about a Thoreau-inspired experiment in a lower greenhouse gas emissions life, Colin Beavan's *Low Impact Man*. But if we turn to a different corner of UMass—the office of Design & Construction Management—we can view the motto, "Dream. Build. Achieve," and then read the construction specs. Among the new projects are a 56,500-square-foot basketball development center and an addition to the football stadium that seems to have in mind a user who is the antithesis of the low impact man. The stadium expansion offers these young men a new lounge, an enlarged locker room, a nutrition center, a film-viewing room, and a spa, among other amenities. Other campus projects sound closer to an academic mission but provide hundreds of thousands of additional square feet for faculty offices, classrooms and dorms.

The college presidents receiving the leadership awards invariably are the same people who support construction projects. If climate award programs are to influence energy consumption overall, they need to praise compact campuses and eliminate from their short lists institutions that have approved large, frivolous, energy-consuming projects. The awards as they now stand do nothing to slow the biggest driver of greenhouse gas emissions in academe: the construction of more and larger campus buildings.

The environmental science departments and environmental clubs might appear to be places that could challenge these developments. The proliferation of sustainability programs in higher education would seem to be a force to reckon with. Today, American higher education offers at least 1,500 environmental studies programs compared to only a handful of formal programs in the 1970s. Even colleges that had resisted the idea, such as my alma mater, Reed College, decided they needed to find a way to combine environmental topics with traditional liberal arts disciplines. In Reed's case, they had received a petition from me in 1980 to start an environmental studies major, and about thirty years later they agreed to launch one.

In the early 1990s many American campuses, with the aid of major philanthropies and especially the Rockefeller Brothers Fund, began sending students to training programs to learn about campus energy conservation. Most colleges set up sustainability offices made up of staff and faculty representatives. In 2006 about forty college presidents joined to form a new network, the American College and University Presidents Climate Commitment. The commitment was to move their institutions toward carbon neutrality, and by 2017 more than six hundred college presidents had signed onto the pledge.[54]

When universities sign on to the American College and University Presidents Climate Commitment, many promise that all their new buildings will receive LEED (Leadership on Energy and Environmental Design) Silver rating or higher. When the New School signed the pledge they did not have any such buildings, but in 2014 they completed their first LEED building, which rated the "Gold" Standard. This building, the University Center, looks very different from all other New School buildings. At 375,000 square feet and 16 stories it towers over the others, and its stairwells and lobbies derive from a monumental tradition. Seven "grand communicating stairs" connect the levels, and adjoining spaces are "sky quads to exchange ideas."[55]

The new center's all-glass walls that span multiple floors are a mainstay of academic and commercial architecture, which has introduced vast atria to existing and new buildings. The glass can help trap heat during the cool winter months in temperate regions, but the huge enclosed spaces often need cooling as well as mechanical ventilation and periodic heating, making for a large overall energy demand. This architectural form sprang up before architects and engineers learned how to manage the energy consumed in these airy spaces.[56] The U.S. Green Building Council, which oversees the LEED certification, admits the glass walls that are seen almost everywhere in new academic buildings waste energy: "The ubiquitous all-glass, unshaded, sealed, flush-skin curtain walls that have significant detrimental effects on energy consumption, indoor environmental quality and occupant comfort and productivity . . . is due as much to the economies of it being a common construction practice as it is to it being an element of architectural modernism, rarely is this choice driven by energy concerns."[57]

The present green building certification makes many ordinary buildings appear to be special, and the various green college guides do little to put a critical eye on a costly construction boom. High school students checking to see if their favored college is green are likely to find it in an edition of *Princeton Review*'s guide to green colleges.[58] The guide haphazardly picks out a vegetable garden here, a solar panel there, or a new ecology course, but in many entries you will find lavish praise for the places that can boast a long list of LEED buildings. For instance, Dickinson College makes the top ten in the 2014 guide because "while the college requires all new buildings to be constructed to LEED Silver standards, every building constructed since 2008 surpassed this goal by achieving LEED Gold certification." The many details about who has these buildings, and how many they have, becomes more comprehensible when it is understood that the guide's cosponsor is none other than the U.S. Green Building Council, the outfit that performs the LEED certification.

What exactly is LEED certification? Obtaining it from the certifier—the U.S. Green Building Council—can ease a building plan past college trustees who may be reluctant to support another building project, and certification can add millions to construction costs. "Bullshit Bingo," according to energy expert Dr. Ozzie Zehner. "LEED has been a successful program from the standpoint of public relations. . . . An institution that has a LEED-certified building is usually not shy about it . . . It is very surprising then, the LEED certification does not require a building to use less energy than a conventional building."[59] As Zehner points out, throughout most of its history the LEED program has awarded certification not on the basis of actual energy use, but based on projections.

Independent researchers wishing to analyze the performance of LEED buildings have been stymied by lack of access to data from the U.S. Green Building Council, but this is changing thanks to new rules for disclosing energy data. Benchmarking laws in New York City, Washington DC and elsewhere mean that data on the energy performance of hundreds of commercial buildings can now be scrutinized and compared with green building claims. When the Green Building Council bestows their Silver- or Gold-level certification, they plant the notion that the buildings will use as much as 40 percent less energy than a typical building. A physicist at Oberlin College, John Scofield, who blogs as the Pragmatic Steward at thepragmaticsteward.com, found that LEED buildings in Washington DC achieved only about half of the 30–40 percent energy savings that they had claimed. The performance for New York City office buildings was poorer, for the LEED buildings did not save energy at all.[60] Echoing Scofield's conclusions, researchers at the University of Florida Gainesville found that the LEED buildings on their campus did not save energy compared with the other buildings.[61]

The shiny promise of green buildings, of course, has been visited on many other types of buildings aside from higher education, including elementary and high schools. A USA Today review of sixty-five schools around the country by Thomas Frank found little correlation between green schools and student performance—or even energy use. It was clear, however, that pursuing LEED certification did add to the cost.[62] DC's first Green Ribbon School project was an expansion of an elementary school that cost $34 million, almost the cost of a new stand-alone school. The project at the Benjamin Stoddert Elementary School accessed a geothermal energy supply and added a modest amount of classroom space, a large gym, and a new lobby atrium. Now, a few years on, parents and staff regret that much of the new space went into the atrium rather than additional classrooms, because the LEED Gold-certified school suffers from crowding and relies on temporary trailer-classrooms. The city does not advertise the school's energy performance, but digging into DC's energy benchmarking database confirms that the school consumes more energy per student than the DC average. In fact, the EPA assigned it an ENERGY STAR score that is in the bottom 1 percent of elementary schools nationally.[63] Stoddert's dismal energy profile is partly due to the challenge of managing the temperature in the new atrium and oversized gymnasium. The gym resembles a college facility, with generous spectator seating and a wall of windows offering views of the neighboring street. Washington DC's other flagship renovation was the expansion of Dunbar High School, bearing a price tag of $122 million and LEED Platinum certification—the highest category. The roof holds a new solar array, and has generated press heralding the outcome as the "greenest school in America," but the school's per-capita carbon dioxide emissions, at 3.5 metric tons per student, is high for a secondary school, and much higher than emissions at the New School.[64]

Although it is heartening that at least some LEED buildings appear to save energy, the new data exposes the basic flaws in the LEED program. The program suffers from an inability to predict behavioral influences on building energy consumption. The latest iteration called LEED v4 promises to have a greater focus on actual performance but loopholes remain; buildings can still receive precertification at the platinum level before the building is completed.[65] For the time being, higher education would do well to just forego LEED certification and instead strive to improve energy use, employing at least two metrics—source energy used per square foot, and greenhouse gas emissions per student. The first metric is essential for improved facility management, and the second is an overall indicator of consumption, priorities, and management.

A promising approach to understanding a building's energy performance is the EPA's ENERGY STAR score, which tries to compare like with like, for example libraries with libraries and dorm rooms with dorm rooms, and only rates buildings after they have been in use for at least a year. The score ranges from 1 to 100, and the resulting number is easier for the public to understand than underlying raw data useful for facility managers such as "weather normalized source energy use per square foot." Unfortunately, in its present form the ENERGY STAR score is plagued by grade inflation. John Scofield, who dismantled many of the LEED green building claims, found that 35 percent of dorms received such a high ENERGY STAR score that they were placed in the top 10 percent of all scores, a statistically impossible result.[66] Other building categories, including medical office buildings, show a similar clustering at the top.[67] The problem with ENERGY STAR may lay not so much with the concept as with the algorithm and data management. If ENERGY STAR can improve its analysis, it may become a useful tool.

The American Institute of Architects (AIA) has taken a step in the right direction in the design of their awards program. Whereas in the past, they chose their "Top Ten" buildings on the basis of design features, for the 2017 award year they revamped the program so that actual building performance on energy use and other factors is taken into consideration.[68] The new award, overseen by AIA's Committee on the Environment (COTE), recommends that all contestants submit at least twelve months of performance data but they can establish an even longer track record because the new contest sets no time limit after a building's completion.

## Conserving Energy

For many college students who reside in dorms, including at the New School, energy conservation ideas only start to come to the fore during an annual energy contest.[69] Typically, the contests set a discrete period of time to monitor electricity use and give a prize to the dorm that has used the lowest kwh during this time. Often, a leaderboard in the lobby or common room gives a real-time reading of kwh used in that particular building, adding a bit of flash to activities that are both hidden and mundane. The intentions are good; American students tend to use more appliances and machines and keep the lights on longer than students in other countries.[70] But do the students continue to save energy after the contest is over? No, according to Princeton professor Sander van der Linden, who found that at the end of the contest energy consumption soon returned to its previous level.[71]

Much rarer are the campuses that incorporate incentives into the price structures of their room and board fees or provide cash incentives to staff, faculty, and students who save energy. Most campus buildings are not metered individually despite the advantages. Metering buildings offers facility managers a view of the savings from energy improvement projects and allows a more rapid response to equipment failures. As the cost of adding metering has declined, the EPA has been encouraging universities to meter individual buildings and dorm rooms, which forms the foundation for such incentives.[72]

Beginning in the early 1990s, the Sustainable Endowments Institute (SEI) supported a nationwide program to improve energy conservation on campuses, an effort that was taken on by many institutions in higher education. Eventually the program called on participants to fill out detailed questionnaires on energy management and other areas of environmental resource usage. Each college received a letter grade from SEI ranging from A to F as part of their Green Report Card project (discontinued in 2012). The surveys revealed vast differences in energy intensity on American campuses, and not surprisingly, the New School's survey answers show a low energy intensity of about 0.008 metric tons $CO_2$ per gross square foot of space. In contrast Vanderbilt University, which has a carbon footprint of about 20 metric tons, uses about three times more energy per square foot. The following chart compares energy management performance for the two schools; Vanderbilt has a poorer showing on all of the following twelve energy savings features except for LED lighting.

The narrative of energy efficiency has a much more complicated through line, of course, than the renewable revolution or divestment from fossil fuels. But the renewable options, especially solar, are still more expensive than most of the energy management tools. The initial solar array installed at Rutgers cost $40 million dollars, but many of their campus buildings remain unmetered, and improving

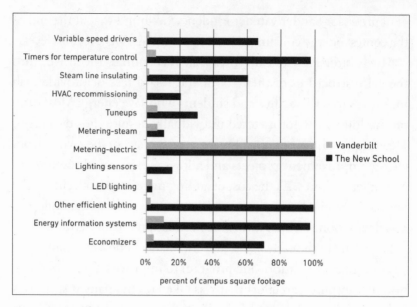

Fig. 17. Energy efficiency at the New School and Vanderbilt. Created by author from Sustainable Endowments Institute, detailed reports circa 2009.

conservation would be cheaper than the solar option. They have saved far more energy through maintaining a cogeneration plant on campus than from all of their renewables combined. In general, while American academia's renewable energy has achieved no more than a few percent in fossil fuel reduction, conservation measures can bring results that surpass a 15 percent drop in the carbon footprint while paying for themselves in a few years. Energy conservation investments have benefited from a variety of local and national rebates and incentives that could be furthered by a bold move such as limiting federal grants and student loans for institutions that are lax on their energy management.

## "Prestigious" Outliers

Caltech happens to be the presumed location for the TV sitcom *The Big Bang Theory*, in which environmentally conscious students occasionally quip about global warming. In one episode an actress walks into the room carrying a handbag that declaims, "A woman can tell a lot about a guy by the size of his carbon footprint." Perhaps it can tell a lot about a university, because Caltech reported their 2009 emissions to be nearly 40 metric tons per student, the highest on record for any university in America. The university was recently shortlisted in *Princeton Review*'s green guide to American colleges for possessing "the second largest rooftop solar installation," but at the root of Caltech's problem is an enormous building plant averaging about 1,800 square feet per student. Science schools tend to use more energy because they need more laboratory space and equipment, but at Caltech much of their new space is hard to pin down. For instance, the ground floor of Caltech's new one-hundred-thousand-square-foot astrophysics and aeronautics building reveals thousands of square feet of empty shelves and glass walls that seeks to "mimic the experience of peering up through a telescope."[73]

Selective universities tend to employ a high number of research staff, which skews the $CO_2$-to-student metric, and universities with graduate science programs expend a great deal of energy in maintaining laboratories and hospitals. Liberal arts colleges tend to have higher per-capita emissions as well because they offer a wide range of departments and amenities without the return to scale of larger universities. Selective institutions admit a more geographically dispersed student body that brings with them mobility-related $CO_2$ emissions. Among the selective colleges that accept fewer than 30 percent of applicants, California's Claremont McKenna had the lowest per-capita emissions at about 3.5 tons, but a new building campaign in the last few years added several new tons and brought them closer to the average carbon footprint for selective institutions—15 metric tons $CO_2$ per student.[74]

At Caltech's East Coast rival, MIT, the Barker Library remains one of the most prominent domed academic buildings in America. Finished during World War I, the dome presides over a vast volume of space that was constructed as a full-scale replica of the Pantheon (Thomas Jefferson had contented himself with a half-scale version for the University of Virginia). In the twenty-first century at MIT we see building campaigns that express the rotunda idea on an ever-larger scale. For instance, MIT's new Brain and Cognitive Sciences Complex boasts a 90-foot atrium. The following description from the university's website lacks any mention of educational function.

All the corridors lead to the monumental atrium in the center, which is the heart of the complex. Subtly sculpted surfaces are illuminated by daylight from the skylight above. Looking up, visitors see the lines of exhaust vents, white against the sky, evoking the sense of being carried on an ocean liner. Flights of stairs, dexterously placed along the periphery, connect the various levels, animating the atrium even when no one is around—a vivid symbol of the human interaction so crucial to cutting-edge scientific research.[75]

MIT's experience of an ocean liner and Caltech's allusion to a telescope are examples of clever architecture, no doubt, and entertaining, at least the first time you see them. But do these allusions to adventure have educational value, and enough to justify the cost to build, heat, cool, and maintain these vast spaces? At 40 metric tons of $CO_2$ per student, Caltech's emissions paint a frightening picture of how high emissions in higher education can go, and only a general slowdown in new campus construction will avoid this scenario.

"Old ideas can sometimes use new buildings. New ideas must use old buildings," wrote Jane Jacobs, but these words are all the more germane when we consider greenhouse gas emissions, in addition to all the human and neighborhood goals behind the historic preservation movements that Jacobs helped to launch.[76]

Life-cycle assessment confirms that it is often better to preserve existing buildings than to build new ones. A recent study of a range of building types in four American cities concluded that choosing renovation instead of new construction reduced $CO_2$ emissions by 7–12 percent in the case of elementary schools and 9–16 percent in the case of commercial offices.[77] Construction activities use large amounts of energy and the construction industry, which makes up about 1.7 percent of total U.S. greenhouse gas emissions, is the largest industry source other than the chemical industry and the oil and gas industry itself.[78]

## A Climate Commitment

One obvious place to start changing the direction of building campaigns and energy use is the college climate commitment, previously known as American and University Presidents Climate Commitment. The network has changed its name (to Second Nature) and modified its approach over time, but it continues to attract membership and an increasing number of college presidents are willing to lend their John Hancock to the pledge to move their institution toward climate neutrality. In their pledge, the college presidents choose a date for reaching neutrality but the self-selected end date means that some places are making promises about what will happen a half century or more into the future, even as late as 2099. More short-term goals would help focus minds and actions on what is realistic, and given the theme of this book, I have a specific number to suggest!

The "tangible action" section of the standard Climate Commitment pledge, as it stands, does not put much of a dent in carbon dioxide emissions. As part of their pledge, colleges promise to implement at least two of the actions, as listed in the table below.[79] The most challenging item on the list is to produce enough renewable energy to make up at least 15 percent of the total electricity used on campus. As of this writing, the top solar producer—Arizona

State—contributes about 7.5 percent of its energy from sunlight, and the top Northern campus—Rutgers University—produces about 3 percent of their energy requirement from solar energy.[80] Carleton College, with its two wind turbines, generates a great deal of wind energy on campus, the equivalent of 31 percent of its electricity needs, but the college finds the load management challenge so formidable that they sell all of the wind output to a utility. Cornell University has the most hydropower but even after expanding their "run of river" system, the hydro contributes only about 2 percent of Cornell's electricity needs.[81] There's certainly a long way to go if renewable energy is to bring campuses to carbon neutrality.

Following the example of the New School's urban form, the greatest achievement that higher education could make would be to practice constraint in building campaigns and to exercise better energy conservation management. The following text box lists ACUPCC's tangible actions as compared with improved actions—the Five-Ton-Life project. Alternative actions may be summed up as follows: Instead of building new and larger buildings through LEED, colleges will place a moratorium on new construction. Rather than buying new and larger appliances that are ENERGY STAR rated, campus administrators will question the need for equipment and/or choose technology that uses less electricity because of scale or simplified features. Instead of purchasing offsets, schools will limit faculty and student air-travel budgets and encourage faculty to conduct meetings via the Internet instead of attending conferences in person. To further reduce high-altitude greenhouse-gas emissions, give an edge to students who live closer to campus. Eliminate subsidized parking and use the freed-up funds to support biking and transit use. These measures would greatly reduce the cost of going to college—costs that have been shouldered by the very generations that stand to suffer more of the severe consequences of climate change.

## Table 1. Five-Ton-Life Project compared with Climate Commitment for higher education goals

| American College and University Presidents Climate Commitment | The Five-Ton Project |
| --- | --- |
| Establish a policy that all new campus construction will be built to at least the U.S. Green Building Council's LEED Silver standard or equivalent. | Place a moratorium on new building construction and lease existing excess space to commercial interests. |
| Adopt an energy-efficient appliance-purchasing policy requiring purchase of ENERGY STAR certified products in all areas for which such ratings exist. | Purchase smaller appliances and/or those with an ENERGY STAR label. |
| Establish a policy of offsetting all greenhouse gas emissions generated by air travel paid for by our institution. | Encourage faculty to conference via Internet; eliminate air travel reimbursement as well as flights for athletics; consider a proximity preference for students. |
| Encourage use of and provide access to public transportation for all faculty, staff, students, and visitors at our institution. | Eliminate subsidized parking on campus. |
| Within one year of signing this document, begin purchasing or producing at least 15 percent of our institution's electricity consumption from renewable sources. | Implement the twenty energy efficiency improvements outlined in the Sustainable Endowments Institute's campus energy program. |
| Establish a policy or a committee that supports climate and sustainability shareholder proposals at companies where our institution's endowment is invested. | Invest in high-quality forest plantations. |
| Participate in the Waste Minimization component of the national RecycleMania competition, and adopt three or more associated measures to reduce waste. | Reduce waste and provide free filtered drinking water in all campus academic buildings and residences. |

# CHAPTER SIX

# Becoming Five Tons

## Anywhere, USA

Standing in a kitchen outbuilding in Colonial Williamsburg one day watching a museum guide demonstrate eighteenth-century cookery, I noticed that the tourists just behind me were wearing clothing that looked only slightly less antiquated than the linen breeches the interpreter wore. They were a group of Amish on vacation. Perhaps they were enjoying the experience of comparing notes on how they handled basic life skills. Maybe they were thinking, "We got it right." If so, how true that is! I looked around. This room might be as close as I was going to get to a reunion of the different strands of low-carbon life. Was that a Manhattan-dwelling college student over there, a bungalow dweller, an urban family?

Probably not. Would a hip, young denizen of the loft, CB2, craft beer culture, choose to be here? Or a Midwestern suburban bungalow resident who looks forward to an extended family barbecue on the weekends, not a history lesson? There may never be a reunion, but that is beside the point. The American tradition gives us multiple points of reference for a more environmentally benign life. The communities are in different places in the Midwest and East Coast, and in different configurations of density. Except for the fossil fuel dissenters—the Amish—the other contemporary neighborhoods are defined by compact living space, small houses, or multi-units. None of the neighborhoods had driveways for cars, freeing up the front of the property for unobstructed walking and greenspace. The exception, the Amish, have driveways maintained as a surface for horseshoes, not pneumatic tires!

Less obviously, the five-ton neighborhoods may appeal to different kinds of people. While some commonality may be found between the residents of Berwyn, Illinois, and central Washington DC, much divides them. The former presents a conforming façade of housing, and it may be no accident that the people who live there tend to be ethnically homogenous even for a Chicago-area neighborhood, and it retains a gritty, blue- and pink-collar identity. On the other hand, the apartment- and condo-dwelling inhabitants of 20009 Washington DC relish the culture of their neighborhoods, where nearly every store and restaurant is one of a kind, local, and family owned. The DC families have embraced a high level of ethnic, linguistic, and socioeconomic diversity in their children's school and social life. The distance between these neighborhoods, however, is nothing compared to their distance from the Amish, who give family and community relationships a place of preeminence, and have no interest in professionalism, let alone in foodie culture or nightlife.

None of the neighborhoods and communities explored in this book relied on new building stock or state-of-the-art construction or design. And none of the places can be described as low-carbon intentional communities that coalesced with shared social and environmental goals that may or may not result in emissions as low as five tons.[1] None of the communities described in this book have been part of concentrated climate-action planning as have other parts of the country, such as Portland, Oregon; Evanston, Illinois; and Pittsburgh, Pennsylvania.[2] Greenhouse gas emissions in the "action" cities happen to be higher than those explored here, and it is fortunate that they are trying to do something about their problems.

The question becomes, therefore, how can other communities and households become more like the examples explored in this book? I would argue that the tools that have been deployed to reduce fossil-fuel consumption, including smart-growth planning and technical improvements in building design and renewable energy, provide us only partial answers. They can be helpful, but they give incomplete guidance on the essential importance of smaller floor plans and lot sizes in general. More broadly, city and community governments have a role to play in expanding opportunities for smaller living spaces by changing zoning laws to allow for more compact development, multi-unit construction, and single-family-house to multi-unit conversions. The federal government has a role to play in expanding credit for building multi-unit housing. This is an area of low-risk lending that has been neglected. At the same time, the enormous subsidy for large houses in the form of the mortgage interest tax credit could be phased out. According to many economists, a phase-out would not reduce the number of home-owners, just the size of the houses.[3] I suggest a twist on the long-standing American subsidy of home ownership—offer the mortgage interest tax deduction only for dwellings that are of a climate-compatible size of, say, 1,500 square feet or less.

And another remit is needed altogether to influence changes in recreational flying, driving, and shopping. The remit to do less of these activities, however, is conversely a call to do more of something else, which invariably brings us out of the realm of specific climate policy measures and into a broad realm of individual values and endeavors. Nevertheless, a number of policy and planning levers are available to support a five-ton life, along with actions that an individual can take autonomously. A summary of desirable actions and policies compared to the status quo appears in the table at the end of this chapter.

Doing less and buying less has some tangible impact on GNP, of course. Many books, including the recently published *Climate of Hope* by Michael Bloomberg and Carl Pope, assume that wealth is desirable and make the claim that green measures can be good for business.[4] Timothy Mitchell, author of *Climate Democracy*, argues that we may lose more than wealth if we cut back on fossil fuels, because these sources of energy have supported the development of democratic institutions in the West.[5] In contrast, the British scholar Tim Jackson makes the case in *Prosperity without Growth* that it is time to forgo conventional notions of success such as a standard work week, a high paycheck, and upward-trending output if we are to be serious about getting on a more sustainable path.[6] Similarly, James Gustave Speth argues in *The Bridge at the Edge of the World* that economic growth and materialism are incompatible with a livable planet.[7]

The likelihood (or lack thereof) of achieving emissions reductions while growing GNP has not been explored in this book aside from the insight that outwardly thriving five-ton communities are found among a broad range of income levels. I cannot say exactly how happy everyone there is on a deep emotional level, but having lived in several of these communities for most of my life, I understand the appeal of these locales. I also understand the theoretical critique of high-consumption lifestyles, which finds little evidence of deep fulfillment in high levels of materialism and mobility. Much of current fossil fuel addiction has unwanted side effects that are hard to shake off, habits related to the shopping-decluttering cycle, the driving-diet cycle, and the binge-flying, post-vacation ennui cycle and other mediocrities of excessive fossil fuel consumption. The question of the psychological value of high-end consumption and wealth has its own literature, and a recent addition is *How to be Alive* written by the original no-impact man, Colin Beavan. Beavan extolls the benefits of trading in some degree of ambition and earning power to pursue a simpler, more environmentally constructive life with diverse local relationships. He offers insights into "each-other help" as opposed to the less green, traditionally self-centered outlook of self-help books.[8]

## A Different Effort

Much of professional climate advocacy has focused not on helping individuals to reduce consumption but on the task of educating the wider public about the dangers of climate change. This effort presumes that the right degree of knowledge will lead to the right kind of action, a hope that has proved to be thoroughly illusory at this point in time. In turn, many thousands of non-experts have been engaging in the task of trying to convince others of the science of global warming. Mike Hulme points out in *Why We Disagree about Climate Change* that this might be a waste of time. Instead, he argues, we can get on with the empowering job of shaping our own world.[9] "Science has universalized and materialized climate change; we must now particularize and spiritualize it," he writes.[10] Paul Bain, a researcher based in Australia, found that even climate-change deniers were willing to take measures to lower their carbon footprints if they thought the changes would "create a more considerate and caring society."[11] The five-ton life gives us examples of the ironies of channeling our efforts into scientific debate. You could spend years trying to convince an Amish person that heat-trapping gases, not God, is causing the rising trend in the earth's average temperature. But to what end? Many Amish are already models of consumption.

From his long experience in climate-change communication, George Marshall explains in *Don't Even Think About It* why thinking about an apocalyptical future makes many people less likely to take practical and effective steps.[12] Dire climate scenarios lack an attractive bridge to the future, and a common response to fear is to comfort oneself with the hope that the outcome will not affect oneself or one's family. Marshall argues for humankind to develop better story-telling to help us on the path to a lower-carbon lifestyle. The communities and traditions in this book offer a skeleton of a story to be filled in, but one that is less fearful than conjuring up a future of (insert dire scenarios here).

Different manifestations of peer pressure, of course, can help advance this narrative. There is the peer pressure that can originate with an eminent individual. The political and agrarian leaders in the early years of the republic took pains to imitate the material and entrepreneurial culture of George Washington and not to exceed it. Consequently, many of America's first leaders developed conservationist projects related to soil improvements and native-species planting. The leadership of George Washington led to restraint in house size and consequently fuel use that carried over into nineteenth-century American emissions, which remained lower than the European trajectory throughout the century. As of this writing, no individual American comes close to this level of eminence and conservationist influence.

In the meantime, we have the tools of decentralized advocacy and community involvement. It is in everyone's power to participate in the thousands of neighborhood-level hearings and public commentary related to zoning and building permitting. People are empowered by right of living somewhere and can elect and sway local officials. People can choose to live in multi-units, build smaller homes, or convert houses. All are empowered to enrich their experiences of local travel and to make long-haul flights to world capitals less frequently, or not at all.

A foundation for this perspective is to learn where one's own residence and commercial buildings fit within the spectrum of emissions: high, low, or in-between. The absence of this knowledge can have detrimental effects on personal agency. In her book *Living in Denial*, Kari Norgaard details a sense of paralysis about global warming expressed by a Norwegian town facing declining winter tourism and by her American students worried about the future. One of her students described "feeling that no matter how hard she tried, she and everyone will go to ecohell."[13] In contrast with a broad-brush sense of guilt, understanding that emissions are differentiated and that a lower-emissions life is within reach encapsulates the idea of carbon capability that I have sought to advance in this book.

Related to that understanding is a new way of communicating that does not shy away from open and frank discussions about consumption that may be construed as rude or inappropriate. Perhaps the Rights Revolution that manifested in the late twentieth century as support for the rights of women, racial minorities, homosexuals, and people with disabilities, is an inspiring precedent because it has succeeded in empowering previously marginalized people and has inspired empathy among people who do not know each other personally.[14] In *The Better Angels of Our Nature*, Steven Pinker reveals how and why a growing number of people with power and privilege came to be concerned about the welfare of people (and animals) very different from themselves. An extension of the Rights Revolution will teach Americans, especially those with resources, to see a direct link between their own actions and the welfare of future generations. A parallel development in environmental culture will find routes to communicate about consumption and emissions, a topic that recent history suggests has been unfairly and dangerously castigated as inappropriate and counterproductive.[15] Part of that change in communication will be to find constructive ways to praise lower-consumption culture, a topic I return to at the end of this chapter.

While writing this book I also took on the challenge of living within a carbon budget and advocating for lower emissions culture and characteristics. It has been a journey of discovery, as I have worked at a hyper-local level within a widening circle, trying to reduce emissions in my immediate surroundings and beyond. I began with my family and condo building, and added on my neighborhood, my child's school, the local library and my alma maters. Conventional activism relies on a larger organization. I pulled in allies here and there who had various motivations, not necessarily environmental.

The climate advocacy proposed in this book is different than contemporary climate-advocacy programs that focus mainly on changing the type of energy we use and the form of electricity-generation technology. The five-ton project calls for a different way of recruiting people and choosing leaders. For instance, several national climate networks such as the Citizens' Climate Lobby and the Moms Clean Air Force bring volunteers to Washington DC to talk to their representatives about the importance of passing legislation to reduce emissions from coal-fired power plants. Moms Clean Air Force brought some dozen parents from Chicago last year to tell their congressional representatives why climate change legislation is important to them. One of the leaders was a mom from a suburb, but not one of the low-carbon-footprint communities discussed in this book. Most residents of Berwyn, Forest Park, or even Oak Park, Illinois, would have much to impart about what is good about their community and how the scale of their homes implies much lower emissions for the country, but this person was from the Chicago suburb with the highest carbon footprint in the region, Highland Park. Her particular house was double the size of the largest bungalows in Berwyn, and Moms Clean Air Force was aggravating her emissions by sponsoring her jet flight to Washington DC and back. The volunteer was empowered to lower her own household emissions, but the agenda was the national legislation that would have a minor effect on her and everyone else's emissions.

Typically, environmental groups remind their members to do relatively easy things like purchase green electricity, use efficient light bulbs, and to recycle. But as George Marshall points out, advising a smoker to cut out one cigarette per day is not a logical answer to the problems of cancer and emphysema.[16] The problem of the large house won't be solved by remembering to turn off the lights more often or stuffing a sock hop under the front door. Our overly mobile lifestyle will not be cured by remembering to keep our tires inflated.

Given the mild prescriptions emanating from many professional environmental organizations, I find the collegiate interest in fossil-fuel divestment understandable, but these campaigns often skirt the difficult questions of consumption. For instance, the fossil-fuel divestment organization at Yale University holds meetings behind the king of glass walls, the new School of Management building. Due to the presence of this new building and many others, Yale's campus building square footage has increased by 14 percent since 2005.[17] In that year, the Yale University president committed to reduce emissions by 43 percent by 2020. Increasingly mild winters have helped the university to reduce energy consumption from buildings, but it looks almost certain that Yale will not meet their original commitment.

Independent of Yale's climate pledge, the student divestment group has pursued their own project. Presumably at the divestment meetings, it is easier to see the extractive parts of the fossil fuel industry as the main culprit and target rather than the endpoint, the electricity and natural gas expended in servicing the room where the activists congregate. Artist Bruce McCall captured the irony of our current cultural blindness in a 2016 cover for the *New Yorker* entitled "Glass Houses" that shows inhabitants of skyscrapers sitting in large, empty rooms while fixated on big screens and tablets.[18] These devices present images of nature and grassy sports venues, while outside the scorched earth looks lifeless and devoid of people. As campuses become more monumental and cocooned in artful, shimmering glass walls, it becomes more difficult to see the destructiveness of our own choices.

Chapter five summarized some of the most important policy levers that could cut greenhouse gas emissions in higher education. A young person choosing a college can consider the fact that part of their tuition will be going toward new building construction and the fossil fuels that will maintain the comfort and utility of the buildings. Some American colleges use much less energy than others and charge less tuition while offering a comparable or better education, albeit with less recreational amenities. A young person worried about climate change can choose to make a statement about all of these attributes at once in choosing a college—all the more so if they write an affirmative letter to their college president or dean after they enroll. The tool for the prospective university student is the institution's greenhouse gas inventory, and if the institution does not have one, that is also an indicator of the school's attitude toward sustainability. Alumni, because they have an entrée into the conversation during the all-too-frequent annual fund drives, can broach these topics on the telephone or via follow-up letter.

Many millennials, older baby boomers, and others already have a preference for urban living, or at least more compact housing. The front lines for supporting these preferences are many thousands of separate building permit applications in the many parts of the country where zoning discourages multi-units. These are small, winnable battles to allow houses to be converted to multi-flats, to prevent small, multi-unit buildings from being deconverted to large houses and to allow new multi-unit housing to be located next to transit and next to single-family neighbors who do not necessarily want them nearby. Similar efforts for the commercial sector present opportunities to moderate our current inclination to monumental, soaring entrances, walls of glass, and other architectural features that are a waste of space and energy. The Green Building Council, through LEED, has helped to save water and materials, but has been a perverse driver or at least rubber stamper of the overbuild in commercial construction.

To be an effective advocate for lowering emissions from commercial and government buildings it is helpful to have building energy-consumption data to compare. Good energy data for commercial and public buildings was once considered confidential information but is now publicly available in more than twenty cities and states.[19] This data comes thanks to benchmarking legislation that requires eligible buildings over a certain size to release data on their energy use per square foot and the square footage of the buildings. In some cities such as Washington DC, residential buildings over a certain size are also required to report this.[20] The new benchmarking data holds the promise of making public involvement in decision making about construction and renovation more effective, allowing for expert localism and increased understanding of how and where greenhouse gas emissions are generated in the community.

Working together on actions that address emissions from educational buildings and in the commercial sector is a worthy goal for any climate activist. It may be psychically easier for volunteers to navigate these projects than to try to work together to reduce each other's personal emissions. For example, citizen-engagement groups like the Climate Rationing Action Groups (CRAGS) that originated in the UK bring together like-minded people to make personal pledges to reduce their emissions.[21] Those who do not meet their targets donate to a kitty that goes toward a group-defined project. Such a setup may work better in cultures outside of the United States, where participants' pledges are more likely to be similar to each other, reflecting a greater conformity in material culture. I suggest instead that groups of like-minded people, especially neighbors, share attendance at local neighborhood zoning, historic preservation, or local government meetings that solicit public commentary about proposed building and transportation plans. An individual's experience and connections can shape their engagement, which may coalesce around faith-based groups, alumni associations, condo associations, and the like. Such individual and group efforts already exist in this country, but the latest scientific news about climate is a wake-up call for broader enlistment.

The millennial generation is not in an enviable position, laden with educational debt, housing made expensive by older generations seeking to maintain housing prices, uncertain employment prospects, and of course worsening impacts from climate change and weather extremes. But the youngest generation of Americans has a special social power and can remake the rules on what is polite and what is important to discuss. I was reminded of this social power when Washington DC neighbors told me they had decided to sell their weekend house. The reason was that their teenage son wanted to spend his family time in and around their city apartment, not driving to and from their larger dwelling in the countryside. His reasons may be unrelated to the household energy use, but the family's reaction had the effect of cutting their household emissions dramatically.

Changing the culture of American housing preferences and options will drive down greenhouse gas emissions from personal mobility. Accelerating a retreat from the large-lot, outer suburb will mean large cuts in emissions from cars. For those in rural areas who aspire to a more local life, there are the examples of the zoning battles that the Amish have won to keep and use horses in jurisdictions that traditionally only allowed the horseless carriage. Some of the bike- and pedestrian-friendly inroads that urbanists have made in the cities can be an example elsewhere. The Amish also give us the example of how wood can be a viable fuel when burned in certified high-combustion wood stoves and used in sparsely settled areas to diffuse the air pollutants. The urban and suburban dweller can emulate their commitment to a local social life where neighbors and family reign supreme, and satisfaction is found in life's shared, quotidian tasks.

## My Efforts

Myself, I have found that the lower-carbon life has felt less like a sacrifice and more like a welcome structure for life choices. I have lived briefly with a rambling floor plan and more often with a compact one, and I prefer the latter to the former. I can relate to the yearning expressed in "The Wish" by seventeenth-century poet Abraham Cowley:

> Ah yet, ere I descend to the grave
> May I a small house and large garden have
> And a few friends, and many books, both true,
> Both wise, and both delightful too! [22]

The author had spent most of his life living in the vast palaces of the English and French monarchs, but in middle age he fulfilled his wish, living fairly simply, immersed in botanical experiments not unlike those of America's founding presidents, who in turn governed a nation of small houses and large gardens, like the modest amount of living space per person embodied in Mount Vernon, and the colorful vegetable plots at Monticello stretching to the horizon over the verdant forests of the Piedmont.

I am not ready to live exactly like an Amish person, but I have no regrets on taking up a more local life. In my case, I have a notion of limiting air travel that works out to be about one domestic flight per year and an international flight every three years or more. We do not have a suburban-style backyard, but we have flowers and trees around our building, a vegetable garden in a different location, a playground two blocks away, and woodlands a few steps from our front door. The main change has been to take the prospect of distant vacations off the drawing board. I haven't ruled them out completely. But I have intentionally not traveled much beyond a radius of a few hours' rail or road journey from DC. My fuel-efficient car averages about three thousand miles per year, less than a third of the national average. More-distant travel to visit relatives we do by overnight sleeping car, a way of traveling that we have come to enjoy a great deal. It's been nagging at me that I haven't visited all the parts of Rock Creek Park and the Potomac River on my list. The more I get to know the local ecosystems, the more I want to stay, though maybe I'll get around to some international travel someday. Maybe I'll check out the nature cams of places that E. O. Wilson describes in *Half Earth* that are best visited remotely, cameras that can show us what is drinking from a watering hole in the Serengeti at dawn.[23]

A less enjoyable, but more lucrative project was to review our condo building's energy usage. With the help of an auditor we found some easy fixes and changed dozens of radiator valves. We saved electricity by changing storage lighting from 24/7 to "as needed." A simple thing that made a big difference was to remove the mandate to overheat the whole building. We gave every resident a short questionnaire that asked whether they thought the building temperature in winter tended to be too hot, too cold, or just about right. Only one person chose "too cold," and after that we had a mandate to cool things a bit, and the boilers were stoked lower. These small steps were in addition to the big step of living in a multi-unit in the first place instead of a larger single-family house.

While I was working on lowering my building's carbon footprint, I invited a solar estimator onto our roof to give us a cost estimate. It was a memorable day that happened to coincide with a ceremony taking place at the White House to commemorate the new solar panels that had just been installed on the president's roof. One of my neighbors, as a prominent solar advocate, was invited to the event. But alas for our building, solar has not yet arrived here. The estimator pointed out that we had so many encumbrances on the roof with air shafts and other interruptions that considerable extra costs would be involved. Five years later, our homeowners' association is still talking solar—the price has come down a lot but the subject still gets punted each year in general talk about when and if the roof will be replaced. The roof seems to be in remarkably great shape considering its age, and plans for a solar roof and green roof plantings are always pushed back. It's much easier to put solar panels on the White House than on a condo building. I asked my renewable-energy guru neighbor whether he would really prefer to see Americans living in single-family houses somewhere with solar panels on the roof instead of here in our highly walkable neighborhood and compact dwelling. He acknowledged, "No."

Energy conservation in apartments and condos has a large potential for savings because most government-subsidized conservation programs are geared toward single-family houses. One of the reasons is the challenge of working with condo boards that have diverse opinions and may see the gains as spread too thinly among all residents. Another reason is that fewer conservation specialists are experienced with multi-unit buildings. The main energy conservation certifier—the Building Performance Institute (BPI)—trains relatively few people in their multi-unit program. But cities that have overcome many of these hurdles, including Boston and New York, have strong track records in reducing the amount of energy wasted in multi-units. I found that in our building we were able to realize savings of about

$25,000 a year from our electricity and natural gas bills, which enabled us to reduce unit owners' monthly fees.

After I worked out my own inventory and then worked on my condo building's energy use, I started to look into the energy being used around me. When the house across the alley was sold to a new owner who wanted to split the building into several condo units, I showed up at the neighborhood hearing, and after listening to one of my neighbors complain that the new project would create too much dust, I volunteered that I lived directly across from the building and had no problem with the conversion. Several other people in the room then allowed that they thought it was okay. To the shock of the owner/developer, who was expecting major NIMBY pushback, the motion was approved.

When our local library held a public meeting to discuss plans to demolish the small library and build a new one, the architect and city officials promised that the new building would use geothermal energy and achieve a net-zero increase in energy consumption, meaning it would not use more energy despite its larger size. Thanks to the energy data revealed in the city's benchmarking database I was able to point out that recent projects by the same architects had not achieved the projected energy savings, and that another geothermal project in the neighborhood had disappointing results. The architects quietly withdrew the heroic claims for geothermal and the historic preservation board made sure that the architects revised the design to reduce the scale of the planned glass walls. I expect that the energy use for the new building will be moderated thanks to these changes, but the planned project still contains the ubiquitous atrium, that twenty-first-century architectural quirk in which design features take precedence over specific functions such as providing space for books.

When working to lower carbon dioxide emissions from my daughter's school I found that the publicly available energy data can be a real eye-opener. Some of the new Green Ribbon LEED-certified renovation projects for Washington DC public schools turned out to have an average or worse performance. Some of DC's government office buildings did not fare so well either. To their chagrin, the city's flagship LEED building had a lackluster result, scoring below average in energy use. This building happens to house the DC Department of General Services (DGS), which is in charge of building and maintaining all of Washington DC's schools and other civic buildings; it also oversees the city's energy conservation program through the Sustainable Energy Utility. When I asked a DGS official the reason why the city government's most celebrated green building used so much energy the reply was, "It is a weird thing that we're looking into."[24]

My undergraduate alma mater, Reed College, has also undergone a building boom and now has performance space about four times larger in square footage than when I attended, and far more parking lots. It has not disclosed a greenhouse gas inventory, though the college says that they have one. For years I brought up the matter during the telephone calls I received from students volunteering for the development office and duly explained to a pleasant undergraduate that I am waiting for the inventory before I send in a contribution. After several years, a student promised me she would look into it, which she did. I have told both the student volunteers and the current president that I think that the campus has enough buildings and does not need any more.

I've also been a tough sales prospect for the callers from the alumni fund at MIT, who listened for years to my pitch about the importance of releasing MIT's missing inventory. Finally in early 2016 they released one, estimating their emissions at the equivalent of about eighteen metric tons carbon dioxide per student, an extremely high emissions rate though not the highest in the country. Recently MIT has been running a series of contests, looking for winning ideas on how to slow global warming. I read through dozens of entries, many very technical, about exploiting new sources of renewable energy, such as a proposal to harness the energy of sand dunes and differential ocean temperature and a floating platform to exploit wind, sun, tidal, and other sources simultaneously. Not surprisingly, MIT alumni tend to see the climate change problem in terms of a technological solution. My proposal to put in place a moratorium on new building construction on MIT's campus certainly did not look very sophisticated. But to my surprise, the judges sent me a letter saying they found my idea "compelling." Unfortunately, they added that my entry did not fit into the subject category of their competition, echoing a problem I have encountered in other contexts while pursuing a cultural approach to reducing emissions.

## Celebrating the Culture

Unlike the Amish, mainstream America provides little social affirmation for those living the lower-emissions life. In my efforts to reduce energy use in my community, I wanted to test out the idea of celebrating lower-emissions lives in some way. My neighborhood has some of the lowest carbon footprint households in America, but who recognizes and honors that? No one, of course! My work with middle school students has been an effort to make some little difference in this regard. I chose a school that I knew would have many students whose emissions were outstandingly low. Before working with the students, I had expected some resistance. I had promised anonymity, but worried that the parents would find the questions to be too personal. Instead, I found that having students collect and report the personal information was—for most of the families—not a big deal. Though some students did not return their surveys, most seemed comfortable with the assignment. Many students reported afterward that the survey had started some new conversations within their family about their activities—questions like whether they could cut down their beef consumption and drive and fly less. Hopefully, the project helped students to start a lifelong understanding of their capabilities. Environmental psychologists who have studied the importance of memory for developing self-identity suggest that if we remind people of past environmental actions they will be more likely to go forward with strengthened environmental self-identity.[25]

People who have never explored a footprint calculator often assume that finding out about their footprint will be technically challenging. Once faced with a basic greenhouse-gas household calculator such as the EPA's, people realize how easy it is.[26] Someone who plugs their utility bill information into the calculator reporting kwhs from electricity and BTUS from gas will get an accurate $CO_2$ estimate for household usage. Some calculators try to calculate emissions specific to a region based on the particular mix of sources used to generate electricity. However, this refinement may not be desirable. Carbon intensities related to electricity are in a state of flux, with the fuel mix changing from year to year as well as changing options for electricity purchase agreements. Considering that the subject at hand is culture and individual agency, I find it preferable to work instead with a simpler, more stable picture of carbon intensity such as the average carbon intensity of electricity generated in America as a whole. For energy used for travel, basic vehicle information, miles traveled each year, and miles per gallon will yield a reasonable estimate. Air miles can be calculated easily with the help of online info on distances between cities, if necessary. A refinement for flying emissions entails multiplying those results by a factor of at least two to take into account other gases emitted by airplanes that are not greenhouse gases, but that affect climate. Completing a useful inventory is far less complicated than filing income taxes, completing a kindergarten enrollment form, or making a cake from scratch.

Justifying the usefulness of calculating one's greenhouse gas emissions, though, may soon be gratuitous, like explaining that standing on a scale may be useful in knowing how much one weighs, or explaining that looking at an odometer is helpful to understand how much one has driven. A shift in attitude to acknowledge that human beings, not companies and fuels, drive greenhouse gas emissions advances the usefulness of calculations. With an increasing number of people knowing their own emissions, the conversation is more likely to flow both in the direction of sharing knowledge and ideas, and in the direction of social cues so that leaders—especially environmental leaders—become subject to ethical standards for their own lifestyle choices.

In the case of the classrooms with which I was engaged, students' climate change education had begun in a way that was not unlike the experience of many students around the country. They had watched *An Inconvenient Truth* and had studied diagrams of how light waves change as they pass the atmosphere and bounce back from the earth, the greenhouse effect. They had absorbed the lesson that Americans are a big part of the problem, with emissions that are higher than most of the rest of the world. They had started the carbon footprint lesson considering themselves as Americans to be a major part of the problem. The students had taken the surveys home and most had worked with their parents to add data about their utility bills, yearly driving rates, miles per gallon, air miles, and beef consumption. I converted their raw numbers into greenhouse gas emissions and returned to their classroom.

Their teacher wrote me the next day, "They were out of their seats, craning to see the numbers." That they would see how they compared with the rest of the class only heightened their curiosity. As emissions in America go, their numbers were fantastic. About three-quarters had emissions from personal mobility far below the average. Many were as low as one-third of the American average. Many lived in apartments, and most spent relatively little time in cars. The pattern held true over successive years and for the additional classes that I reached. Some of the students looked very happy. Except for this type of exercise, there isn't anyone or anything giving them a bit of a pat on the back and urging them to stay the course. Were it not for this project, these same students would have been swept into the guilty lot of American emissions in general, for they had no way of knowing how they compared with the rest of the world. "You are rock stars!" I told them, and they seemed to take it in.

A recent college classroom experiment suggests that the "warm glow" of finding out that one's footprint is lower than the average can mean that the room actually feels warmer to those individuals with a lower footprint.[27] I did not take any temperature readings in the classroom, but the body language seemed to indicate that something had happened. With every class, the room moved from apprehension to applause and foot stomping, resembling a herd of elephants! These teens, dwellers of small homes, liberated from a car-centric existence, were energized with a new sense of prestige, a sense of consequence that has often perversely been accorded instead to our biggest consumers. It is our challenge for the future to endow our projects with the perspective of the carbon conscious, to pursue a path of understanding our own physical impact on the world, in the tradition of the experiments of our founding president. Once enlightened, the paths forward are endless, and as varied as our own traditions.

Table 2. Five-Ton Life culture compared with the status quo

|  | *Status Quo* | *Five-Ton Project* |
| --- | --- | --- |
| Household Accounting | Footprint? What's that? | Treat the physical impact of our own household as a vital scientific question (see chapter 1). |
| Mansions and McMansions | Admire or at least tolerate large and very large houses. | Root a social upper limit to house size (7,000 square feet) in the American tradition (see chapter 1). |
| Social Life | Widely dispersed. | People within biking or horse/buggy distance are a priority (see chapter 2). |
| Material Culture | Cheap, trendy, and prodigious are okay. | Focus on fewer but high-quality, durable goods (see chapter 2). |

| | | |
|---|---|---|
| Tax Code | Mortgage interest tax deduction. | Mortgage Interest Tax Deduction on homes 1,500 square feet or smaller (see chapter 3). |
| | Vacation/second home— mortgage interest tax deduction. | No deduction or credit. |
| Federal Lending | Favors single-family houses. | Favor multi-unit buildings (see chapter 3). |
| Zoning rules | Maintain single-family house districts. | Permit house conversion to multi-units, preserving exterior in historically significant buildings (see chapters 3 and 4). |
| Spatial Planning | Wide residential lot frontage with driveway. | Narrow residential lot frontage with alleys (see chapter 4, Berwyn). |
| Road and traffic engineering in suburban locales | Encourage the efficient movement of vehicles. | Pedestrian safety and experience a priority (see chapter 4, Forest Park). |
| Commercial Building Construction | Use LEED and Green concepts and build away! | Repurpose existing space with better management of occupancy/flow (see chapter 5). |
| Progressive Diet | Meatless Mondays. | Meaty Mondays or Sundays (vegetarian other days). |
| Frequent Flying | 52 international destinations for the new year. | Nature, culture, and people within 150 miles. |

# Acknowledgments

This book had an inauspicious beginning, sitting on the lawn at Mount Vernon in a daydream thinking about a future in which the nineteenth and twentieth centuries had never taken place. The steam turbine had not been invented, coal and petroleum had been left in the ground, the genocides of the twentieth century had not occurred. Walking the grounds and mansion of George Washington's home, I experienced a degree of comfort comparing this relatively compact building with the sprawling residences of the English kings and aristocracy I had visited while working as an environmental researcher at a British university. Before me, the Potomac River looked pristine, with the wooded shoreline stretching as far as the eye could see. Despite our profligate consumerism and a carbon footprint about double that of the UK's, at times we have veered from a sharply escalating trajectory of greenhouse gas emissions. Could this happen again? Where were America's best examples of lower carbon culture?

In this way, my quest to find and understand these strands of American culture began, but the project would have faltered were it not for the people willing to share their perspectives and practical details like their utility bills and what they enjoy about inner-city life. The data compilation undertaken by the Sustainable Endowments Institute and the Chicago-based Center for Neighborhood Technology were vital sources for finding the lower-carbon colleges and communities.

This book stands separate from the literature of technological optimism and faith in pricing signals, and my own interest in culture as a driver of emissions benefited from a variety of sources. The writings of David Owen and Ozzie Zehner convey—with wit and insight—this perspective of critique and helped me to consolidate my broader thinking about consumption and modern environmentalism. Andrea Wulf's work on the founding president's biophilic, citizen-science endeavors was an inspiring find while searching for the cultural roots of greenhouse gas emissions reduction. City planners Andres Duany, Elizabeth Plater-Zyberk, and Jeff Speck taught me a lot about streets and buildings. The University of East Anglia's School of Environmental Sciences, especially Jean Palutikof and Mike Hulme, helped me to better understand the disciplinary boundaries of the climate problem and how to seek to remove them.

Friends, family members, and veteran writers graciously read chapters and excerpts and offered comments: Rick Bailey, Anton Cipriani, Mimi Kolesar, Lauren Markoe, Emily Mechner, Thomas Pfister, David Plotz, Carl Subak, Jon Subak, and Ozzie Zehner. My father, nearing the century of his birth, read and commented on rough drafts of all the chapters. UNP's Emily Wendell was very helpful and speedy. My copyeditor, Ana Balka, did an insightful edit. Two anonymous reviewers contributed interesting and constructive suggestions. Heather Lundine commented on the entirety of an early draft.

I'd also like to thank Bennett Barsk for his support and Tom Bassett Dilley, Bob Trezevant, and Jerry Jacknow for their help on the suburban chapter. Michael Visser provided coffee and a good writing venue. Patricia Badiali and Ken Addison helped make my own building both pleasant and sustainable. My friend of more than three decades, Tracey Dewart, showed steadfast faith in the project, making its difficult, protracted moments fewer than they would otherwise have been. My daughter, Diana, an eco-spirit in her own right, put up with everything and was a constant reminder of what is at stake.

At the University of Nebraska Press, I have had the good fortune to work with a complete editor, Bridget Barry, who supported the manuscript, marshaled the drafts through review, and offered her own many astute comments and improvements.

# Notes

## Introduction

1. Weber, "Perception and Expectation," 314–41. Doing one thing, or "single action bias," is discussed in social science research as a common response to a threat or risk that exaggerates the importance of the single action while excluding additional and more effective actions. Van der Werff, Steg, and Keizer, "Follow the Signal," 273–82. A counterweighting idea sometimes called "the foot in the door" argues that the first action can lead to an adjustment in personal identity that can lead to more effective action in the future.

2. U.S. Environmental Protection Agency (EPA), *Inventory*, ES-11.

3. U.S. EPA, "Fast Facts from the Inventory of U.S. Greenhouse Gas Emissions and Sinks: 1990–2014," accessed September 14, 2017, https://www.epa.gov/sites /production/files/2016–06/documents/us_ghg_inv_fastfacts2016.pdf.

4. U.S. EPA, *Inventory*, ES-24.

5. Josh Katz and Jennifer Daniel, "What You Can Do About Climate Change," *New York Times*, December 2, 2015.

6. "Fact Sheet Clean Power Plan Overview," discontinued and archived content from EPA website, https://archive.epa.gov/epa/cleanpowerplan/fact-sheet-clean -power-plan-overview.html, accessed September 14, 2017. The Clean Power Plan sought to reduce electricity generations emissions by 30 percent below 2005 levels by 2025. Since U.S. emissions were much higher in 2005 than in subsequent years, these cuts are more modest from the standpoint of today's emissions. The Clean Power Plan's focus on electricity generation means that the majority of emissions sources are not addressed in the plan. For these reasons, the expected greenhouse gas emissions reduction from national 2014 emissions levels would be only 10.7 percent.

7. *Annual European Union Greenhouse Gas Inventory 1990–2014*, European Environment Agency, published 2016, https://www.eea.europa.eu/publications /european-union-greenhouse-gas-inventory-2016#tab-data-references.

8. Favaro, *The Carbon Code*, 33.

9. U.S. EPA, *Inventory*, ES-4.

10. U.S. Energy Information Administration (EIA), *Monthly Energy Review*, July 26, 2016. https://www.eia.gov/totalenergy/data/monthly/archive/00351607.pdf.

11. Ronald B. Mitchell, "Technology is Not Enough," 24–27.

12. Cohen, Hingham, and Cavaliere, "Binge Flying," 1070–89.

13. Zehner, *Green Illusions*, 150.

14. Pinker, *Better Angels*, 465–74.

15. *Licensed Drivers, By Sex and Age Group, 1963–2014*, Table DL-220, Office of Highway Policy Information, Federal Highway Administration, last modified November 17, 2016. https://www.fhwa.dot.gov/policyinformation/statistics /2014/dl220.cfm. *National Household Travel Survey*, Oak Ridge National Laboratory. In 2011, only one car was sold for every 222 adults age 18–24, compared to one car per fifteen drivers age 55–64. Sivak, "Marketing Implications," http:// umich.edu/~umtriswt/PDF/UMTRI-2013_14_Abstract_English.pdf. According to transportation researchers who surveyed more than six hundred Americans aged 18–39, common reasons stated for not obtaining a license include lack of time, the expense of owning and operating a vehicle, being able to get transportation from others, and preferring to bike or walk. Schoettle and Sivak, "Recent Decline," 6–9.

16. U.S. EPA, *Inventory*, ES-24.

17. Entranze Enerdata of the EU 2013–2015 for the year 2008, https://www .entranze.enerdata.eu. U.S. Energy Information Administration (EIA), "2009 Residential Energy Consumption Survey," released in 2013 for the year 2009, https://www.eia.gov/consumption/residential/data/2009/.

18. Shui and Harriss, "U.S.-China Trade," 4063–68. Jiang et al, "Firm Ownership," 466–74.

19. Weber and Matthews, "Household Carbon Footprint," 379–91.

20. Druckman and Jackson, "How Much Household Carbon Do We Really Need?" 1794–1804. A study in the UK sought to understand what minimum carbon footprint level would fulfill basic needs and identified a level about 37 percent below UK's current per-capita emissions of 9.47 metric tons $CO_2e$. Since the UK's current emissions are similar to the five-metric-ton notion (emissions that are counted directly), the UK minimum revealed in the UK study translates to about 3–4 metric tons of $CO_2$ equivalent.

21. Brown et al, *Shrinking the Carbon Footprint of Metropolitan America*, 20, accessed September 14, 2017, https://www.brookings.edu/research/shrinking -the-carbon-footprint-of-metropolitan-america/.

22. Brown et al, *Carbon Footprint*, 20. The highest emitters were identified as the cities of Lexington-Fayette, KY, and Indianapolis, IN.

23. Kalle Huebner, "2,000 Watt Society," *Our World*, June 2, 2009, https://ourworld .unu.edu/en/2000-watt-society, accessed August 10, 2016.

24. Wackernagel and Rees, "Perceptual and Structural Barriers," 3.

25. The household calculator currently available at https://www3.epa.gov/carbon -footprint-calculator/ has been supported by both Democratic and Republican administrations, but as of early 2017, its future is uncertain.

26. Subak, "Accountability for Climate Change"; Subak and Clark, "Accounts for Greenhouse Gases"; Subak, "Assessing Emissions," 51–69.

27. Gruebler and Fujii, "Inter-Generational and Spatial Equity Issues," 1397–1416; Smith et al., "Joint $CO_2$ and $CH_4$ Accountability," E2865-E2874.

28. For the most recent reporting year (2015), the U.S. EPA reports end use greenhouse gas emissions as follows (million metric tons carbon dioxide equivalent): residential sector: 1,072, agriculture: 612, commercial sector: 1,115, transportation sector: 1,810. U.S. EPA, 2017, ES-25, https://www.epa.gov/sites/production/files/2017–02/documents/2017_executive_summary.pdf. Emissions from the "agriculture" sector are used to approximate diet. The agriculture emissions category that EPA reports in their inventory includes some energy used to grow corn for ethanol and it does not include energy used to manufacture and transport food. The transportation sector category includes non-personal transportation. For this analysis, emissions from personal transportation were distinguished from the sector as a whole taking into account the following data: passenger cars: 758, light trucks: 325, buses 20, motorcycles 4, commercial air 120, rail 47, yielding a subtotal of 1,274. U.S. EPA, 2017, 2–30–2–31, https://www.epa.gov/sites/production/files/2017–02/documents/2017_chapter_2_trends_in_greenhouse_gas_emissions.pdf. The 2015 U.S. population was 323 million. https://www.census.gov/quickfacts/fact/table/US/PST045216.

29. Demographic data related to the conversions is not currently available. The author conducted an informal survey of residents in three converted buildings in the 2000 block of Ashmead Place, Washington DC, in July 2016 that yielded this range.

30. Plutzer et al., "Climate Confusion," 665.

31. Whitmarsh, Seyfang, and O'Neill, "Public Engagement," 56–65.

32. Rayner and Prins, "Wrong Trousers"; Stripple and Bulkeley, Governing the Climate.

33. Dennis Rodkin, "Why So Many Two-Flats are Turning into One-Flats," Chicago Real Estate Daily, July 7, 2015.

34. Jay Koziarz, "A Local Expert's Guide to Chicago's Lincoln Park Neighborhood," Curbed Chicago, April 12, 2016, https://www.chicago.curbed.com/2016/4/12/11414006/chicago-neighborhood-guide-lincoln-park.

35. The average air travel per person among the DC middle school families was 6,700 miles in a year, about 3,000 miles more than the average for American air flights as derived from Bureau of Transportation Statistics, U.S. Department of Transportation data for 2014, accessed September 14, 2017, https://www.rita.dot.gov/bts/press_releases/bts018_16.

36. Kraybill, Johnson-Weiner, and Nolt, The Amish, 139. The New Order Amish, who permit airplane travel, live in Holmes County, Ohio, and make up less than 5 percent of the Amish population.

37. Bill McKibben, "Embarrassing Photos of Me, Thanks to My Right-Wing Stalkers," *New York Times*, August 5, 2016.

38. Marshall, *Don't Even Think About It*, 202.

39. Wilson, *Consilience*, 278.

## 1. Founding Mitigator

1. Mary V. Thompson, "Hospitality at Mount Vernon," Mount Vernon Digital Encyclopedia, http://www.mountvernon.org/digital-encyclopedia/article /hospitality-at-mount-vernon/. After the American Revolution overnight guests were present at Mount Vernon most days of the year. Current visitors are approximately one million, according to the Mount Vernon Ladies' Association (MVLA) *Annual Report for 2015*, 32. http://www.mountvernon.org /preservation/mount-vernon-ladies-association/2015-annual-report/. Peter Baker, "The White House Will Disclose Visitor Logs," *New York Times*, September 24, 2009. Visitors to the White House averaged 70,000 to 100,000 per month during the Obama administration.

2. Chernow, *Washington*, 904.

3. The paintings are by William Winstanley (1775–1806) and George Beck (1749–1812).

4. Diaries of George Washington (GW), March 13, 1748, *Founders Online*, National Archives, last modified November 26, 2017, http://founders.archives .gov/documents/Washington/01–01–02–0001–0002–0003.

5. Vincent, "Fine Arts," 164–185; Manca, *George Washington's Eye*. George Washington collected landscape paintings already in the 1730s.

6. Diaries of GW, March 1785, *Founders Online*, National Archives, last modified November 26, 2017, http://founders.archives.gov/documents/Washington /01–04–02–0002–0003. George Washington planted tulip poplar and poplar species in 1784, which are among the fastest-growing hardwood species native to North America.

7. Adam Erby, "The Vaughan Mantel," digital video, 2014, 05:41, Mount Vernon historic estate website, http://www.mountvernon.org/video/view/144/.

8. "A Map of General Washington's Farm from a Drawing Transmitted by the General," (1801), Library of Congress Geography and Map Division, Washington DC, https://lccn.loc.gov/99466780, image. With his extensive landholdings, Washington may have been able to source much of his fuel from his own woodlands, because as much as a third of his land was not tilled.

9. "Notes and Queries," *Virginia Magazine of History and Biography* 1, no. 1 (1893), 98. 1763–1764: 11,542 bushels of coal from the James River upper district. Peterson, "Commerce of Virginia," 302. 1789–1791: 28,719 bushels of coal from England.

10. Martha W. McCarthy, "Historical Overview of the Midlothian Coal Mining Company Tract," Midlothian, VA, Midlothian Mines Park website, www .midlomines.org/historic-overview.html, accessed March 4, 2017.

11. Goodwin, "Coal and Fire Grates."

12. Graham, "Report on Heating," 9. Lord Botetourt shipped 200 bushels of coal to George Wythe at 10 dollars each in 1770.

13. "Inventory and Appraisement of the Estate of Peyton Randolph," (January 5, 1776), Colonial Williamsburg Digital Library, http://research.history .org/DigitalLibrary/view/index.cfm?doc=Probates\PB00064.xml&highlight =Randolph. Upon his death in 1775, Peyton Randolph, the president of the Continental Congress, had stocks of wine and rum valued at ten times the worth of his one hundred bushels of fuel. "100 bushels dust coal (2 pounds 10 shillings); 30 gallons rum (7 pounds 15 shillings); 1 pipe of wine (60 pounds)."

14. "Appraisment [sic] of the Estate of Thomas Hobday decd.," 18 May 1752, York County Estate Inventories, Colonial Williamsburg Digital Library, http:// research.history.org/DigitalLibrary/view/index.cfm?doc=Probates\PB01111.xml &highlight=Thomas%20hobday.

15. Diaries of GW, October 1770, *Founders Online*, National Archives, last modified November 26, 2017, http://founders.archives.gov/documents/Washington /01–02–02–0005–0027.

16. See Cash Accounts, November 1771, *Founders Online*, National Archives, last modified November 26, 2017, http://founders.archives.gov/documents /Washington/02–08–02–0357; October 1772, *Founders Online*, National Archives, last modified November 26, 2017, http://founders.archives.gov /documents/Washington/02–09–02–0079; January 1774, *Founders Online*, National Archives, last modified November 26, 2017, http://founders.archives .gov/documents/Washington/02–09–02–0323. Over a period of three years beginning in 1771, George Washington made annual orders of between two hundred and five hundred bushels of coal for use in the Mount Vernon blacksmith shop that supplied the estate and enterprises with nails and farm tools.

17. GW to Bartholomew Dandridge Jr., December 3, 1797, *Founders Online*, National Archives, last modified November 26, 2017, http://founders.archives.gov /documents/Washington/06–01–02–0443. On November 27, 1797, George Washington paid $33.58 for "200 bushl coal to William Dandridge," but other orders after the Revolutionary War, if they existed, do not appear in the accounts.

18. Adam Erby, "The Vaughan Mantel," digital video, 05:41, Mount Vernon historic estate website, http://www.mountvernon.org/video/view/144/.

19. Two Nerdy History Girls blog February 4, 2010, "Keeping Warm: Buzaglo Stoves," http://twonerdyhistorygirls.blogspot.com/2010/02/keeping-warm -buzaglo-stoves.html, quoting from J.C.T. Oates, "Hot Air from Cambridge," The Library v; volume s5-XVIII Issue 2, June 1963, 141.

20. Richard Kay, "Queen Goes Green to Light Windsor Castle with Hydro Electric Power," the *Daily Mail* online, July 11, 2013, http://www.dailymail.co.uk /news/article-2361347/Richard-Kay-Queen-goes-green-light-Windsor-Castle -hydro-electric-power.html.

21. Marland, Boden, and Andres, "Fossil Fuel"; Jeffries, "U.K. Population," 3; U.S. Census Bureau, *Historical Statistics*, A-18; Pfister and Fertig, "Population History," 5; L'Atelier du Centre de Recherches Historiques, "Territoire et population de 1800 a 1890," posted February 06, 2011, http://acrh.revues.org/3410.

22. Andreae and Ramanathan, "Climate's Dark Forcings."

23. Greenberg, "Architecture: The Mansion House," 55.

24. Jim Buckley, "What is a Rumford Fireplace, Anyway?" quoting from The Collected Works of Count Rumford, Sanborn Brown ed. vol. 2, accessed September 15, 2017, http://www.rumford.com/articleWhat.html.

25. Buckley, "Rumford Fireplace," accessed February 20, 2014.

26. Griffin, *Catalogue*, 65.

27. Charles Pettit to GW, November 6, 1787, *Founders Online*, National Archives, last modified November 26, 2017, http://founders.archives.gov/documents /Washington/04–05–02–0382.

28. "The Weather Watch." Library of Congress website. Accessed September 15, 2017, https://www.loc.gov/collections/george-washington-papers/articles-and -essays/introduction-to-the-diaries-of-george-washington/the-weather-watch/. *OSHA Technical Manual*, Section III, Chapter 2, accessed September 15, 2017, http://www.osha.gov/dts/osta/otm/otm_iii/otm_iii_2.html#5.

29. GW to Lafayette, June 8, 1786, *Founders Online*, National Archives, last modified November 26, 2017, http://founders.archives.gov/documents/Washington /04–04–02–0105.

30. Lafayette to GW, January 13, 1787, Paris, *Founders Online*, National Archives, last modified November 26, 2017, http://founders.archives.gov/documents /Washington/04–04–02–0442.

31. Chickens were typically left in the open to forage, but picked off by foxes and birds of prey. Accordingly, poultry were a much smaller part of the eighteenth-century American diet than it is today. Interview with farm manager, Great Hopes Plantation, Colonial Williamsburg, November 2011.

32. Martha Washington to Fanny Bassett Washington, July 1, 1792. The Martha Washington site, a project of MVLA and George Mason University, http:// marthawashington.us/items/show/462.

33. The economic historian Lorena Walsh concluded that vegetable sales made up only 3 percent of the value of transactions in Chesapeake food markets. Walsh, Martin, and Bowen, "Provisioning Early American Towns," 141. Today, by comparison, Americans spend at least 10 percent of their food budget on vegetables. Average annual expenditures and share for the U.S. and regions 2014–15, Bureau of Labor Statistics, Consumer Expenditure Survey, 2016, https://www.bls.gov/cex/2016/standard/multiyr.pdf.

34. Jefferson, *Garden Book*, 245.

35. Laing, "Cattle in Early Virginia," 199. Observed for the years 1813–16 and 1818–19.

36. Rifkin, *Beyond Beef*, 55.

37. Walsh, "Whence the Beef?" 279.

38. Walsh, Martin and Bowen, "Provisioning Early American Towns," 108–111.

39. Patrick, "Partitioning the Landscape," 35. GW to William Strickland, July 15, 1797, at Mount Vernon.

40. Patrick, "Partitioning the Landscape," 35.

41. GW to Anthony Whitting, October 28, 1792, from Philadelphia, *Founders Online*, National Archives, last modified November 26, 2017, http://founders .archives.gov/documents/Washington/05–11–02–0155–0001.

42. GW to James Anderson, December 10, 1799, cited in Fusonie and Fusonie, *George Washington*, 32.

43. Fusonie and Fusonie, *George Washington*, 30.

44. GW to James Anderson, December 13, 1799, "From George Washington to James Anderson, 13 December 1799," *Founders Online*, National Archives, last modified November 26, 2017, http://founders.archives.gov/documents /Washington/06–04–02–0403–0001.

45. GW to Samuel Vaughan, February 5, 1785, *Founders Online*, National Archives, last modified November 26, 2017, http://founders.archives.gov/documents /Washington/04–02–02–0235.

46. "Servants and Laborers," *George Washington Digital Encyclopedia*, Mount Vernon website, http://www.mountvernon.org/digital-encyclopedia/subject /servants-and-laborers/. Record of meat rations for the following: Alexander Cleveland, James Boyd, James Donaldson, John Neale, John Violet, Joseph Cash, Patrick Callahan, William Roberts, William Stuart.

47. Walsh, Martin, and Bowen, "Provisioning Early American Towns," 69–73, 140–43, 175–77; Walsh, "Whence the Beef?" 269.

48. Miles, "The Mysterious Gas," 255.

49. GW to Lafayette, May 10, 1786, *Founders Online*, National Archives, last modified November 26, 2017, http://founders.archives.gov/documents/Washington /04–04–02–0051.

50. GW to Lafayette, November 19, 1786, *Founders Online*, National Archives, last modified November 26, 2017, http://founders.archives.gov/documents /Washington/04–04–02–0342.

51. Bixby, *Inventory of the Contents of Mount Vernon*, 50–57.

52. Intergovernmental Panel on Climate Change (IPCC), *Guidelines*, 10.28.

53. U.S. Department of Agriculture, "Table 2: Livestock on farms and ranches—Farms reporting, 1900 to 1935; number, 1840 to 1935; and value, 1850 to 1935; of specified species in the United States," 1935 Census Publications, *Volume 3: General Report*, Part 5. http://agcensus.mannlib.cornell.edu/AgCensus /getVolumeTwoPart.do?volnum=3&year=1935&part_id=784&number=5&title =Livestock and Livestock Products.

54. Intergovernmental Panel on Climate Change, *Climate Change Fifth Assessment Report Synthesis*, 2014. Global Warming Potential for methane of 28 over

100-year time horizon used to convert methane emissions to carbon dioxide equivalent units.

55. "Inventory and Appraisment of M. William Rind," Estate inventories for York County, Colonial Williamsburg Digital Library, http://research.history.org /DigitalLibrary/View/index.cfm?doc=Probates%5CPB00040.xml.

56. Walsh, "Whence the Beef?" 273.

57. Diaries of GW, July 1, 1786, *Founders Online*, National Archives, last modified November 26, 2017, http://founders.archives.gov/documents/Washington /04–04–02–0342.

58. *Lafayette in the Age*. Lafayette to Adrienne de Noailles de Lafayette, August 20, 1784, 237–39.

59. Weld, *Travels through the State*. 39.

60. J. F. D. Smyth quoted in "Trees on the Duke of Gloucester Street in the Eighteenth Century," essay on Colonial Williamsburg website, http://www.history .org/history/cwland/resrch5.cfm, accessed March 2, 2017.

61. Bentley Boyd, "60 Years Later, Governor's Palace Gets Its Trees," *Daily Press* (Williamsburg, VA), September 15, 1993. http://articles.dailypress.com /1993–09–15/news/9309140344_1_planting-six-trees-governor-s-palace.

62. Diaries of GW, March 24, 1785, *Founders Online*, National Archives, last modified November 26, 2017, http://founders.archives.gov/documents/Washington /01–04–02–0002–0003–0024.

63. John Roach, "George Washington Tree Cloned for Arbor Day Plantings." *National Geographic News*, April 29, 2004. http://news.nationalgeographic.com /news/2004/04/0427_040427_arborday.html.

64. Wulf, *Founding Gardeners*, 52.

65. John Adams to Abigail Adams, April 5, 1786, *Founders Online*, National Archives, last modified November 26, 2017, http://founders.archives.gov /documents/Adams/04–07–02–0041.

66. Wulf, *Founding Gardeners*, 52.

67. Wulf, *Brother Gardeners*, 74.

68. M. K. Anderson, "Prehistoric," 913–94.

69. Van Doren, *Travels of William Bartram*, 149.

70. Day, "Indian as an Ecological Factor," 334.

71. Craven, *Soil Exhaustion*, 9.

72. Sherwood, "Soils and Land Use." https://www.montpelier.org/library/media /sherwood_soil_history.pdf. Accessed April 16, 2014. Site discontinued.

73. Sookhdeo and Druckenbrod, "Effect of Forest Age on Soil Organic Matter," 1–4.

74. Dierauf, "Montpelier Landmark Forest," accessed November 2011.

75. Land owners who pursued experimentation in the late eighteenth century include the Maryland planter John Beale Bordley and Virginia planters Landon Carter and John Taylor of Caroline. Craven, *Soil Exhaustion*, 99–100.

76. Thomas Jefferson to Walter Jones, January 2, 1814, *Founders Online*, National Archives, last modified November 26, 2017, http://founders.archives.gov /documents/Jefferson/03–07–02–0052.

77. GW to Arthur Young, December 4, 1788, Mount Vernon, *Founders Online*, National Archives, last modified November 26, 2017, http://founders.archives .gov/documents/Washington/05–01–02–0120.

78. GW to Arthur Young, December 5, 1791, *Founders Online*, National Archives, last modified November 26, 2017, http://founders.archives.gov/documents /Washington/05–09–02–0153.

79. "Draft of George Washington's Eighth Annual Address to Congress, [10 November 1796]," *Founders Online*, National Archives, last modified November 26, 2017, http://founders.archives.gov/documents/Hamilton /01–20–02–0255.

80. GW to Lafayette, 18 June 1788, *Founders Online*, National Archives, last modified November 26, 2017, http://founders.archives.gov/documents/Washington /04–06–02–0301.

81. Chernow, *Washington*, 142. Lee, *Experiencing Mount Vernon*, 33.

82. Schreiner, "Early Fertilizer Work," 39–48.

83. Richard Peters to GW, April 27 1788, *Founders Online*, National Archives, last modified November 26, 2017, http://founders.archives.gov/documents /Washington/04–06–02–0208.

84. Farm Reports, August 16–22, 1789, *Founders Online*, National Archives, last modified November 26, 2017, http://founders.archives.gov/documents /Washington/05–03–02–0271.

85. Fageria, Baligar, and Bailey, "Role of Cover Crops."

86. Thomas Jefferson to Jonathan Williams, July 3, 1796, *Founders Online*, National Archives, last modified November 26, 2017, http://founders.archives.gov /documents/Jefferson/01–29–02–0105.

87. Dan Barber, "What Farm-to-Table Got Wrong," *New York Times*, May 17, 2014.

88. Subak, "Soil Carbon Accumulation," 185–95.

89. GW to David Stuart, June 15, 1790, *Founders Online*, National Archives, last modified November 26, 2017, http://founders.archives.gov/documents /Washington/05–05–02–0334.

90. GW to George Augustine Washington, October 25, 1786, "From George Washington to George Augustine Washington, 25 October 1786," *Founders Online*, National Archives, last modified November 26, 2017, http://founders.archives .gov/documents/Washington/04–04–02–0279.

91. Murtaugh and Schlax, "Carbon Legacies," 14–20.

92. "Abigail Adams to Abigail Adams Smith, 7 July 1788," *Founders Online*, National Archives, last modified November 26, 2017, http://founders.archives .gov/documents/Adams/04–08–02–0135.

93. The merchant and privateer Elias Hasket Derby was believed to be the wealthiest American contemporaneous with George Washington. His mansion was completed in 1799 and at 8,757 square feet was larger than Mount Vernon. Elias Derby's descendants viewed the mansion as impractical and had it demolished in 1815. Soltow, *Distribution of Wealth*, 62; Kimball, *Early American Architecture*, 18.

94. Binder, *Coal Age Empire*, 16.

95. Marsha Mullin, chief curator, the Hermitage, personal communication, October 10, 2014.

96. Frank, "Ford Orientation Center," 881.

97. In the late eighteenth century, greenhouse gas emissions from Mount Vernon were dominated by methane emissions from livestock, which is estimated as 380 metric tons carbon dioxide equivalent based on the following assumptions. Mount Vernon's 1799 estate inventory lists the relevant livestock population as follows: cattle: 329, sheep: 600–1000, mules: 58, horses: 25. http://www.mountvernon.org/george-washington/farming/animals/the-animals-of-mount-vernon/.

Emission factors were applied using IPCC Tier 1 default emissions factors: cattle: 26 kg CH$_4$/year, sheep: 5 kg CH$_4$/year, mules 10 kg CH$_4$/year, horses, 18 kg CH$_4$/year. A developing country default emission factor for cattle was chosen because of the slower weight gain characterized by eighteenth-century breeds. An assumption that half of the cattle stock were immature animals was selected to reflect husbandry intended for dairy as well as beef. Intergovernmental Panel on Climate Change (IPCC), *Guidelines*, 10.28, 10.79. A global warming potential of 28 was used to convert methane units to carbon dioxide units. Intergovernmental Panel on Climate Change, *Climate Change Fifth Assessment Report Synthesis*, 2014.

Current greenhouse gas emissions from energy consumption at Mount Vernon is estimated as 1,293 metric tons of carbon dioxide equivalent based on the following assumptions. According to recent tax filings, expenditures for utilities for the Mount Vernon Ladies Association were $634,645 in 2012, the most recent year available for this line item. "Return of Organization Exempt from Income Tax: Form 990," 2012, 10. https://pp-990.s3.amazonaws.com/2013_12_EO/54-0564701_990_201212.pdf?X-Amz-Algorithm=AWS4-HMAC-SHA256&X-Amz-Credential=AKIAI7C6X5GT42DHYZIA%2F20180205%2Fus-east-1%2Fs3%2Faws4_request&X-Amz-Date=20180205T215140Z&X-Amz-Expires=1800&X-Amz-SignedHeaders=host&X-Amz-Signature=6c49a886dd9b60e718495d8e4e949f991e1c3a23947759309f1665ed9268e411.

Because expenditures for the sub-items of natural gas, electricity, and water were not itemized within this budget category, commercial sector-wide averages for expenditures from electricity compared with natural gas, fuel oil and district heat were applied to apportion the budget data into fuel categories. U.S. EIA, "2012 CBECs Survey Data," Table C2, *Commercial Building Energy Consumption Survey*, https://www.eia.gov/consumption/commercial/data/2012/c&e/pdf/c2.pdf.

The expenditure share of electricity is 82 percent as a proportion of all energy sources on average in the U.S. commercial sector. Because the utilities budget category for Mount Vernon would have included non-energy charges such as water usage, which usually make up the minority of commercial sector utilities, a conservative assumption was applied that half of the Mount Vernon utilities budget was not fuel related. The fuel consumption estimate may be conservative considering that the tax year 2012 expenditures did not reflect fuel consumption in the library building completed in the following year. Estimated expenditures for electricity and natural gas were converted to greenhouse gas emissions using EPA's carbon footprint calculator. https://www3.epa.gov/carbon-footprint-calculator/, accessed December 4, 2017.

## 2. Carbon Dissenters

1. Kraybill, Johnson-Weiner, and Nolt, *The Amish*, 185.
2. Kraybill, Johnson-Weiner, and Nolt, *The Amish*, 153. The more traditional groups such as the Swartzentruber and Andy Weaver groups, which use less technology, are growing the fastest due to larger family size.
3. Biswas-Diener, Vitterso, and Diener, "Most People," 205–26.
4. Kraybill, *Riddle of Amish Culture*, 84.
5. Wetmore, "Amish Technology." 6.
6. Igou, *Their Own Words*, 130, letter-writer E. Still.
7. Scott and Pellman, *Living Without Electricity*, 77–78.
8. In Lancaster County and parts of Ohio, Amish families are installing radiant floor heating by placing pipes in the ceiling of the basement to carry heated air to warm the floor above. The space heating allows family members to become more dispersed during the cold weather months, and it remains to be seen whether the practice is challenged by the traditional adherents of the Old Order Amish. This form of space heating, which is fueled by propane, involves much higher greenhouse gas emissions than the wood-burning stove.
9. Schoenauer, *6,000 Years of Housing*, 171.
10. While more than 87 percent of U.S. households have air conditioning, in India only about 2 percent of households do. "India's Power Consumption to Grow on Rise in AC Sales," *The Economic Times*, October 28, 2015, http://economictimes.indiatimes.com/industry/energy/power/indias-power-consumption-to-grow-on-rise-in-ac-sales/articleshow/49569791.cms.
11. As of the late 1990s, about 20 percent of Amish districts allowed propane and fewer still permitted natural gas. Scott and Pellman, *Living Without Electricity*, 9.

12. Scott and Pellman, *Living Without Electricity*, 17.

13. Scott and Pellman, *Living Without Electricity*, 24.

14. Kraybill, *Riddle*, 206

15. U.S. Energy Information Administration (EIA), *Residential Energy Consumption Survey* (RECS), Table HC7.7: "Air Conditioning in homes in the Northeast and Midwest regions, 2015," February 2017, https://www.eia.gov/consumption /residential/data/2015/hc/php/hc7.7.php.

16. McNary and Berry, "Using Energy."

17. Scott and Pellman, *Living Without Electricity*, 9.

18. Scott and Pellman, *Living Without Electricity*, 9.

19. Author's calculation of the wringer washer machine compared with a 280 kwh and 350 kwh conventional, ENERGY STAR-rated washing machine in 2015.

20. Bendt, "Clothes Dryers?" 1.

21. U.S. EIA, RECS, "2009 RECS Survey Data," Table CE1.2, https://www.eia.gov /consumption/residential/data/2009/index.php?view=consumption. Sixty percent of American households have dishwashers.

22. Scott and Pellman, *Living Without Electricity*, 9. About 25 percent of districts accept power lawn mowers.

23. J. L. Banks and Robert McConnell, "National Emissions from Lawn and Garden Equipment," September 2015, study results paper, U.S. EPA, https://www .epa.gov/sites/production/files/2015–09/documents/banks.pdf.

24. Based on estimated average annual natural gas usage from the distributor, Lehman Hardware and Appliances, Dalton, Ohio. By contrast, the lowest emissions for a conventional electricity-powered refrigerator is found with a 2016 model consuming 280 kwh a year, which would be about 0.12 metric tons $CO_2$ annually, or about one-sixth as much $CO_2$ as the natural gas fridge. New regular models consume an average of 350 kwh. "ENERGY STAR: Most Efficient 2016—Medium, Large, and X-Large Refrigerators." U.S. EPA ENERGY STAR website, https://www.energystar.gov/most-efficient/me-certified-refrigerators.

25. Ad Crable, "Cell Phones, Computers More and More Part of Lancaster County Amish's Real World," *Lancaster Online*, May 18, 2014, http:// lancasteronline.com/news/local/cell-phones-computers-more-and-more-part -of-lancaster-county/article_432d645c-def6–11e3–9e84–001a4bcf6878.html.

26. Bergman et al., "Carbon Impacts," 220.

27. Slade, *Made to Break*, 336.

28. Kraybill and Nolt, *Amish Enterprise*, 66.

29. Schumacher, *Small Is Beautiful*, 305.

30. Hurst and McConnell, *An Amish Paradox*, 217. An estimated 80 percent of Old Order in Holmes County use solar; Phil McKenna, "Amish Are Surprise Champions of Solar Technology," *The New Scientist Blogs* (blog), *New Scientist*, June 1, 2007, https://www.newscientist.com/blog/environment/2007/06/amish -are-surprise-embracers-of-solar.html.

31. Lehman's store catalogue, also available online at https://www.lehmans.com/, specializes in goods and machines that support traditional households that do not use conventional technology and electricity and that do not purchase contemporary designs in furnishings.

32. Terry Johnson, "Amish Technique for Stacking Firewood," *Mother Earth News*, December 2014. https://www.motherearthnews.com/homesteading-and -livestock/sustainable-farming/stacking-firewood-technique-zm0z14djzkin.

33. Lehmans.com, Cookstoves, see Baker's Choice model, invented by Mark Stoll.

34. Andreae and Ramanathan, "Climate's Dark Forcings," 280–281.

35. U.S. EPA, *Inventory*, 6–23–24, https://www.epa.gov/sites/production/files /2017–04/documents/us-ghg-inventory-2016-main-text.pdf.

36. "Selected Housing Characteristics," 2015, American Community Survey, U.S. Census Bureau, https://factfinder.census.gov/faces/tableservices/jsf/pages /productview.xhtml?pid=ACS_15_5YR_DP04&src=pt.

37. Michael Wilson, "'Letters to Answer, and Logs to Split,'" *New York Times*, October 1, 2010.

38. Eric McConnell, "Ohio's Forest Economy," Fact Sheet, F-80–12, Ohio State University Extension; 2012. https://ohioline.osu.edu/factsheet/F-80; Pennsylvania Forest Products Association, "Forest Ownership," fact sheet, 2004, http://www .paforestproducts.org/files/OWNERSHIP1.pdf; Bratkovich et al., "Forests of Indiana."

39. McConnell, "Forest Economy"; Pennsylvania Forest Products Association, "Forest Ownership"; Bratkovich et al., "Forests of Indiana."

40. 2015 New Source Performance Standards for New Residential Wood Heaters brings the allowable particulate emissions to 4.5 grams per hour or less. Many stove manufacturers now offer products that emit 1.0 or fewer grams of particulates per hour, a large difference from earlier stove models that emitted at 15–30 grams/hour. Federal Register, Vol. 80, No. 50, p. 13678, March 16, 2015. https://www.gpo.gov/fdsys/pkg/FR-2015-03–16/pdf /2015–03733.pdf.

41. CDC, Community Health Status Indicators, Holmes County, 2015, http://www .countyhealthrankings.org/app/ohio/2017/rankings/holmes/county/outcomes /overall/snapshot. The national average annual pm2.5 concentration is 10.7 microns/m3.

42. CDC, Community Health Status Indicators, Lancaster County, 2015, http:// www.countyhealthrankings.org/app/pennsylvania/2017/rankings/lancaster /county/outcomes/overall/snapshot.

43. Amish averaged 1.7 servings of red meat daily compared with 1.9 daily servings for non-Amish. Carter, "Food Intake," 1.

44. CDC, Community Health Status Indicators, Holmes County, 2015.

45. Kraybill, *Riddle of Amish Culture*, 215, 223.

46. Scott and Pellman, *Living Without Electricity*, 115.

47. The return per acre has been calculated as small grains: $126 Amish, $28 Non-Amish; alfalfa hay: $233 Amish, $124 non-Amish; corn: $65 Amish, $9 non-Amish. James, "Horse and Human Labor"; Bender, "Economic Comparison," 2–15.

48. Kraybill and Nolt, *Amish Enterprise*, 20. More than half of farms in Lancaster County are Amish.

49 Mary Jackson, *Amish Agriculture*, 483.

50. "Selected Economic Characteristics 2015," American Community Survey (ACS), U.S. Census Bureau, https://factfinder.census.gov/faces/tableservices/jsf/pages/productview.xhtml?src=CF.

51. Johnson-Weiner, "Technological Diversity," 1; Scott and Pellman, *Living Without Electricity*, 98.

52. Kraybill and Nolt, *Amish Enterprise*, 119.

53. Scott and Pellman, *Living Without Electricity*, 9.

54. U.S. EPA, *Inventory*, Table 3–8, page 3–11.

55. CDC, "Community Health Status Indicators, 2015," Violent crime rate per 100,000: Nation: 199.2; Holmes County 36.4, Lagrange County 42.0.

56. Kraybill, Johnson-Weaver, and Nolt, *The Amish*, 355–56.

57. Elkhart County Sheriff's Department, *Horse and Buggy Driver's Manual*.

58. "Amish Buggy Accidents 2015," Mission to Amish People website, www.mapministry.org/news-and-testimonies/amish-buggy-accidents.

59. Kraybill, Johnson-Weaver, and Nolt, *The Amish*, 46.

60. Kraybill, *Amish Enterprise*, 113.

61. "Annual Vehicle Distance Traveled 2014," Office of Highway Policy Information, Federal Highway Administration, 2015, https://www.fhwa.dot.gov/policyinformation/statistics/2014/vm1.cfm; data in comparison with Mission to Amish People data.

62. "US Business Travel," National Household Travel Survey, 2001–2002, Bureau of Transportation Statistics, https://www.rita.dot.gov/bts/sites/rita.dot.gov.bts/files/publications/america_on_the_go/us_business_travel/html/entire.html.

63. According to a Lancaster Amish source, in practice, some families do not host because they do not have enough space, but the exceptions are few.

64. Kraybill, Johnson-Weaver, and Nolt, *The Amish*, 165.

65. Defection rates: Stephen Scott, *Ohio Amish Directory, Holmes County and Vicinity*, 2010, cited in Kraybill, Johnson-Weaver, and Nolt, 163; Nolt and Meyers, *Plain Diversity*, 83.

66. Kraybill, Johnson-Weiner, Nolt, *The Amish*, 157.

### 3. Urban Families

1. "A Kalorama 'Pic-Nic' With Wild, Romantic Scenery," January 16, 2013, Ghosts of DC website, http://ghostsofdc.org/2013/01/16/a-kalorama-pic-nic-with-wild-romantic-scenery/, accessed March 10, 2017. The article cited was from the *Baltimore Sun*, August 6, 1844.

2. Occupation by sex for the civilian employed, American Community Survey 2015, U.S. Census Bureau. https://factfinder.census.gov/faces/tableservices/jsf /pages/productview.xhtml?src=CF. About 75 percent of the residents work in white-collar professions.

3. EIA, *Residential Energy Consumption Survey* (RECS), "2009 RECS Survey Data," Table CE4.12, https://www.eia.gov/consumption/residential/data/2009/index .php?view=consumption#undefined. Over half of American households with incomes of $120,000 report that their ceilings are "unusually high." Wealthy households in this income bracket spend an average of $1,960 per household member on energy each year, about double that spent by households with earnings $20,000–40,000. Expenditures for U.S. households earning less than $20,000 were $900; those earning $20,000–$40,000 were $1,090.

4. Mazur and Wilson, "Housing Characteristics," 4. Washington DC has less of a tradition of second-home ownership compared to some of America's largest cities. New York and Michigan each have about a quarter of a million seasonal homes, many of which are owned by apartment dwellers in New York City and Chicago. Seasonal/vocational homes in 2010: New York 289,000, Michigan 263,000.

5. Selected housing characteristics, American Community Survey, 2014, U.S. Census Bureau, https://factfinder.census.gov/faces/tableservices/jsf/pages /productview.xhtml?src=CF.

6. Johnson et al., "Lives of U.S. Children."

7. Anonymous correspondent, "Do independent school families live in condos?" dcurbanmoms.com forum, June 22, 2010.

8. Anonymous correspondent, dcurbanmoms.com forum, June 22, 2010.

9. District of Columbia Energy Consumption and Production Estimates, 2015, U.S. Energy Information Administration, https://www.eia.gov/state/?sid=DC#tabs-3.

10. "OSSE Announces Eligibility for 2014–15 Free and Reduced Priced Meals," Office of the State Superintendent of Education, January 14, 2015, https://osse .dc.gov/release/osse-announces-eligibility-2014-2015-free-and-reduced-priced -meals. The low economic status student in Washington DC is characterized by a household income of less than $45,000 for a family of four.

11. "DC 2010 Tract Profile: Population," U.S. Census Bureau, https://www .neighborhoodinfodc.org/censustract10/Nbr_prof_trct58.html. Washington DC tracts 40.1 (Kalorama Triangle); 40.2 (Adams Morgan).

12. Anonymous contributor, "Talk to Me About Regret," dcurbanmom.com forum, August 30, 2016, http://www.dcurbanmom.com/jforum/posts/list/30 /579765.page.

13. "Uniform Crime Report," 2014, FBI, https://www.ucrdatatool.gov/Search /Crime/State/RunCrimeStatebyState.cfm. Reported violent crime in the District of Columbia dropped by 53 percent between 1995 and 2014.

14. Hansen, *Kalorama Triangle*, 3.

15. Cook, *Little Old Oak Park*, 79.

16. Putnam, *Bowling Alone*.

17. Gallagher, *End of the Suburbs*, 272 (citing Sarah Susanka).

18. Joyce Anderson-Maples, "Experts Discuss New Trend of Eating Out vs. Eating at Home," *Medical Xpress*, May 25, 2015, https://medicalxpress.com/news/2015–05-experts-discuss-trend-home.html.

19. Gallagher, *The End of the Suburbs*, 157.

20. Belden, Russonello & Stewart, *The 2011 Community Preference Survey: What Americans are looking for When Deciding Where to Live*, survey conducted for the National Association of Realtors, March 2011, http://www.brspoll.com/uploads/files/2011%20Community%20Preference%20Survey.pdf.

21. U.S. Census, "Highlights of Annual 2016 Characteristics of New Housing," Survey of Construction, https://www.census.gov/construction/chars/highlights.html.

22. Van Boven and Gilovich, "To Do or To Have?" 1193.

23. Pamela Druckerman, "The Clutter Cure's Illusory Joy," *New York Times*, February 15, 2015.

24. Weber and Matthews, "Household Carbon Footprint," 379.

25. Stephen S. Fuller, *The Trillion Dollar Apartment Industry: How the Apartment Industry and Its 35 Million Residents Drove a Trillion Dollar Contribution to the National Economy*. Report by the National Apartment Association and the National Multi Housing Council in partnership with the author, February 2013. https://www.naahq.org/sites/default/files/naa-documents/government-affairs/Fuller-Report-Trillion-Dollar-Apt-Industry.pdf.

26. Virge Temme, architect, Door County, WI, in conversation with the author, August 30, 2016.

27. Harriet Edleson, "In Northeast DC, Brian Levy seeks to Spark a Revolution with his Innovative Micro-House," *Washington Post*, December 4, 2014.

28. Society of Certified Senior Advisors, "State of the Senior Housing Industry," 2011, 6. http://www.helpathomecares.com/uploads/3/4/2/3/34234986/stateoftheseniorhousingindustryreport.pdf.

29. U.S. Census Bureau, "New Privately Owned Housing Units Completed in the United States by Intent and Design," August 16, 2017. https://www.census.gov/construction/nrc/pdf/quarterly_starts_completions.pdf.

30. National Multifamily Housing Council, "Apartment Industry Opposes Plan to Restrict Multifamily Lending," October 10, 2013. https://www.nmhc.org/News/Apartment-Industry-Opposes-Plan-to-Restrict-Multifamily-Lending/.

31. Glaeser and Shapiro, "Mortgage Interest Deduction," 4.

32. Hanson, "Size of Home," 195–210.

33. Russell, *Agile City*, 78.

34. U.S. Census. Characteristics of New Multifamily Buildings, Housing Survey, 2017. https://www.census.gov/construction/chars/mfu.html, accessed October 2, 2017.

35. Harak, "Up the Chimney," 1.
36. National Grid, "Energy Saving Programs," 2017. https://www.nationalgridus
.com/energy-saving-programs; McKibbin et al., "Engaging as Partners," 1.
37. "Defining the Urban Boomer," KRC Research for Zipcar, May 2015. https://
www.slideshare.net/Zipcar_PR/zipcar-urban-boomersstudyfinal. Car sharing
program Zipcar reports that their membership by customers aged fifty-plus
has been growing by about 10 percent each year.
38. Einberger, *A History of Rock Creek Park*, 253.
39. Chris Mooney, "E. O. Wilson Explains Why Parks and Nature Are Really
Good For Your Brain," *Washington Post*, September 30, 2015.
40. Stevens, *Under the Oaks*.
41. Leonor Vivanco, "Chicago Ranks 11th on List of U.S. Cities with Best Parks,"
*Chicago Tribune*, May 24, 2017.
42. U.S. EIA, *RECS*, "2009 RECS Survey Data," Table CE1.2. https://www.eia.gov
/consumption/residential/data/2009/index.php?view=consumption#summary.
43. U.S. EIA, *RECS*, "2009 RECS Survey Data," Table CE1.2. In the U.S. Northeast a
single-family attached house consumes 50.3 thousand BTUs per square foot on
average, compared with the 80.1 thousand BTUs per square foot in an apartment that is part of a two- to four-unit building.
44. Ian Shapira, "It's Pop-Ups vs. Solar Panels on Shepherd Street NW in Columbia Heights," *Washington Post*, July 20, 2014.
45. David Whitehead, "More Housing is Now Banned from Lanier Heights.
Organizing is What Won the Day," *Greater Greater Washington*, April 12, 2016.
Comment by a reader who signed as "Matt."
46. "Frequently Asked . . . ," City Bike NYC. https://help.citibikenyc.com/hc/en-us,
accessed October 2, 2017.
47. Cabi_addict, comment, "Earthquake!" *Greater Greater Washington*, August 23,
2011. https://ggwash.org/view/10499/earthquake.
48. Jonathan Maus, "Behind the Scenes of Capital Bike Share," *Bike Portland*,
March 10, 2013, https://bikeportland.org/2013/03/10/behind-the-scenes-of
-capital-bikeshare-84006.
49. LDA Consulting, *Capital Bikeshare*, ii. Regarding bike sharing, savings assume
that members drive 158 miles less than they would have, aggregating to 4.4
million miles saved by the 27,600 bike share members.
50. Ashley Halsey III, "DC is the Wild West When Enforcing Tickets for Traffic
Violators, Audit Finds," *Washington Post*, September 8, 2014.
51. "NYC Collected $1.9B in Fines, Fees through 2015," *CBS New York* online,
March 24, 2016, http://newyork.cbslocal.com/2016/03/24/traffic-fines-new-york
-city/; Ross Barkan and Will Bredderman, "City Council Approves $78.5 Bil-
lion Budget for New York City," Observer.com, June 26, 2015. http://observer
.com/2015/06/city-council-approves-78-5-billion-budget-for-new-york-city/.

52. Zipcar Overview, http://www.zipcar.com/press/overview, accessed July 5, 2016.

53. "Millennials and the New American Dream: A Survey Commissioned by Zipcar," January 2014. https://www.slideshare.net/Zipcar_PR/millennials-2013-slide-share.

54. MacLean and Lave, "Life Cycle Assessment," 5448.

55. Martin and Shaheen, "Greenhouse Gas Emissions," 1074.

56. Nina Casalena, "How often do Americans Eat Vegetarian Meals? And how many adults in the U.S. are Vegetarian?" Vegetarian Research Group, May 18, 2012, http://www.vrg.org/blog/2015/05/29/how-often-do-americans-eat-vegetarian-meals-and-how-many-adults-in-the-u-s-are-vegetarian-2/, accessed March 16, 2017.

57. "Poultry Slaughter," Reports by USDA National Agricultural Statistics Service, 2017. http://usda.mannlib.cornell.edu/MannUsda/viewDocumentInfo.do ?documentID=1131.

58. U.S. EPA, *Inventory*, 5–8–5–15. In 2014, poultry manure contributed an estimated 0.076 percent of total U.S. greenhouse gas emissions. While poultry and swine manure have increasingly been managed as liquid waste, giving rise to both methane and nitrous oxide, the scale of these emissions is believed to be extremely small.

59. Michael Allison Chandler, "DC Public Schools Plans to Offer International Trips to Middle Schoolers," *Washington Post*, March 24, 2015.

60. Hawken, *Drawdown*, 150–55

61. Susan Gilbert, "Practical Traveler; Study Abroad: Getting Younger," *New York Times*, March 31, 2002.

62. "DCPS is Going Places. Come With Us," dcpsglobaled.org/why-study-abroad/, accessed September 27, 2017.

## 4. The Greenest Suburb

1. Chicago Metropolitan Area Planning (CMAP), *Homes for a Changing Region*, http://www.cmap.illinois.gov/livability/housing/homes. Rather than modeled carbon dioxide data, Chicago area data includes actual energy-use data from utility records compiled by the nonprofit Center for Neighborhood Technology (CNT) for the year 2009. I used CNT energy consumption data published in the series *Homes for a Changing Region*, published by Chicago Metropolitan Area Planning (CMAP) and sponsored by the Metropolitan Mayors Caucus and the Metropolitan Planning Council. The series includes reports for the West Cook County Housing Collaborative, the South Suburban Housing Collaborative, the Northwest Suburban Housing Collaborative, and the Fox Valley Housing Upper Cluster.

2. CMAP, *Homes . . . Year Five*, 100.

3. Ron Pazola, "A Tour of Chicago's Native American Sites," *Chicago Tribune*, November 15, 1991, http://articles.chicagotribune.com/1991–11–15 /entertainment/9104120534_1_native-americans-indian-legacy-potawatomi.

4. U.S. Census Bureau, "Selected Housing Characteristics," American FactFinder, 2014. https://factfinder.census.gov/faces/tableservices/jsf/pages/productview .xhtml?src=CF.

5. CMAP, *Homes . . . Year Five*, 63.

6. CMAP, *Homes . . . Year Five*, 45. CMAP, *Homes . . . Year Seven*, 25. The CNT energy data published in CMAP's *Homes for a Changing Region* series includes twenty-three Chicago suburbs. A town in Kane County, Carpentersville, has the next-lowest per-capita emissions after Berwyn. Like Berwyn, Carpentersville is a majority Hispanic community with a relatively large household size.

7. U.S. EIA, "Annual Energy Review," September 2012, https://www.eia.gov /totalenergy/data/annual/showtext.php?t=ptb0109. The Chicago area $CO_2$ emissions are not meant to be strictly compared with those in communities in other parts of the country with different heating and cooling demands and a different carbon intensity. The Chicago area has cold winters and needs about 45 percent more heating than average in America, a fact that drives up its $CO_2$ emissions. On the other hand, Illinois has one of the lowest carbon intensities of any state because of its heavy reliance on nuclear power. In this respect Chicago may be seen as having a fairly average carbon intensity.

8. Deuchler, *Berwyn*, 7.

9. Deuchler, *Berwyn*, 63.

10. Mary Daniels, "The Haunting Legends of Lobstein House," *Chicago Tribune*, October 29, 2006.

11. Kathleen Donohue, "Living Green in a Historic Chicago Bungalow," *American Bungalow* 78 (Summer 2013), https://www.americanbungalow.com/living-green/.

12. Deuchler, *Berwyn*, 62.

13. City of Homes Organization, "Central Berwyn Bungalow Historic District Added to National Register of Historic Places," *Chicago Tribune*, September 12, 2015. http://www.chicagotribune.com/suburbs/daily-southtown/community /chi-ugc-article-central-berwyn-bungalow-historic-district-add-2015–09–11 -story.html.

14. Mike Williams, "Berwyn: Chicagoland's Hidden Treasure," American Bungalow, April 11, 2011, 88.

15. Berwyn Historical Society, http://berwynhistoricalsociety.org/2017/06/11th -bungalows-and-more-tour-september-24–2017/, accessed October 2, 2017.

16. Under Illinois law, if a homeowner spends at least 25 percent of a property's value on qualifying rehabilitation projects, property assessments may be frozen for eight years. Rental properties on the National Register may receive a 20 percent tax credit. "Landmarks," Berwyn Historic Preservation Commission, http://www.berwynpreservation.org/landmarks.html, accessed March 7, 2017.

17. See for instance Rowan, *Compact Houses*; Tolpin, *New Cottage Home*.

18. U.S. Census Bureau, "Square Feet of Floor Area in New Single-Family Houses Completed," 2014. https://www.census.gov/construction/chars/pdf/squarefeet.pdf.

19. Sharon Daly, "The 2-Flat De-Conversion Game: Reasonable Strategy or Wishful Thinking?" *Forest Park Review*, January 7, 2014. http://www.forestparkreview.com/News/Articles/1-7-2014/The-2_flat-de_conversion-game%3A--Reasonable-strategy-or-wishful-thinking%3F-/.
20. CMAP, *Homes . . . Year Five*, 48.
21. Hackl, "John S. Van Bergen," 1.
22. "New Type of Apartment Building," *Oak Leaves*, December 4, 1915, 23.
23. Annette Frost-Jensen, correspondence with author, February 7, 2015.
24. U.S. EIA. "Illinois Electric Power Industry Generation by Primary Energy, Table 5," 2015. https://www.eia.gov/electricity/state/illinois/.
25. U.S. EIA. "Ohio Electricity Profile 2015," Table 1. https://www.eia.gov/electricity/state/ohio/.
26. Loomis and Pagan, "The Illinois RPS," 13.
27. "2012 Past Award Winners: EPA Green Power Purchaser Awards," Green Power Partnership, U.S. EPA, 2012. https://www.epa.gov/greenpower/2012-past-award-winners#oakp.
28. Timothy Inklebarger, "Oak Park Scraps Green Energy Program," *Wednesday Journal*, April 14, 2014.
29. "Still Time to Opt Out of the Brown Energy Default," http://www.greencommunityconnections.org/tag/oak-park-energy/, accessed September 26, 2017.
30. Household size in Berwyn is somewhat larger than the national average, about 15 percent higher than Chicago's and 50 percent larger than Forest Park's household size. U.S. Census Bureau, "Profile of General Population and Housing Characteristics," American FactFinder, 2010, https://factfinder.census.gov/faces/tableservices/jsf/pages/productview.xhtml?src=CF.
31. Duany and Plater-Zyberk, *Suburban Nation*. 254.
32. "Living in Oak Park," Walk Score website, https://www.walkscore.com/IL/Oak_Park, accessed September 26, 2017.
33. CMAP, *Homes . . . Year Five*, 104.
34. "Children's Food Environment State Indicator Report, 2011," CDC. https://www.cdc.gov/obesity/downloads/childrensfoodenvironment.pdf.
35. *Oak Park Telephone Directory*, 1957, accessed at Oak Park Historical Society, December 2012.
36. John McDermott, "Corner Grocery Closes Door," *Wednesday Journal*, July 19, 1989.
37. Oak Park Zoning Update, September 2016, Village of Oak Park, https://oakparkzoning.com/2016/10/07/september-2016-draft-zoning-ordinance-draft-zoning-map-now-available/.
38. "South of the Border," *Wednesday Journal*, May 24, 2005.
39. Walcott, "Chicago's Avenues." 357.
40. Speck, *Walkable City*, 82; Hart and Spivak, *Elephant in the Bedroom*.
41. CMAP, *Berwyn Comprehensive Plan*. http://www.cmap.illinois.gov/programs-and-resources/lta/Berwyn.

42. U.S. Census Bureau, "Selected Housing Characteristics."

43. Hoagland, *Historical Survey*.

44. Cook, *Little Old Oak Park*. 100.

45. Davis et al, *Transportation Energy Data Book*.

46. Bob Stigger, "A Few Modest Proposals for Hiking Revenue," Letter, *Wednesday Journal*, April 11, 2017.

47. "Former Oak Leaves Columnist Dies," *Oak Leaves*, August 28, 2002. Harriet Vrba's weekly column "Oak Chips" ran for thirty years in Oak Park's weekly newspaper, *Oak Leaves*.

48. Forest Park unemployment at 8.7 percent, Berwyn at 8.8 percent. U.S. Census Bureau, 2014.

49. CMAP, *Homes . . . Year Five*, 80.

50. CMAP, *Homes . . . Year Five*, 45.

51. CMAP, *Berwyn Comprehensive Plan*. http://www.cmap.illinois.gov/programs -and-resources/lta/berwyn.

52. Rosenberg, *Join the Club*, 162.

53. Rybczynski, *Makeshift Metropolis*, 83.

54. CMAP, *Homes . . . Year Five*, 63. When we consider Forest Park's commercial build-ings, the town's per capita emissions jump up to about 15 metric tons $CO_2$ per person, about 19 percent higher than the per capita average in Cook County. The town of River Forest, which borders on Forest Park, relies on Forest Park for shopping and dining because it has almost no commercial areas of its own.

55. CMAP, *Homes . . . Year Four*, 45.

56. Mike Nolan, "Southland Groups Clean Up Flood of Foreclosures in the Chicago Area," *Chicago Tribune*, May 26, 2015. http://www.chicagotribune .com/suburbs/daily-southtown/news/ct-sta-southland-foreclosed-homes-st -0524–20150526-story.html.

57. CMAP, *Homes . . . Year Four*, 59.

58. Nelson. "Mass Market," 811–26.

59. Shyam Kannan, "Suburbia, Soccer Moms, SUVs, and Smart Growth," http:// www.rclco.com/pub/doc/presentation-2012–02–02-Suburbia_Soccer_Moms _SUVs_and_Smart_Growth.pdf, accessed March 7, 2017.

60. "Berwyn: Redesigning the Campaign for a Singular City," Firebelly Designs. https://www.firebellydesign.com/work/berwyn, accessed October 4, 2017.

## 5. College, Commercial Carbon

1. *The College Sustainability Report Card*, Sustainable Endowments Institute web-site, http://www.greenreportcard.org/index.html, accessed September 28, 2017. I calculated average $CO_2$ emission per student after consulting about 150 greenhouse gas emissions inventories years 2005–2009.

2. Space heating consumes more energy in the United States than cooling. ASU's solar contribution is calculated based on its greenhouse gas inventory for fiscal

year 2015 reported to the American College President's Climate Commitment (ACUPCC) at http://reporting.secondnature.org/institution/detail!146##146 and on ASU's March 2017 updated ASU Solar site, https://cfo.asu.edu/solar.

3. U.S. EIA, *Residential Energy Consumption Survey (RECS)*, "2009 RECS Survey Data," Table CE3.1, https://www.eia.gov/consumption/residential/data/2009/index.php ?view=consumption#undefined. In 2009, air conditioning consumed 6.3 percent of home energy use compared to 41.5 percent for space heating.

4. Rutgers University, "Addressing Climate Change in the Rutgers Community," http://climatechange.rutgers.edu/rutgers-climate-stewardship#energy-use-and -generation, accessed September 28, 2017.

5. Andrews, "America's Greenest Colleges."

6. U.S. EIA, "2003 CBECS Survey Data," *Commercial Buildings Energy Consumption Survey*, https://www.eia.gov/consumption/commercial/data/2003/.

7. U.S. EIA, "2012 CBECS Survey Data," *Commercial Building Energy Consumption Survey*, https://www.eia.gov/consumption/commercial/data/2012/.

8. *The State of Sustainability in Higher Education: Emissions Metrics, Consumption Trends and Strategies for Success*, Report by the Sustainability Institute at the University of New Hampshire and *Sightlines*, 2015, http://www.sightlines.com/wp-content /uploads/2016/01/The-State-of-Sustainability-in-Higher-Education-2015.pdf.

9. *Five Year Energy Management Plan 2013 Update*, McGill University, https://www .mcgill.ca/facilities/files/facilities/emp_2013_update.pdf; Stephanie Joyce, "University of Wyoming's Utility Bill Climbs as Budget Falls," *Inside Energy*, August 29, 2016. For instance, McGill University (Montreal, Quebec) energy costs per student are about $510 (U.S. $392). Energy expenditures in the United States average about $855 per student.

10. Christopher McCready, "School Design: Making Adaptive Reuse Work," *American School & University magazine*, July 1, 2011. http://www.asumag.com /constructionplanning/school-design-making-adaptive-reuse-work.

11. "Report Card 2011," *The College Sustainability Report Card*, Sustainable Endowments Institute, http://www.greenreportcard.org/report-card-2011 /surveys.html. Like many other universities, The New School compiles its own greenhouse gas emission inventory, organized into categories starting with the most certain data (Scope 1)–direct emissions from fossil fuel consumption—mainly natural gas and petroleum for heating and cooking and any campus fleet, followed by (Scope 2) estimated emissions from purchased electricity. The university consultant, or whoever does the inventory, usually has easy access to this data. The third category (Scope 3) relates to commuting to campus, as well as staff and student air travel, data that is hard to put together accurately. Therefore, for the campus comparisons I have used the Scope 1 and Scope 2 data, but not the transport (Scope 3) data. The inventory data is drawn from detailed surveys compiled by the Sustainable Endowments Institute.

12. Between 105 and 159 institutions reported emissions to the Sustainable Endowments Institute for these years, according to author's compilation of data.

13. Owen, *Conundrum*, 61.

14. Selingo, *College (Un)Bound*, 240.

15. Iosue and Mussano, *College Tuition*. Between 2000 and 2006, higher education doubled spending on construction, although student enrollment only grew by 16 percent during this time.

16. Richard Fry and Andrea Caumont, "Five Key Findings about Student Debt," in *Factank: News in the Numbers*, Pew Research Center online, May 14, 2014. http://www.pewresearch.org/fact-tank/2014/05/14/5-key-findings-about -student-debt/.

17. The "top ten" list included the University of Oregon and the University of Washington. *Princeton Review, Guide to 322 Green Colleges 2014. Princeton Review* offers current green guides at their website, https://www .princetonreview.com/college-rankings/green-guide.

18. American residential colleges and universities averaging 5 metric tons $CO_2$ eq. or less per student, excluding diet or personal transportation, as compiled by the author based on surveys submitted to the Sustainable Endowments Institute by 2011 or the American College and University Presidents Climate Commitment by 2015, http://www.greenreportcard.org/report-card-2011/surveys .html. Public universities are noted *: University of Alabama*, University of Alaska, Anchorage*, American University, Anna Maria, University of Arizona*, Arizona State University*, Bentley, Bowie State*, Bryant, Berkeley*, University of Buffalo*, California Polytechnic State*, Colgate, College of the Atlantic, De Paul, Evergreen College*, Fordham, Frostburg State*, George Mason*, Goucher, University of Hawaii at Manoa*, Hocking, University of Houston*, Ithaca, Loyola Marymount, University of Massachusetts Amherst*, McMaster, University of Memphis*, Western Michigan University*, Mills, University of Montana*, University of New Hampshire*, New York University, University of North Carolina at Greensboro*, University of North Texas*, University of Oregon*, University of Puget Sound, Ramapo*, Richard Stockton*, Rider, University of Rochester, Rutgers*, St. Joseph's, University of San Francisco, University of South Dakota*, Southern Oregon State*, Clark, Stevens Institute of Technology, Syracuse, University of Texas, Austin*, Valdosta State*, George Washington University, The New School, University of the Pacific, University of Toledo*, University of Vermont*, Virginia Commonwealth*, University of Washington*, Willamette, Worcester Polytechnic.

19. Andrew Martin, "Building a Showcase Using an I.O.U.," *New York Times*, December 13, 2012.

20. Rachel Yeager, "Razorback Stadium Electricity Bill Topped $500,000 Last Year," *Razorback Reporter*, December 2013. http://razorbackreporter.uark.edu /2013/12/razorback-stadium-electricity-bill-topped-500000-last-year/.

21. William Hobson and Steven Rich, "Playing in the Red," *Washington Post*, November 23, 2015. http://www.washingtonpost.com/sf/sports/wp/2015/11/23/running-up-the-bills/?utm_term=.5d9da3b0edbb.

22. William Hobson and Steven Rich, "The Latest Extravagances in the College Sports Arms Race? Laser Tag and Mini Golf," *Washington Post*, December 21, 2015.

23. William Hobson and Steven Rich, "Why Students Foot the Bill for College Sports, and How Some are Fighting Back." *Washington Post*, November 30, 2015.

24. Roman Stubbs, "Maryland Releases New Plans, Photos for Cole Field House Project," *Washington Post*, October 19, 2016.

25. *Swimming Pools and the Energy Star Score in the United States and Canada*, ENERGY STAR website, July 2013, https://www.energystar.gov/sites/default/files/buildings/tools/ENERGY%20STAR%20Score%20for%20Swimming%20Pools.pdf. Olympic-sized outdoor pool 597,821 kBTUs, indoor pool 6,266,009 kBTUs.

26. "The 30 Best College Pools," College Rank, http://www.collegerank.net/best-college-pools/, accessed September 29, 2017.

27. Laurier Nichols, "Improving Efficiency," 6. A general survey shows that a standard ice rink uses 1,500,000 kwh/year, and the most energy-efficient rinks use 800,000 kwh/year.

28. Lawrence Biemiller, "Bowdoin's New Ice Arena Wins LEED Certification — but It's the Zamboni You'll Notice," *The Chronicle of Higher Education*, July 27, 2009. http://www.chronicle.com/blogs/buildings/bowdoins-new-ice-arena-wins-leed-certification-but-its-the-zamboni-youll-notice/7479.

29. James S. Russell, "On Elite Campuses, an Arts Race," *New York Times*, November 13, 2014.

30. National Endowment for the Arts, *Arts Engagement*, 5.

31. National Endowment for the Arts, *Arts Engagement*, 5.

32. District of Columbia Department of the Environment and Department of General Services District Public Building Benchmarking Report FY 2009–2013; Martin Luther King Library, flush glass building form 330 kBTU/gsf compared with ~150 kBTU/gsf for older DC libraries, https://doee.dc.gov/sites/default/files/dc/sites/ddoe/publication/attachments/DDOE-DGS_PublicBenchmarking_013113.pdf.

33. Larry Milstein, "New SOM Building Sparks Controversy," *Yale Daily News*, January 16, 2014. http://yaledailynews.com/blog/2014/01/16/new-som-building-sparks-controversy/.

34. "Parking," section in *Guidebook*, Reed College Office of the Dean, www.reed.edu/academic/gbook/comm_pol/parking.html, accessed 7/15/16.

35. MIT, Department of Facilities, Ray and Maria Stata Center, http://web.mit.edu/facilities/construction/completed/stata.html, accessed September 28, 2017.

36. Universal Access Transit Pass. Wikipedia. https://en.wikipedia.org/wiki/Universal_transit_pass, accessed September 28, 2017.

37. T. Hayden Barnes, letter to the editor of vsu *Spectator*, April 19, 2007. https://www.thefire.org/t-hayden-barnes-letter-to-the-editor-of-vsu-spectator/.

38. https://www.valdosta.edu/academics/library/depts/archives-and-special-collections/vsu-history/presidents/zaccari.php.

39. James Highsmith, "Students Gather 300 signatures to Oppose New Parking Structure," *Washtenaw Voice*, May 8, 2010. http://archive.washtenawvoice.com/tag/molly-indura/.

40. Greg Lukianoff, "A Crucial Courtroom Victory for College Student's Rights," *Huffington Post*, September 23, 2010. http://www.huffingtonpost.com/greg-lukianoff/a-crucial-courtroom-victo_b_736253.html.

41. Andy Thomas, "Former Valdosta State U. Student's Free-Speech Lawsuit Ends in $900,000 Settlement," *The Chronicle of Higher Education*, July 23, 2015. http://www.chronicle.com/blogs/ticker/valdosta-state-u-will-pay-900000-to-settle-students-free-speech-lawsuit/102355.

42. 2016 Colgate University, "State of Sustainability Report," http://www.colgate.edu/docs/default-source/default-document-library/2016-state-of-sustainability-report.pdf?sfvrsn=0, accessed September 28, 2017. Colgate has received 5,000 tons of carbon offsets since 2012 through Patagonia Sur LLC. Patagonia Sur Carbon Offset Project. Offset Network. http://offsetnetwork.org/patagonia-sur-carbon-offset-project/ accessed September 28, 2017.

43. Hobson and Rich, "Playing in the Red." Auburn University reportedly sent 370 staff members and their spouses, and Florida State sent 237 people to a recent title game.

44. "Greenhouse Gas Report for Duke University, 2015," Second Nature, Inc. website, http://reporting.secondnature.org/ghg/ghg-public!3779.

45. Bill Pennington, "Rise of College Club Teams Creates a Whole New Level of Success," *New York Times*, December 1, 2008.

46. Mark Schapiro, "GM's Money Trees," *Mother Jones*, November/December 2009. http://www.motherjones.com/environment/2009/11/gms-money-trees/; Chris Lang, "David Nilsson: Carbon Cowboy," November 22, 2011. https://chrislang.org/2011/11/22/david-nilsson-carbon-cowboy/, accessed March 22, 2017.

47. Anderson, "Truth of Carbon Offsets."

48. Le Quere et al., "Low-Carbon Research," 161.

49. Kevin Anderson, "Hypocrites in the Air: Should Climate Change Academics Lead by Example?" from the author's website, August 12, 2013. http://kevinanderson.info/blog/hypocrites-in-the-air-should-climate-change-academics-lead-by-example/.

50. Parke Wilde, F.A.Q. for #Flyingless. https://docs.google.com/document/d/1URRRh4zMSpvtZY08F9-Rkbx0qkNNmfzIzqOlqZWKxkE/edit *Flying Less: Reducing Academia's Carbon Footprint*, www.academicflyingblog.wordpress.com.

51. Adam Taylor, "Meteorologist Breaks Down in Tears after Climate Change Report, Says He Will Never Fly Again," *Business Insider*, September 28 2013. http://www.businessinsider.com/meterologist-eric-holthaus-quits-air-travel-2013-9.

52. U.S. Department of Transportation, "U.S. Air Carrier Aircraft Departures, Enplaned Revenue Passengers, and Enplaned Revenue Tons," Bureau of Transportation Statistics. Last updated May 21, 2017. https://www.bts.gov/archive /publications/national_transportation_statistics/table_01_37.

53. U.S. EPA, *Inventory*, Table 3–12, page 3–19.

54. "A Diverse Network of Leaders," Second Nature, Inc. website, http:// secondnature.org/wp-content/uploads/Network-Snapshot-3_Diverse-Network .pdf, accessed October 1, 2017.

55. Skidmore, Owings & Merrill, "The New School's University Center to Open January 23," January 22, 2014. http://www.som.com/news/the_new_schools _university_center_to_open_january_23.

56. L. Moosavi, "Thermal Performance," 655.

57. Brager, et al., *Building Research Agenda*, 27.

58. "Guide to 375 Green Colleges, 2017," *Princeton Review*. https://www .princetonreview.com/college-rankings/green-guide.

59. Zehner, *Green Illusions*, 404.

60. Scofield, "Efficacy of LEED-Certification," 517–524.

61. Agdas et al., "Energy Use Assessment," 15–21.

62. Thomas Frank, "Green Schools: Long on Promise, Short on Delivery," *USA Today*, December 11, 2012. https://www.usatoday.com/story/news/nation/2012 /12/10/green-schools-construction-leed/1753823/.

63. "District Public Building Benchmarking Report: Fiscal Years 2009–2012," Report by District Department of the Environment (DDOE) and the Department of General Services (DGS), January 18, 2013. https://ddoe.dc .gov/sites/default/files/dc/sites/ddoe/publication/attachments/DDOE-DGS _PublicBenchmarking_013113.pdf.

64. Dunbar High School annual carbon dioxide emissions data from Department of General Services District Public Building Benchmarking Report. Perry Stein, "The 'Greenest' School Building in the World is in Washington," *Washington Post*, March 12, 2015, https://www.washingtonpost.com/news/local /wp/2015/03/12/the-greenest-school-building-in-the-world-is-in-washington/ ?utm_term=.e7fcd944b50d.

65. Olivia Pulsinelli, "Bank of America Signs Lease in New Downtown Tower, Kicking Off Construction," Houston Business Journal, April 12, 2017. https:// www.bizjournals.com/houston/news/2017/04/12/bank-of-america-signs-lease-in -new-downtown-tower.html.

66. John H. Scofield, "Energy Star Scores for Dormitories are Skewed," July 25, 2013, from author's blog, the Pragmatic Steward, https://thepragmaticsteward .com/2013/07/25/energy-star-scores-for-dormitories-are-skewed/.

67. John H. Scofield, "Energy Star Scores for Medical Office Buildings Exhibit 'Grade Inflation,'" author's blog, July 24, 2013, https://thepragmaticsteward.com/2013/07 /24/energy-star-scores-for-medical-office-buildings-exhibit-grade-inflation/.

68. AIA and COTE Top Ten Awards, 2017 Call for Entries, 2. http://aiad8.prod
.acquia-sites.com/sites/default/files/2016–11/COTE_2017TopTenAwardsEntry
_final_1.pdf, accessed October 4, 2017.

69. Contests may be organized by individual institutions or by programs such as
the EPA's ENERGY STAR program.

70. Natural Resources Canada, *Benchmarking and Best Practices*, 4. Canadian universities spent only $130 million (CDN dollars) annually on higher education
energy costs (circa 2000) for their 175 associated colleges, a per student cost of
only about $88 in U.S. currency.

71. van der Linden, "Intrinsic Motivation."

72. U.S. EPA, "Best Management Practices for Colleges and Universities:
Energy, Sub-Metering Campus Buildings," updated January 2007. https://
sftool.gov/Content/attachments/SCSUSubmetering1–8-07.pdf; "Sub-
Metering Energy Use in Colleges and Universities Incentives and Chal-
lenges," U.S. EPA, 2002. https://www.energystar.gov/ia/business/higher_ed
/Submeter_energy_use.pdf.

73. "Caltech's Newest Shining Star: the Cahill Center for Astronomy and Astrophysics," Caltech news online, January 26, 2009. http://www.caltech.edu/news
/caltechs-newest-shining-star-cahill-center-astronomy-and-astrophysics-1503.

74. Claremont McKenna completed construction of the 162,000-square-foot Kra-
vis Center in 2013 and the 130,000-square-foot Roberts Pavilion in 2016.

75. Long, "Cognitive Sciences Complex."

76. Jacobs, *Death and Life*.

77. Preservation Green Lab of the National Trust for Historic Preservation, *The
Greenest Building: Quantifying the Environmental Value of Building Reuse*,
2011, vi, https://living-future.org/wp-content/uploads/2016/11/The_Greenest
_Building.pdf.

78. U.S. EPA, *Potential for Reducing Greenhouse Gas Emissions in the Construction Sector*, February 2009, 3–4, https://archive.epa.gov/sectors/web/pdf/construction
-sector-report.pdf.

79. "Tangible Actions and Early Successes," Second Nature website, http://
secondnature.org/climate-guidance/tangible-actions-early-successes/#Example
_Tangible_Actions, accessed October 2, 2017.

80. "Rutgers Powers Campus with Largest Solar Canopy in Nation," Green Sports
Alliance website, September 13. 2013. http://greensportsalliance.org/rutgers
-powers-campus-with-largest-solar-canopy-system-in-nation/. About 5 percent
of Rutgers-enrolled students live at the Livingston campus, the location of
the solar array that is expected to reduce power use by 63 percent in those
buildings.

81. "Hydroelectric Plant," Cornell University website, https://
energyandsustainability.fs.cornell.edu/util/electricity/production/hydroplant
.cfm, accessed October 1, 2017.

## 6. Becoming Five Tons

1. Barbara Bogaev, host, "New technologies to save the planet," *Sustainability Hour*, 53:54, Minnesota Public Radio, April 22, 2009. https://www.mprnews.org/story/2009/04/22/midday2. Intentional environmental communities range from urban examples such as Takoma Village Cohousing in Washington DC, which resembles the lower-carbon lifestyle of conventional multi-unit residences, or rural examples such as Hundredfold Farm in southern Pennsylvania, which is a small rural community that pursues rooftop solar, carpooling, and tree-planting.

2. Boswell, Greve, and Seale, *Local Climate Action Planning*, 199–226.

3. Roger Lowenstein, "Who Needs the Mortgage Interest Deduction?" *New York Times*, March 5, 2006.

4. Bloomberg and Pope, *Climate of Hope*.

5. Timothy Mitchell, *Carbon Democracy*.

6. Jackson, *Prosperity Without Growth*.

7. Speth, *Edge of the World*.

8. Beavan, *How to be Alive*, 19.

9. Hulme, *Why We Disagree About Climate Change*, 392.

10. Hulme, *Why We Disagree About Climate Change*, 330.

11. Bain et al., "Promoting Pro-Environmental Action," 600–603.

12. Marshall, *Don't Even Think About It*, 95.

13. Norgaard, *Living in Denial*, 195.

14. Pinker, *Better Angels*, 832.

15. Klein, *This Changes Everything*, 117.

16. George Marshall, "Can this Really Save the Planet?" *Guardian*, September 12, 2007.

17. "Greenhouse Gas Emissions Reduction Progress 2016," Yale University leaflet, accessed March 9, 2017. http://sustainability.yale.edu/sites/default/files/2016_greenhouse_gas_reduction_report.pdf. In 2005, Yale University's president signed a pledge to reduce campus emissions by 43 percent by 2020. As of 2016, Yale reported reductions of 24 percent from the 2005 baseline.

18. Bruce McCall, "Glass Houses," *New Yorker*, November 7, 2016.

19. "U.S. Building Benchmarking Policy Landscape," September 2017. https://www.buildingrating.org/graphic/us-building-benchmarking-policy-landscape. As of 2017, these cities include Austin; Boulder; Atlanta; Denver; Cambridge; Boston; Chicago; Evanston; Minneapolis; Kansas City; New York City; Orlando; Philadelphia; Pittsburgh; Portland, Maine, Portland, Oregon; Salt Lake City; Washington DC; and also Montgomery County, Maryland; and the states of California and Washington.

20. 2015 Building Benchmarking Dataset, DC Department of Energy & Environment, September 28, 2017. https://doee.dc.gov/node/1203042.

21. "Start Your Own CRAG!" September 14, 2009. http://carbonday.com/get-involved/crag/.

22. Cowley, "The Wish," 353.

23. Wilson, *Half Earth*, 272.

24. Author interview with Sam Brooks, former Director of Sustainability and Energy Division at the DC Department of General Services, April 4, 2014.

25. Van der Werff, Steg, and Keizer, "I am What I am," 273–82.

26. At this point in time the EPA footprint calculator offers a useful, simple format to calculate emissions from residences and mobility. www3.epagov/carbon-footprint-calculator, accessed March 24, 2017.

27. Taufik, Bolderdijk, and Steg, "Acting Green," 37–40.

# Bibliography

## Archives

Adams Family Papers: An Electronic Archive. Massachusetts Historical Society. Boston, 2017. http://www.masshist.org/digitaladams.

George Washington Papers. *The Diaries of George Washington*. Donald Jackson, Dorothy Twohig, eds. Charlottesville: University of Virginia Press, 1976–1979. Library of Congress Digital Collections. https://www.loc.gov /collections/george-washington-papers/?fa=segmentof%3Amgwd.wd01%2F %7Ccontributor%3Ajackson%2C+donald&st=gallery&sb=shelf-id.

The Papers of George Washington. Digital Edition. Theodore J. Crackel, ed. (Charlottesville: University of Virginia Press, 2017). http://rotunda.upress .virginia.edu/founders/GEWN.

The Papers of Thomas Jefferson. Digital Edition. James P. McClure and J. Jefferson Looney, eds. (Charlottesville: University of Virginia Press, 2017). http:// rotunda.upress.virginia.edu/founders/TSJN.

York County Estate Inventories, Colonial Williamsburg digital library. http:// research.history.org/DigitalLibrary/inventories/.

## Published Works

Agdas, Duzgun, Ravi S. Srinivasan, Kevin Frost, and Forrest J. Masters. "Energy Use Assessment of Educational Buildings: Toward a Campus-Wide Sustainable Energy Policy." *Sustainable Cities and Society* 17 (September 2015): 15–21.

Anderson, Kevin. "The Inconvenient Truth of Carbon Offsets." *Nature* 484 No. 7392 (April 4, 2012) 7.

Anderson, M. K. "Prehistoric Anthropogenic Wildland Burning by Hunter-Gatherer Societies in the Temperate Regions." *Chemosphere* 29, no. 5 (1994): 913–94.

Andreae, Meinrat O., and V. Ramanathan. "Climate's Dark Forcings," *Science* 340, no. 6130 (2013): 280–81.

Andrews, Avital. "America's Greenest Colleges: Cool Schools 2014." *Sierra*. http:// www.sierraclub.org/sierra/coolschools-2014.

Bain, Paul G., Matthew J. Hornsey, Renata Bongiorno, and Carla Jeffries. "Promoting Pro-Environmental Action in Climate Change Deniers." *Nature Climate Change* 2 (2012): 600–603.

Beavan, Colin. *How to be Alive: A Guide to the Kind of Happiness that Helps the World*. New York: Dey Street Books, 2016.

Bender, M. H. "An Economic Comparison of Traditional and Conventional Agricultural Systems at County Level." *American Journal of Alternative Agriculture* 16, no. 1 (2001): 2–15.

Bendt, P. "Are we Missing Energy Savings in Clothes Dryers?" Paper Presented at the 2010 ACEEE Summer Study on Energy Efficiency in Buildings. August 2010. http://aceee.org/files/proceedings/2010/data/papers/2206.pdf.

Bergman, Richard, Maureen Puettmann, Adam Taylor, and Kenneth E. Skog. "The Carbon Impacts of Wood Products." *Forest Products Journal* 64, nos. 7–8 (2014): 220–31.

Binder, Frederick Moore. *Coal Age Empire: Pennsylvania Coal and its Utilization to 1860*. Harrisburg: Pennsylvania Historical and Museum Commission, 1974.

Biswas-Diener, Robert, Joar Vitterso, and Ed Diener. "Most People are Pretty Happy, but There Is Cultural Variation. The Inughuit, the Amish and the Maasai." *Journal of Happiness Studies* 6 (2005): 205–26.

Bixby, W. K. *Inventory of the Contents of Mount Vernon, 1810*. Cambridge: Cambridge University Press, 1909.

Bloomberg, Michael, and Carl Pope. *Climate of Hope: How Cities, Businesses, and Citizens Can Save the Planet*. New York: St. Martin's Press, 2017.

Bogaev, Barbara. "New Technologies to Save the Planet." *Sustainability Hour*. 50:53. Minnesota Public Radio, April 22, 2009.

Boswell, Michael R., Adrian L. Greve and Tammy Seale. *Local Climate Action Planning*. Washington DC: Island Press, 2012.

Brager, Gail, Drury Crawley, John Fernandez, Rich Haut, Judith Heerwagen, Michael Holtz, Bruce Hunn, et al. *A National Green Building Research Agenda*. U.S. Green Building Council. February 2008. https://www.usgbc.org/resources/national-green-building-research-agenda.

Bratkovich, Stephen, Joey Gallion, Earl Leatherberry, William Hoover, William Reading, Glenn Durham. *Forests of Indiana: Their Economic Importance*. USDA Forest Service and Indiana Department of Natural Resources, 2004. https://www.na.fs.fed.us/spfo/pubs/forestprod/indiana_forest04/forests_of_IN04.htm.

Brown, Marilyn A., Andrea Sarzynski, and Frank Southworth. *Shrinking the Carbon Footprint of Metropolitan America*. Brookings Institution, May 2008. https://www.brookings.edu/wp-content/uploads/2016/06/carbonfootprint_report.pdf.

Carter, Gebra Cuyun. "Food Intake, Dietary Practices, and Nutritional Supplement Use Among the Amish." PhD diss., Ohio State University, 2008. http://rave.ohiolink.edu/etdc/view?acc_num=osu1211898334.

Centers for Disease Control and Prevention (CDC). *Children's Food Environment State Indicator Report, 2011*. Department of Health and Human Services, 2011. https://www.cdc.gov/obesity/downloads/childrensfoodenvironment.pdf.

Chernow, Ron. *Washington: A Life*. New York: Penguin, 2010.

Chicago Metropolitan Agency for Planning (CMAP). *City of Berwyn Comprehensive Plan*. August 2012. http://www.cmap.illinois.gov/documents/10180/22894 /FY13–0009%20BERWYN%20LTA%20PLAN.pdf/7a7df885–876d-4977-a878 -e32b4e0a0fc6.

Chicago Metropolitan Agency for Planning (CMAP), Metropolitan Mayors Caucus, and Metropolitan Planning Council. *Homes for a Changing Region: Phase 3: Implementing Balanced Housing Plans at the Local Level, Year Four: Hazel Crest, Lansing, Olympia Fields and Park Forest*. January 2012. http://www.cmap.illinois.gov /documents/10180/10818/SOUTH_SUBURBAN_HOUSING_COLLAB_HOMES _FOR_A_CHANGING_REGION.pdf/fede9eea-1e4e-416c-bae1-ff8e6069d238.

———. *Homes for a Changing Region: Phase 3: Implementing Balanced Housing Plans at the Local Level, Year Five: Bellwood, Berwyn, Forest Park, Maywood, and Oak Park*. April 2012. http://www.cmap.illinois.gov/documents/10180/10818 /WEST_COOK_COLLAB_HOMES_FOR_A_CHANGING_REGION.pdf /64da5665–0cae-4ebd-9416–1217953a3cf8.

———. *Homes for a Changing Region: Phase 3: Implementing Balanced Housing Plans at the Local Level, Year Six: Arlington Heights, Buffalo Grove, Mount Prospect, Palatine, and Rolling Meadows*. January 2013. http://www.cmap.illinois.gov /documents/10180/10818/NW_HOMES_FOR_A_CHANGING_REGION.pdf /80f2b323-f7d0–43c8-b6f1-c0694e09fc27.

———. *Homes for a Changing Region: Phase 3: Implementing Balanced Housing Plans at the Local Level, Year Seven: Carpentersville, East Dundee, Elgin, and West Dundee*. May 2014. http://www.cmap.illinois.gov/documents/10180 /10818/FY14–0016%20HOMES%20FOR%20A%20CHANGING%20REGION %202014%20lowres.pdf/bd368215-df74–4152–9dcc-cd4b3762a7b9.

Cohen, Scott A., James E. S. Higham, and Christina T. Cavaliere. "Binge Flying: Behavioural Addiction and Climate Change." *Annals of Tourism Research* 59, no.3 (2011): 1070–89.

Cook, May Estelle. *Little Old Oak Park*. Oak Park IL: privately printed, 1961.

Cowley, Abraham. "The Wish." In *The Oxford Book of English Verse 1250–1900*, edited by Arthur-Quiller-Couch. Oxford: Oxford University Press, 1919.

Craven, Avery O. *Soil Exhaustion as a Factor in the Agricultural History of Virginia and Maryland: 1606–1860*. Champaign: University of Illinois Press, 1925.

Davis, Stacy C., Susan W. Diegel, and Robert G. Boundy. *Transportation Energy Data Book*. U.S. Department of Energy. Edition 34. 2011.

Day, Gordon M. "The Indian as an Ecological Factor in the Northeastern Forest." *Ecology* 34 no.2 (1953): 329–46.

Deuchler, Douglas. *Berwyn: Images of America*. Charleston SC: Arcadia, 2005.

Dierauf, Thomas A. "History of the Montpelier Landmark Forest: Human Disturbance and Forest Recovery." University of Virginia Library, 2011. www .montpelier.org/sites/default/files/FM-landmark-forest.pdf, accessed November 2011, (site discontinued).

Druckman, Angela, and Tim Jackson. "How Much Household Carbon do we Really Need?" *Ecological Economics* 69, no. 9 (2010): 1794–1804.

Duany, Andres, and Elizabeth Plater-Zyberk. *Suburban Nation: The Rise of Sprawl and the Decline of the American Dream* (10th anniversary edition). New York: North Point Press, 2010.

Einberger, Scott. *A History of Rock Creek Park: Wilderness & Washington DC.* Charleston SC: The History Press, 2014.

Elkhart County Sheriff's Department. *Horse and Buggy Driver's Manual.* Elkhart IN. http://www.elkhartcountysheriff.com/resources/horse-buggy-manual/, accessed October 3, 2017.

Etemad, B., J. Luciani, P. Bairoch, J. C. Toutain. *World Energy Production: 1800–1985.* Centre d'Histoire Economique International: University of Geneva, 1991.

Fageria, N. K., V. C. Baligar, and D. A. Bailey. "Role of Cover Crops in Improving Soil and Row Crop Productivity." *Communications in Soil Science and Plant Analysis* 36, no. 19–20 (2005): 2733–57.

Favaro, Brett. *The Carbon Code: How You Can Become a Climate Change Hero.* Baltimore: Johns Hopkins University Press, 2017.

Frank, Steve. "Ford Orientation Center and Donald W. Reynolds Museum and Education Center, Mount Vernon." *Journal of American History* 94, no. 3 (2007): 881–85.

Fusonie, Alan, and Donna Jean Fusonie. *George Washington: Pioneer Farmer.* Mount Vernon: Mount Vernon Ladies' Association, 1998.

Gallagher, Leigh. *The End of the Suburbs: Where the American Dream is Moving.* New York: Portfolio Reprints, 2014.

Glaeser, Edward L., and Jesse M. Shapiro. "The Benefits of the Home Mortgage Interest Deduction." *Tax Policy and the Economy* 7 (2003).

Goodwin, Mary R.M. *Use of Coal and Fire Grates in Eighteenth Century Virginia: A Research Report.* Colonial Williamsburg Foundation Library, 1963.

Graham, Eleanor. "Report on Heating," Colonial Williamsburg Foundation Library, 1945. Colonial Williamsburg Foundation Library Research Report Series 0154, 1990. http://research.history.org/DigitalLibrary/view/index.cfm?doc=ResearchReports\RR0154.xml&highlight=report%20on%20heating.

Greenberg, Allan. "Architecture: The Mansion House of Mount Vernon." In *George Washington's Mount Vernon.* Wendell Garrett (ed.). New York: Monacelli Press, 1988.

Griffin, Appleton P.C., ed., *A Catalogue of the Washington Collection in the Boston Athenaeum*, The Boston Athenaeum, 1900.

Grubler, Arnulf, and Yasumasa Fujii. "Intergenerational and Spatial Equity Issues of Carbon Accounts." *Energy* 16, no. 11–12 (1991): 1397–1416.

Hackl, Martin. *The Work of John S. Van Bergen, Architect.* Oak Park, Illinois: Martin Hackl, 2001.

Hansen, Stephen A. *Kalorama Triangle: The History of a Capital Neighborhood.* Charleston SC: The History Press, 2011.

Hanson, Andrew. "Size of Home, Home Ownership, and the Mortgage Interest Reduction." *Journal of Housing* 21, no.3 (2012): 195–210.

Harak, Charlie. *Up the Chimney: How HUD's Inaction Costs the Taxpayers Millions and Drives up the Utility Bills for Low Income Families.* Boston: National Consumer Law Center, August 2010. https://www.nclc.org/images/pdf/pr-reports /up_the_chimney_082610.pdf.

Hart, Stanley, and Alvin Spivak. *The Elephant in the Bedroom: Automobile Dependence and Denial: Impacts on the Economy and Environment.* Carol Stream IL: Hope Publishing House, 2010.

Hawken, Paul. *Drawdown: The Most Comprehensive Plan Ever Proposed to Reverse Global Warming.* London: Penguin Books, 2017.

Hoagland, Gertrude Fox, ed. *Historical Survey of Oak Park.* Compiled under the Federal Works Progress Administration, 1937.

Hulme, Mike. *Why We Disagree About Climate Change.* Cambridge: Cambridge University Press, 2009.

Hurst, Charles E., and David L. McConnell. *An Amish Paradox: Diversity and Change in the World's Largest Amish Community.* Baltimore: Johns Hopkins University Press, 2010.

Igou, Brad, ed. *The Amish in Their Own Words: Amish Writings from 25 Years of Family Life Magazine.* Scottsdale PA: Herald Press, 1999.

*Intergovernmental Panel on Climate Change. Climate Change 2014 Synthesis Report.* R. K. Pachauri and L. A. Meyer, eds. *Fifth Assessment Report.* Geneva, Switzerland.

Intergovernmental Panel on Climate Change. *2006 IPCC Guidelines for National Greenhouse Gas Emissions Inventories.* Eggleston, Simon et al., eds. Vol. 4, Ch. 10, "Emissions from Livestock and Manure Management." Hayama, Japan: 2006. http://www.ipcc-nggip.iges.or.jp/public/2006gl/pdf/4_Volume4/V4_10_Ch10 _Livestock.pdf.

Iosue, Robert V., and Frank Mussano. *College Tuition: Four Decades of Financial Deception.* Indianapolis: Blue River Press, 2014.

Jackson, Mary. "Amish Agriculture and No-Till: The Hazards of Applying the USLE to Unusual Farms." *Journal of Soil and Water Conservation* 43 No. 6 (1988).

Jackson, Tim. *Prosperity Without Growth: Economics for a Finite Planet.* London: Routledge, 2011.

Jacobs, Jane. *The Death and Life of Great American Cities.* New York: Modern Library Reissue, 1993.

James, Randall E. "Horse and Human Labor Estimates for Amish Farms." *Journal of Extension* 45, no. 1, (2007).

Jefferson, Thomas. *Thomas Jefferson's Garden Book, 1766–1824: With Relevant Extracts from His Other Writings.* Philadelphia: American Philosophical Society, 1944.

Jeffries, Julie. "The U.K. Population Past, Present, and Future." In *Focus on People and Migration.* R. Chappell (ed.). London: Palgrave Macmillan, 2005.

Jiang, Xuemei, Dabo Guan, Jin Zhang, Kunfu Zhu, Christopher Green. "Firm Ownership, China's Export Related Emissions, and the Responsibility Issue." *Energy Economics* 51 (2015): 466–74.

Johnson, Julia Overturf, Robert Kominski, Kristin Smith, and Paul Tillman. "Changes in the Lives of U.S. Children: 1990–2000." Working Paper no. 78, Population Division, U.S. Census Bureau, Washington DC, November 2005. https://www.census.gov/population/www/documentation/twps0078/twps0078.html.

Johnson-Weiner, Karen. "Technological Diversity and Cultural Change Among Contemporary Amish Groups." *Mennonite Quarterly Review* 88, no 1, (2014).

Kannan, Shyam. "Suburbia, Soccer Moms, SUVs, and Smart Growth." Visual data presentation. RCLCO Public Strategies Group, 2012. http://www.law.du.edu/documents/rmlui/conference/powerpoints/2012/KannanS-WhatAmericansReallyWant.pdf.

Kimball, Fiske. *Regional Types in Early American Architecture, Architects Emergency Committee, Great Georgian Houses of America, Volume 2*. Mineola NY: Dover, 1970.

Klein, Naomi. *This Changes Everything*. New York: Simon & Schuster, 2015.

Kraybill, Donald B. *The Riddle of Amish Culture*. Baltimore: Johns Hopkins University Press, 2001.

Kraybill, Donald, Karen Johnson-Weiner, and Steven Nolt. *The Amish*. Baltimore: Johns Hopkins University Press, 2013.

Kraybill, Donald B., and Stephen Nolt. *Amish Enterprise: From Plows to Profits*. Baltimore: Johns Hopkins University Press, 2004.

Lafayette, Marquis de. *Lafayette in the Age of the American Revolution, Selected Letters and Papers, 1776–1790*. Vol. 5. Stanley J. Idzerda and Robert R. Crout, eds. Ithaca: Cornell University Press, 1983.

Laing, Wesley Newton. "Cattle in Early Virginia." PhD diss., University of Virginia, 1952.

LDA Consulting. *Capital Bike Share 2014 Member Survey Report*. Washington DC: April 3, 2015. https://d21xlh2maitm24.cloudfront.net/wdc/cabi-2014surveyreport.pdf?mtime=20161206135936.

Lee, Jean B. *Experiencing Mount Vernon: Eyewitness Accounts, 1784–1865*. Charlottesville: University of Virginia Press, 2006.

Leonard, Annie. *The Story of Stuff: The Impact of Overconsumption on the Planet, Our Communities and Our Health—And How We Can Make it Better*. With Ariana Conrad. New York: Free Press, 2011.

Le Quéré, Corinne, et al. "Towards a Culture of Low-Carbon Research for the 21st Century." Working Paper 161, Tyndall Centre for Climate Change Research. Norwich, UK: March 2015. http://tyndall.ac.uk/sites/default/files/publications/twp161.pdf.

Long, Phillip D. "MIT: The Brain and Cognitive Sciences Complex." In *Learning Spaces*, Diana G. Oblinger, ed. EDUCAUSE, 2006. http://www.educause.edu/res earch-and-publications/books/learning-spaces/chapter-26-mit-brain-and-cognitive-sciences-complex.

Loomis, David, and Antonio Pagan. "The Illinois RPS: Context, Structure and History of the Policy." Center for Renewable Energy, Illinois State University. 2011. https://renewableenergy.illinoisstate.edu/downloads/publications/2011%20TheIllinoisRPS%200411.pdf.

MacLean, Heather L. and Lester B. Lave. "Life Cycle Assessment of Automobile/Fuel Options." *Environmental Science & Technology* 37, no. 23 (2003): 5445–52.

Manca, Joseph. *George Washington's Eye: Landscape, Architecture, and Design at Mount Vernon.* Baltimore: Johns Hopkins University Press, 2012.

Marland, G., T. A. Boden, and R. J. Andres. "Global, Regional, and National Fossil-Fuel $CO_2$ Emissions." *In Trends: A Compendium of Data on Global Change.* 2008. Carbon Dioxide Information Analysis Center, Oak Ridge National Laboratory, U.S. Department of Energy, Oak Ridge TN. http://cdiac.ess-dive.lbl.gov/trends/emis/overview.

Marshall, George. *Don't Even Think About It: Why our Brains are Wired to Ignore Climate Change.* New York: Bloomsbury, 2014.

Martin, Elliot W., and Susan A. Shaheen. "Greenhouse Gas Emission Impacts of Car Sharing in North America." *IIEE Transactions on Intelligent Transportation Systems* 12 no. 4 (2011): 1074–86.

Mazur, Christopher, and Ellen Wilson. "Housing Characteristics: 2010" Report, U.S. Census Bureau, October 2011. https://www.census.gov/prod/cen2010/briefs/c2010br-07.pdf.

McKibbin, Anne, Anne Evens, Steven Nadel, Eric Mackres. "Engaging as Partners in Energy Efficiency: Multifamily Housing and Utilities," Center for Market Transformation and ACEEE, 2013. http://aceee.org/research-report/a122.

McNary, Bill, and Chip Berry. "How Americans are Using Energy in Homes Today." American Council for an Energy-Efficient Economy (ACEEE). Summer study on energy efficiency in buildings, 2012. http://aceee.org/files/proceedings/2012/data/papers/0193-000024.pdf.

Miles, Wyndham D., ed. "The Mysterious Gas of the New Jersey Lakes." Proceedings of the New Jersey Historical Society 74, no. 4 (1956): 255–59.

Mitchell, Ronald B. "Technology is Not Enough: Climate Change, Population, Affluence and Consumption." *The Journal of Environment & Development* 21, no. 1 (2012): 24–27.

Mitchell, Timothy. *Carbon Democracy: Political Power in the Age of Oil.* London and New York: Verso, 2013.

Moosavi, Leila, Norhayati Mahyuddin, Norafida Ab Ghafar, and Muhammad Azzam Ismail. "Thermal Performance of Atria: An Overview of Natural Ventilation Effective Design." *Renewable and Sustainable Energy Reviews* 34 (June 2014): 654–70.

Murtaugh, Paul, and Michael Schlax. "Reproduction and the Carbon Legacies of Individuals." *Global Environmental Change* 19, no. 1 (2009): 14–20.

National Endowment for the Arts. *A Decade of Arts Engagement: Findings from the Survey of Public Participation in the Arts, 2002–2012.* NEA Research Report no. 58, January 2015. https://www.arts.gov/sites/default/files/2012-sppa-feb2015.pdf.

Natural Resources Canada. *Benchmarking and Best Practices Guide for College Facility Managers.* Office of Energy Efficiency, 2000. http://www.ertc.deqp.go.th /ertc/images/stories/user/ct/ct1/cp/water_and_energy_conservation/Energy %20Efficiency%20for%20Colleges.pdf.

Nelson, Arthur C. "The Mass Market for Suburban Low-Density Development is Over." *The Urban Lawyer* 44, no. 4 (2012): 811–26.

Nichols, Laurier. "Improving Efficiency in Ice Hockey Arenas," *ASHRAE Journal* 51, no. 6 (June 2009): 16–20.

Nolt, Steven M., and Thomas J. Meyers. *Plain Diversity: Amish Cultures and Identities.* Baltimore: Johns Hopkins University Press, 2007.

Norgaard, Kari Marie. *Living in Denial: Climate Change, Emotions, and Everyday Life.* Cambridge: MIT Press, 2011.

Oates, J. C. T. "Hot Air from Cambridge." *The Library* s5-XVIII, no. 2 (1963): 140–42.

Olmert, Michael. "Cool, Calm, and Clean: Dairies Were the Most Elaborate of Out Buildings and the Cleanest," *Colonial Williamsburg Journal* (Winter 2005–2006). http://www.history.org/foundation/journal/winter05–06/dairies.cfm.

Owen, David. *The Conundrum: How Scientific Innovation, Increased Efficiency, and Good Intentions can Make Our Energy and Climate Problems Worse.* New York: Riverhead Books, 2011.

Patrick, Vanessa E. *Partitioning the Landscape: The Fence in Eighteenth Century Virginia.* December 6, 1983. Colonial Williamsburg Foundation Library Research Report series no. 0134. Colonial Williamsburg Digital Library. http://research .history.org/DigitalLibrary/view/index.cfm?doc=ResearchReports%5CRR0134 .xml&highlight=.

Peterson, Arthur G. "Commerce of Virginia, 1789–1791," *William and Mary Quarterly* 10, no. 4 (1930): 302–9.

Pfister, Ulrich, and Georg Fertig. "The Population History of Germany: Research Strategy and Preliminary Results." MPIDR Working Paper WP 2010–035, Laboratory of Historical Demography, Max Planck Institute for Demographic Research, Rostock, Germany, December 2010. http://www.demogr.mpg.de /papers/working/wp-2010–035.pdf.

Pinker, Steven. *The Better Angels of Our Nature: Why Violence has Declined.* New York: Viking, 2011.

Plutzer, Eric, Mark McCaffrey, A. Lee Hannah, Joshua Rosenau, Minda Berbeco, and Ann H. Reid. "Climate Confusion Among U.S. Teachers." *Science* 351, no. 6274 (2016): 665.

Putnam, Robert. *Bowling Alone: The Collapse and Revival of American Community.* New York: Simon & Schuster, 2001.

Rayner, Steve, and Gwyn Prins, "The Wrong Trousers: Radically Rethinking Climate Policy," Discussion Paper, University of Oxford and London School of Economics, 2007. http://eprints.lse.ac.uk/24569/?from_serp=1 and the actual text here: http://eureka.sbs.ox.ac.uk/66/.

Rifkin, Jeremy. *Beyond Beef: The Rise and Fall of Cattle Culture*. New York: Plume, 1993.

Rosenberg, Tina. *Join the Club: How Peer Pressure Can Transform the World*. New York: W. W. Norton, 2012.

Rowan, Gerald. *Compact Houses: 50 Creative Floor Plans for Well-Designed Small Homes*. North Adams MA: Storey, 2013.

Russell, James S. *The Agile City: Building Well-Being and Wealth in an Era of Climate Change*. Washington DC: Island Press, 2011.

Rybczynski, Witold. *Makeshift Metropolis: Ideas About Cities*. New York: Scribner, 2010.

Salatin, Joel. *Salad Bar Beef*. Stanton VA: Polyface, 1996.

Schoenauer, Norbert. *6,000 Years of Housing*. New York: W. W. Norton & Company, 2000.

Schoettle, Brandon, and Michael Sivak. "The Reasons for the Recent Decline in Young Driver Licensing in the United States." *Traffic Injury Prevention* 15, no. 1 (2014): 6–9.

Schreiner, Oswald. "Early Fertilizer Work in the United States," *Soil Science* 40, no. 1 (1935): 39–48.

Schumacher, E. F. *Small Is Beautiful: Economics as if People Mattered*. New York: Harper & Row, 1975.

Scofield, John H. "Efficacy of LEED-Certification in Reducing Energy Consumption and Greenhouse Gas Emissions for Large New York City Office Buildings." *Energy and Buildings* 67 (2013): 517–24.

Scott, Stephen, and Kenneth Pellman. *Living Without Electricity: Lessons from the Amish*. New York: Good Books, 1999, 2016.

Selingo, Jeffrey J. *College (Un)Bound: The Future of Higher Education and What it Means for Students*. Amazon reprint edition, 2015.

Shui, Bin, and Robert C. Harriss. "The Role of $CO_2$ Embodiment in U.S.-China Trade." *Energy Policy* 34, no. 18 (2006): 4063–68.

Sivak, Michael. "Marketing Implications of the Changing Age Composition of Vehicle Buyers in the U.S." University of Michigan, Ann Arbor, Transportation Research Institute. UMTRI-2013-14.

Slade, Giles. *Made to Break: Technology and Obsolescence in America*. Cambridge: Harvard University Press, 2007.

Smith, Kirk R., Manish A. Desai, Richard A. Houghton, and Jamesine V. Rogers. "Joint $CO_2$ and $CH_4$ Accountability for Global Warming." *Proceedings of the National Academy of Sciences* 110, no. 31 (2013): E2865-E2874.

Soltow, Lee. *Distribution of Wealth & Income in 1798*. Pittsburgh: University of Pittsburgh Press, 1989.

Sookhdeo, Christine, and Daniel L. Druckenbrod, "Effect of Forest Age on Soil Organic Matter at Mount Vernon va." *Bulletin, NJ Academy of Science* 57, no. 1 (January 2012): 1–4.

Speck, Jeff. *Walkable City: How Downtown Can Save America, One Step at a Time.* New York: North Point, 2013.

Speth, James Gustave. *The Bridge at the Edge of the World: Capitalism, the Environment, and Crossing from Crisis to Sustainability.* New Haven CT: Yale University Press, 2009.

Steg, Linda, and Kees Keizer. "Follow the Signal: When Past Pro-Environmental Actions Signal Who You Are." *Journal of Environmental Psychology* 40 (2014): 273–82.

Stevens, William K. *Under the Oaks: The Revival of Nature in America.* New York: Pocket Books, 1995.

Stripple, Johannes, and Harriet Bulkeley, eds. *Governing the Climate: New Approaches to Rationality, Power and Politics.* Cambridge: Cambridge University Press, 2014.

Subak, Susan. "Accountability for Climate Change." Report, Stockholm: Stockholm Environment Institute, 1990.

———. "Agricultural Soil Carbon Accumulation in North America: Considerations for Climate Policy." *Global Environmental Change* 10, no. 3 (2000): 185–95.

———. "Assessing Emissions: Five Approaches Compared." In *The Global Greenhouse Regime: Who Pays?* Kirk. R. Smith and Peter Hayes, eds. London and Tokyo: Earthscan and United Nations University Press, 1993.

———. "Global Environmental Costs of Beef Consumption." *Ecological Economics* 30, no. 1 (1999): 79–91.

Subak, Susan, and William C. Clark. "Accounts for Greenhouse Gases: Toward the Design of Fair Assessments." In *Usable Knowledge for Managing Global Climatic Change.* William C. Clark, ed. Advisory Group on Greenhouse Gases, Stockholm Sweden. Stockholm Environment Institute, 1990.

Taufik, Danny, Jan W. Bolderdijk, and Linda Steg. "Acting Green Elicits a Literal Warm Glow." *Nature Climate Change* 5 (2015): 37–40.

Thompson, Mary V. *Dining with the Washingtons at Three Periods of their Lives.* Mount Vernon Ladies' Association, 2003.

Tolpin, James L. *The New Cottage Home: A Tour of Unique American Dwellings.* Newtown CT: Taunton, 1998.

U.S. Census Bureau. *Historical Statistics of the United States, Colonial Times to 1970.* Bicentennial Edition, Part 1. Washington DC, September 1975.

U.S. Environmental Protection Agency (EPA). *Inventory of U.S. Greenhouse Gas Emissions and Sinks: 1990–2014.* Washington DC. April 15, 2016. https://www.epa.gov/sites/production/files/2017–04/documents/us-ghg-inventory-2016-main-text.pdf.

Van Boven, Leaf, and Thomas Gilovich. "To Do or To Have?" *Journal of Personality and Social Psychology* 85, no. 6 (2003): 1193–1202.

Van der Linden, Sander. "Intrinsic Motivation and Pro-Environmental Behaviour." *Nature Climate Change* 5, (2015): 612–13.

Van der Werff, Ellen, Linda Steg, and Kees Keizer. "Follow the Signal: When Past Pro-Environmental Actions Signal Who You are." *Journal of Environmental Psychology* 40 (December 2014): 273–82.

———. "I Am What I Am, by Looking Past the Present: The Influence of Biospheric Values and Past Behavior Values and Past Behaviour on Environmental Self-Identity." *Environmental Behavior* 46 no. 5 (2014): 626–57.

Van Doren, Mark. *The Travels of William Bartram, 1791*. New York: Dover, 1955.

Vincent, Gilbert T. "Fine Arts: A Collection Fitting the Nation." In *George Washington's Mount Vernon*, edited by Wendell Garrett, 164–85. New York: The Monticello Press, 1998.

Wackernagel, Mathis, and William E. Rees. "Perceptual and Structural Barriers to Investing in Natural Capital: Economics from an Ecological Footprint Perspective." *Ecological Economics* 20 no.1 (1997): 3–24.

Walcott, Derek. "Chicago's Avenues as White as Poland." *The Poetry of Derek Walcott, 1948–2013*. New York: Farrar, Straus & Giraux, 2014.

Walsh, Lorena S. "Feeding the Eighteenth-Century Town Folk, or Whence the Beef?" *Agricultural History* 73, no 3, (1999): 267–80.

Walsh, Lorena S., Ann Smart Martin, and Joanne Bowen. "Provisioning Early American Towns: The Chesapeake: A Multidisciplinary Case Study." September 30, 1997. Colonial Williamsburg Digital Library Research Report Series 0404. http://research.history.org/DigitalLibrary/view/index.cfm?doc=ResearchReports%5CRR0404.xml&highlight=.

Weber, Christopher L., and H. Scott Matthews. "Quantifying the Global and Distributional Aspects of American Household Carbon Footprint." *Ecological Economics* 66, nos. 2–3 (2008): 379–91.

Weber, E. U. "Perception and Expectation of Climate Change: Precondition for Economic and Technological Adaptation." In *Psychological Perspectives to Environmental and Ethical Issues in Management*. M. Bazerman, David Messick, Ann Tenbrunsel, and Kimberly Wade-Benzoni, eds. 314–341. San Francisco: Jossey-Bass, 1997.

Weld, Isaac. *Travels through the State of Northern America, and the provinces of Upper and Lower Canada during the years 1795, 1796, and 1797*. London: John Stockdale, Piccadilly, 1799.

Wetmore, Jameson. "Amish Technology: Reinforcing Values and Building Community. *IEEE Technology and Society Magazine* 26, no. 2 (2007): 10–21.

Whitehead, David. "More Housing is Now Banned from Lanier Heights. Organizing is What Won the Day." Comment by Matt. *Greater Greater Washington*, April 12, 2016.

Whitmarsh, Lorraine, Gill Seyfang, and Saffron O'Neill. "Public Engagement with Carbon and Climate Change: To What Extent is the Public 'Carbon Capable'?'" *Global Environmental Change* 21, no.1 (2011): 56–65.

Wilson, Edward O. *Consilience: The Unity of Knowledge*. New York: Vintage, 1999.
———. *Half Earth: Our Planet's Fight for Life*. New York: Liveright, 2016.
Wulf, Andrea. *Brother Gardeners: A Generation of Gentleman Naturalists and the Birth of an Obsession*. New York: Vintage, 2010.
———. *Founding Gardeners: The Revolutionary Generation, Nature, and the Shaping of the American Nation*. New York: Vintage, 2012.
Yoder, Elmer. *The Beachy Amish Mennonite Fellowship Churches*. Hartville OH: Diakonia Ministries, 1987.
Zehner, Ozzie. *Green Illusions: The Dirty Secrets of Clean Energy and the Future of Environmentalism*. Lincoln: University of Nebraska Press, 2012.

# Index

Amish subgroups: Andy Weaver, 84, 221n2; Nebraska Group, 67; New Order, 82–83, 213n36; Old Order, 59, 78, 84, 222n30; Swartzentruber, 67, 69, 84, 221n2

Amish technology: appliances, 66–68, 70, 76, 223n31; cell phones, 62, 68–69; compressed air, 64, 67; electricity use, 59, 65–67, 76; lighting, 64–65; refrigeration, 68; renewables, 69–70; scooters, 77, 79; solar panels usage, 13, 69–70, 83, 222n30; stoves, 59, 63–64, 72; washing machines, 67

Amtrak. *See* transportation: trains and railways travel

Anacostia Watershed Society, 107

Anderson, Kevin, 171–72

Anna Maria College, 233n18

Annapolis MD, 27, 53

apartments. *See* multi-unit residences

appliances, prevalence of, 66–67, 76

architecture: atria, 54–55, 174, 181–83, 201; Georgian, 53; gothic, 53–54; monumental, 55, 155, 174, 196; Prairie School, 22, 131, 134–35; small cool, 22, 100–104; Victorian, 96–99, 128, 131. *See also* American Institute of Architects

Arizona State University, 153, 183–84, 231–32n2, 233n18

Arlington Heights IL, *125*

Arts and Crafts design, 89, 129

Atlanta, 123, 143, 238n19

Auburn University, 235n43

Austin TX, 238n19

automobiles. *See* car ownership; car-sharing; transportation: cars

Babauta, Leo, 102

baby boomers, 104, 227n37

Bain, Paul, 191

Barnes, Hayden, 166–68

Beachey Amish Mennonites, 78

Beavan, Colin, 102, 172–73, 190

Beck, George, 214n3

Becker, Joshua, 102

beef consumption, 5, 7, 35, 39, 42, 57, 115–17

Bellwood IL, 124, *125*

benchmarking, energy, 176–77, 201

Bentley University, 233n18

Bertram, John, 45

Berwyn bungalows, 19, 22, 124, *126*, 128–29

Berwyn IL, 13, 124–30, 131–33, 136, 137–40, 187–88, 231n48; $CO_2$ emissions, 123, *125*, 138, 147; car-pooling,144; commercial development, 127, 147; comprehensive plan, 151–52; demography, 123, 127, 230n30; history, 125–27; transit, 141–44, 147

Berwyn IL, neighborhoods: Cermak Plaza, 137–38, 147; Cermak Road, 127; Depot District, 147, 152; Ogden Road, 138, 152; Proksa Park, 140

*The Better Angels of Our Nature* (Pinker), 193

bicycles: paths, 145–46, 152; sharing, 107, 111–12, 227n49; usage, 95, 111–12, 144–46. *See also* Capitol Bike Share

big box stores, 147–50

bilingual education, 13, 94–95, 132

biomass. *See* wood fuel

biophilia, 107–8

black carbon, 30, 70

blacksmiths, 28, 29, 215n16

blind pedestrians, 141, *142*, 145

Bloomberg, Michael, 189

Bogaev, Barbara, 238n1

Bordley John Beale, 218n,75

Boston MA, 90, 200, 238n19

Boulder CO, 238n19

Bowdoin College, 162

Bowie State University, 233n18

brain development, 94–95

Brando, Marlon, 155–56

Britain. *See* United Kingdom
Bryant University, 233n18
Buffalo Grove IL, *125*
bungalows. *See* Berwyn bungalows
burden sharing, 11
bus ridership, 113, 134
Buzaglo stove, 29

California, 9, 238n19
California Polytechnic State, 233n18
Cal Tech, 13, *169*, 180–81
Cambridge MA, 166, 238n19
Canada, 3, 11, 155, 158, *159*, 232n9, 237n70
Capitol Bike Share, 111–12
carbon capability, 14, 192, 203–7
*The Carbon Code* (Favaro), 3
carbon dioxide emissions. *See* greenhouse gas emissions
carbon footprint: Amish, *85*; calculator, 10, 15, 21, 203–4, 212n25, 239n26; education, 14–15, 196, 204–6; Europe, 3, 4, 14; knowledge about, 14, 20, 157, 192; survey, 92–93, 117–19; United Kingdom, 197; United States, 3, 4, 11. *See also* greenhouse gas emissions
carbon neutrality, 2, 167, 171, 174, 183
carbon offsets, 171–72, *185*
carbon sequestration: soils, 47–50, 75, 117; trees, 43–47, 71
car ownership: alternatives, 86–87, 111–15, 117–18; Amish, 77–80; compact, 113–14; demographic characteristics, 212n15; historical, 144
car sharing, 107, 114–15, 227n37
Carleton College, 165, 184
Carpentersville IL, *125*, 229n6
Carter, Jimmy, 32
Carter, Langdon, 218n75
Casey Trees Foundation, 107
cattle, 5, 32–33, *33*, 35–39, 41
Center for Neighborhood Technology, *125*, 228n1

Centers for Disease Control and Prevention (CDC), 139
charcoal, 28
chemical contamination, 13
Chesapeake region. *See* Maryland; Virginia
Chicago, 121–23, 138, 142, 154, 225n4, 238n19; climate, 229n7; $CO_2$ emissions, *125*, 228n1, 229n7; electricity fuel mix, 136, 229n7; natural gas, 136; neighborhoods, 17. *See also* Berwyn bungalows
Chicago Metropolitan Area Planning (CMAP), *125*
Chicago Transit Authority (CTA), *122*, 141–43
child obesity, 139
China, 7, 69
cities greenhouse gas targets, 188
Citizens Climate Lobby, 193
civil liberties, 167–68
Claremont McKenna College, 181–82, 237n74
Clark University, 233n18
Clean Power Plan, 3, 8, 211n6
climate activism: carbon neutrality, 174, 183–85, 201; federal climate legislation, 3, 193–94, 211n6; footprint advocacy, 195, 202; fossil fuel divestment, 166–68, 194–95; neighborhood, 192–203
climate change, 21; communication, 191–93, 197; denial, 20; education, 14, 15, 190–91, 205. *See also* activism
Climate Rationing Action Groups, 196–97
clothes dryers, 67
clutter. *See* material goods
coal, 8, 59; eighteenth century, 27–30, 43, 214n9, 215n12, 215n13, 215n16, 215n17; Illinois fuel mix, 136–37; nineteenth century, 53–55, *54*

cogeneration, 180
cognitive dissonance, 20
Colgate University, 170–71, 233n18, 235n42
College of the Atlantic, 233n18
Colonial Williamsburg. *See* Williamsburg
colonial workforce: enslaved labor, 34, 44, 48–49; free labor, 39; rations, 39, 217n46
Colorado College, 169
Columbia University, 155, 160, 165
commercial sector: architectural trends, 57, 174–75, 196; benchmarking data, 174–75, 196; Canadian, 154; construction trends, 56, 57, 154, 158–59; $CO_2$ emissions, 7, 11, 157–58, *159*, 231n1; defined, 157–58; energy consumption, 149–50, 175–76; libraries, 56; museums, 55, 56, 57
commuting: biking, 17, 145–46; carpooling, 76, 144; driving alone, 143–44; transit, 17, 141–43, 146
compact housing. *See* house size
condos. *See* multi-unit residences: condos
construction moratorium, 184–85, *185*, 203
construction trends, 100, 129–30, 158–59
consumption denial, 17, 18, 20
convenience, 66–67, 86
conversions. *See* house construction: conversion
Cook, May Estelle, 98, 144–45
Cook County, 147
Cornell University, 167, 184
corner grocery store, 139–40
corn production, 5, 48, 117
Cowley, Abraham, 198
crime rates, 95, 224n55, 225n13
crop rotation, 48–50
Czech American, 123
Czech Republic, 8

*Daudy Haus*. *See* accessory units
DC Department of General Services, 202, 234n32, 236n64, 239n24
DC Public Schools, 92–95
decarbonizing, 4
deforestation, 5, 116–17
Denmark, 6, 8
density, 89, 125, 133, 156, 187
Denver CO, 238n19
DePaul University, 154, 156, 166, 233n18
DePauw University, 169
Derby, Elias Hasket, 220n93
Dickinson College, 175
diet: Amish, 73; contemporary, 216n33; eighteenth century, 34–35, *43*, 216n31, 216n33, 217n46; greenhouse gas emissions, 11, 33–35, 42, 116, 213n28, 228n58; meat consumption, 5, 7, 42, 116–17, 223n43. *See also* vegetarian
*Don't Even Think About It!* (Marshall), 191
draft animals, 41–43, 74–75
driveways, 138–39, 187–88, 207
driving: Amish prohibitions, 77–80; driver's license prevalence, 6, 212n15; emissions trends, 5–6; vehicle miles traveled, 80, 141–44
Duke University, 164, *169*, 169–70, 171
Dunbar High School, 177, 236n36
duplexes, 130

Earthjustice, 168
East Dundee IL, *125*
Eckersley, Lauren, 155
eco-equity, 11
ecological footprint, 10
Eden, Robert, 27
Egan, Andrea, 95–96, 102
electricity: Amish applications, 65–68, 76; consumption trends, 66; fuel mix, 204; generation, 2, 136–37, 211n6. *See also* Clean Power Plan

greenhouse gas emissions (*continued*) *159*, 159–60, 180, 183; higher education, 154–55, 157–59, *159*, 160–61, 231–32n1–2, 232n11; historical, 11, 42–43, 53–54, *54*; household, *85*; personal targets, 2, 8–11; sector, 5, 11, *85*, 158, 213n28; suburban, *125*, 146–47, 229n6, 231n54; transportation, 7, 117; trends, 3, 4, 5, 7, *54*, *159*; urban families, 92–93, 109, 117–19; George Washington, 39, 42–43, 50

*Green Illusions* (Zehner), 5

green-ribbon schools, 176–77, 201–2

Greenwich Village, 155–57

Grinnell College, 156

Gross National Product, 189–90

happiness, 61

Harvard University, 104, 105, 163

Hawaii, 9

Hazel Crest IL, *125*

hedgerows, 37

higher education: amenities race, 160–64, 195; buildings and operations, 159, 161, 173; class size, 160; construction costs, 158–59, 233n15; energy expenditures, 225n3, 232n9, 234n25, 234n27, 237n70; energy surveys, 232n11, 233n12, 233n18; enrollment trends, 158, 233n15; floorspace, 13, 181, 194; geographic diversity, 169–70, 181; liberal arts colleges, 181; parking subsidies, 164–68; public universities, 160; research universities, 171–72; selective colleges, 158, *159*, 169–70, 181; sports, 160–63, 170–71, 173, 234n25, 234n27; student debt, 159, 197 transit subsidies, 166; tuition, 159–61, 165, 195 *See also* greenhouse gas emissions

Highland Park IL, 124, *125*, 144, 150, 194

Highway 66, 137–38

Hill, Graham, 102

Hispanic, 116, 123, 127, 229n6. *See also* Berwyn IL; Carpentersville IL

historic preservation, 17, 110, 135, 182–83, 197, 201, 229n16

Hoboken NJ, 121

Hobson, William, 161

Hocking College, 233n18

Holmes County OH. *See* Amish settlements

Holthaus, Eric, 172

horses, 41, 60, 74–75, 77–79, 86. *See also* Amish culture: transportation; draft animals; transportation: horse and buggies

house, single family: functions, 98–100; maintenance, 102; second homes, 51, 90, 131, 197, 207, 225n4. *See also* house size

house construction: conversion, 12, 89–90, 99, 108–11, 130–33, 189, 196, 201, 207, 213n29; deconversion, 17, 133, 196; owner-built, 129–30; trends, 6

household size, 85, 98, 132, 230n30

house size, 6–8, 90; eighteenth century, 25–26, 52–53, 58, 98; mansions, 17, 20, 25, 96–99, 206, 220n93; McMansions, 18, 81, 151–52, 206; nineteenth century, 53–55, 58, 96–99; small houses, 6, 19, 99, 124–25, 128, 189; tiny houses, 103; trends, 7. *See also* palaces

HUD. *See* U.S. Housing and Urban Development (HUD)

Hulme, Mike, 191

human rights. *See* inter-generational equity

Hundredfold Farm, 238n1

hypocrisy, 20

ice rinks. *See* higher education: sports

Illinois commuters, 143, 147

University of New Hampshire, 155, 233n18
University of North Carolina, Greensboro, 233n18
University of North Texas, 233n18
University of Oregon, 160, 233n18
University of Puget Sound, 233n18
University of Rochester, 233n18
University of San Francisco, 233n18
University of South Dakota, 233n18
University of Texas, Austin, 233n18
University of the Pacific, 233n18
University of Toledo, 233n18
University of Vermont, 233n18
University of Virginia, 161–62, 182
University of Washington, 160, 233n18
urban families, 8–9, 90–96, 109, 116–19, 187–88
urban naturalism, 107–8, 199
urban parks, 22, 133; the High Line, 155; Proksa Park, 140; Rock Creek Park, 89, 107, 108, 199
U.S. EPA: carbon calculator, 10, 204, 212n25, 221n97, 239n26; Energy Star, 222n19, 222n24, 237n69; greenhouse gas inventory, 213n28; position on consumption, 20; wood stove certification, 31, 223n40
U.S. Green Building Council, 174–76. See also LEED
U.S. Housing and Urban Development (HUD), 133
U.S. News and World Report, 160

Valdosta State University, 166–68, 233n18
Van Bergen, John, 134–35
Vanderbilt University, 179–80, 180
van der Linden, Sander, 178–79
vegetable gardens, 34–35, 73
Vegetarian Research Group, 116
vegetarian, 35, 73, 86, 115–17, 207

vehicles. See car ownership; car sharing; transportation
veterans, 130–31, 141
Victorian house. See architecture
Virginia, 89
Virginia, colonial: Lord Botetourt, 29; coal mining, 27, 214n9; diet, 34, 39, 42, 43, 216n31, 216n33; Lord Dunmore, 27; mansions, 26; plantations, 24, 26, 36, 43; Richmond, 27; Virginia Gazette, 28, 42; Williamsburg, 27, 36; Yorktown, 28, 36
Virginia Commonwealth University, 233n18
Vrba, Harriet, 145

Walcott, Derek, 143
walkability: characteristics, 137–41, 207; concept shortcomings, 1, 17, 138–39; walk score, 138
warm-weather states, 9
washing machines, 67, 222n19
Washington, George: agricultural experiments, 21, 24, 38, 47–50; animal breeding, 24, 37; conservation ethic, 25, 37, 38, 46, 47, 48; diet, 24, 33–35, 39–40, 42–43, 43, 56; draft animals, 41–42; fuel use, 24, 27–28, 30, 32, 43, 214n9, 215n12, 215n13, 215n16, 215n17; greenhouse gas emissions, 42–43, 43, 46, 50, 57; hospitality, 23, 24; house size, 25, 26, 30; landscape design, 43, 44; landscape paintings, 23–24, 214n3, 214n5; legacy, 22, 52–58, 191–92; livestock husbandry, 32–33, 33, 36–39, 43; weather diary, 32. See also colonial workforce; Mount Vernon
Washington, Martha, 34
Washington (state), 238n19
Washington DC, 89–119, 205–6, 225n2, 225n10, 225n13, 238n19; air travel incentives, 15; bilingual education,

13, 94–95; crime, 95; energy supply, 93; government, 201–2; housing stock, 89–91; transportation, 22, 111–15, 145–46; zoning revision, 109–11

Washington DC neighborhoods: Adams Morgan, 89, 96, 107; Columbia Heights, 89, 107; Dupont Circle, 90–91, 92, 115; Kalorama Triangle, 89–90, 92–93, 96–97, 107, 108; Lanier Heights, 96, 107; Northeast, 103; U Street corridor, 107

*Washington Post*, 161

Washtenaw Community College, 167

water consumption, 13, *185*

watts, as consumption metric, 10

wealth, 89–90, 93, 124, 146, 151, 189–90, 225n3

Weber, Elke, 211n1

West Dundee IL, *125*

Western Michigan University, 233n18

white flight, 95, 127, 156

White House, 200, 214n1

Whitmarsh, Lorraine, 14

Willamette College, 233n18

Williamsburg, 27, 29, 36, 42–44, 187

Wilson, E. O., 21, 107, 199

wind energy, 4, 136–37, 184

Windsor Castle, 26, 29

Winstanley, William, 214n3

Wisconsin, 131

wood fuel, 63, 70, 198; eighteenth century, 28–30; national consumption, 71; rural health, 72. *See also* forests

wood products, 69, 71

wood stoves, 63–64, 70–71, 198, 223n40

Worcester Polytechnic, 233n18

Wright, Frank Lloyd, 121, 128, 134, 144. *See also* Prairie School

Wulf, Andrea, 45

Wythe, George, 27

Yale University, 163, 164, *165*, *169*, 194–95, 238n17

York county VA, 42–43, *43*, 214n9

Young, Arthur, 47, 48

Zaccari, Roland, 167

Zehner, Ozzie, 5, 175

zero emissions, 2, 9, 201

Zipcar, 114, 227n37

zoning, 192, 197; accessory units, 109–10; commercial, 140; commissions, 17, 110; horse barns, 198; housing, 189, 196, 207